MW01253551

PSYCHOLOGY OF SELF-REGULATION

PSYCHOLOGY OF EMOTIONS, MOTIVATIONS AND ACTIONS

Additional books in this series can be found on Nova's website
under the Series tab.

Additional E-books in this series can be found on Nova's website
under the E-book tab.

PSYCHOLOGY OF SELF-REGULATION

VASSILIS BARKOUKIS
EDITOR

Nova Science Publishers, Inc.
New York

LIBRARY OF CONGRESS CATALOGING-IN-PUBLICATION DATA

Psychology of self-regulation / editor, Vassilis Chatzi.
    p. cm.
Includes index.
ISBN 978-1-61470-380-8 (hardcover)
1. Self-control. 2. Cognition. I. Chatzi, Vassilis.
BF632.P75 2011
155.2'5--dc23

               2011022220

Published by Nova Science Publishers, Inc. † New York

CONTENTS

Preface		vii
Chapter 1	Adaptive Metacognitive Self-regulation and Functional Resilience-related Assets in the Midst of Challenging Tasks: A Qualitative Analysis *Nils Beer, Giovanni B. Moneta*	1
Chapter 2	Monitoring, Control and the Illusion of Control *Magda Osman*	37
Chapter 3	Learning about Non-dogmatic Thinking *Daniel Favre and Lionel Simonneau*	61
Chapter 4	About the Fuels of Self-regulation: Time Perspective and Desire for Control in Adolescents Substance Use *Nicolas Fieulaine, Frédéric Martinez*	83
Chapter 5	The Promotion of Self-Regulation through Parenting Interventions *Matthew R. Sanders and Trevor G. Mazzucchelli*	103
Chapter 6	Cognitive Persistence: Refining the Role of Consciousness within Self-regulation *Derek Dorris*	121
Chapter 7	Antecedents and Consequences of Self-Regulated Learning in Physical Education *Vassilis Barkoukis, Kondilenia Katsani, and Despoina Ourda*	129
Chapter 8	Self-Control, Self-Regulation, and Juvenile Delinquency *Martha Frías-Armenta', Jorge Borrani, Pablo Valdez, Hugo Tirado and Xochitl Ortiz Jiménez*	147

Chapter 9   Hypnosis, Absorption and the Neurobiology
                  of Self-Regulation   **169**
                  Graham A. Jamieson

Index   **183**

PREFACE

This book presents topical research in the study of the psychology of self-regulation with a focus on topics including adaptive metacognitive self-regulation and functional resilience-related assets during challenging tasks; self-regulation resources and their application to improved learning, social behavior and cognitive processes; self-regulation and substance abuse; the promotion of self-regulation through parenting interventions and self-control, self-regulation in juvenile delinquency.

Chapter 1 - Metacognition(s) can be conceptualized as knowledge and beliefs about one's own cognitive processes (Flavell,1979) and the individual's ability to deconstruct and understand their own cognitive processes involving reflection and awareness of various types of problem- solving (Milne, 2003). The concept of metacognition has been applied to educational settings with positive connotation, e.g. in Wang's (1992) metacognitive competence as the ability to reflect and exhibit advantageous self-regulation (self-regulated learners) and Sternberg's (1984) link between metacognition and adaptive behavior. In psychopathology the focus has been on maladaptive metacognition. In extending schema theory, which predominantly emphasizes content rather than explaining mechanisms, Wells and Matthews' (1994, 1996) Self-Regulatory Executive Function (S-REF) Model has been a valuable and novel attempt to uncover the underlying cognitive processes in psychological disorders. Wells and Matthews' potential explanation of dysfunctional metacognitive processes provided the basis for amending, i.e. partially reversing, this model to derive and test a theoretical framework for core processes with respect to functional, adaptive metacognition (and meta-emotions) within this study.

Chapter 2 - Adaptive control in the face of uncertainty involves making online predictions about events in order to plan actions to reliably achieve desirable outcomes. However, we often face situations in which the effects of our actions are probabilistic (e.g., returns on our investments), and the environment itself is dynamic, - it can change irrespective of any action we decide to take, and in a relatively stable or unstable way (e.g., economic climate). Therefore, the problem of control concerns learning to isolate the effects that are generated directly by our actions, from those that occur independently of them. We face this problem in a host of uncertain dynamic environments: ecological (using fertilizers to increase crop yield), economic (investing in real estate), industrial (operating nuclear power plants), mechanical (driving cars) and medical (stemming outbreaks of disease). The aim of this review is to bring together empirical research from disparate disciplines spanning Social and Cognitive Psychology as well as Neuroscience all of which are concerned with adaptive control. In order to achieve this, this chapter presents a general framework (Monitoring and control- MC framework) which is used to integrate two central ideas (agency, uncertainty) that have important ramifications for understanding self regulatory processes and their relationship to control processes. In sum, the chapter proposes that control processes involve self-regulatory mechanisms (Task Monitoring and Self Monitoring) that enable us to make subjective estimates of success, which help to anchor the authors' interpretation of uncertain events to expected ones. In addition, these estimates are integrated with estimations of rates of change of the events in the environment which helps us track the outcomes we aim to control. The chapter ends with a discussion on the illusion of control and the possible mechanisms that give rise to it.

Chapter 3 - Very often, teaching the sciences still tends to set out stabilized knowledge and not the cognitive processes and values which lead to its collective elaboration. Consequently, the epistemic postures which characterize the scientific process and the scientific mind are not the subject of learning at school or at the university. In this chapter, the authors try to understand what type of learning, including scientific and epistemological education, should be developed. An epistemo-historical survey will first show the stages which have enabled Western philosophers to work out new epistemic postures to objectify the world. They developed models for these postures, in language and texts, with linguistic indicators to distinguish "dogmatism" from "non-dogmatism" and applied these models to various contexts. The authors suggest that knowing about these postures should help to self-regulate one's thinking and learning by facilitating the "destabilization/stabilization" cycle of ideas. Indeed, when people become perceptive to the linguistic indicators identifying dogmatic and non-dogmatic modes of thought, and are able to grasp the shifts between these two modes, they also become able to regulate their own thoughts and, consequently, their behaviour. Various experiments on pupils, students and teachers have shown how learning about these postures can modify pupils' behaviour (violence, school learning). They have also shown the difficulties encountered by adults in regular Master's degree learning. As an attempt to explain these data and difficulties, the authors suggest that learning about the epistemic postures of the scientific process could be an intermediary between Level two and Level three learning as described by Gregory Bateson.

Chapter 4 - In this chapter, the authors focus on the role of time perspective (TP) and desire for Control (DC) in self-regulation theory (SRT). Whereas self-control is the muscle of self-regulatory processes, time and control, as distal factors in self-regulation, may be considered as the fuels of this activity. The authors present results from a study investigating how SRT and TP frameworks can be related empirically, and to evaluate the role played by DC in the context of an extended model of the theory of planned behavior (TPB). The study was designed to explore the intervention of Desire for Control (DC) in the relation of TP to substance use, and to evaluate the contribution of these constructs to the TPB model and SRT. Participants were randomly recruited in high schools (N=690) and the study was prospective in design with an assessment of behaviors one week later. Findings showed the moderating role of DC in the relation of TP to substance use, suggesting the impact of those constructs on cannabis use behaviors, through their impact on proximal predictors. Findings of this research program offer some perspectives to integrate further TP research in the framework of self-regulation, and have some practical implications for promotion-or prevention-focused intervention related to substance use behaviors. They also open perspectives for a more "social" view on self-regulation.

Chapter 5 - The capacity for a parent to self-regulate their own performance is argued to be a fundamental process underpinning the maintenance of positive, nurturing, non-abusive parenting practices that promote good developmental and health outcomes in children. Deficits in self-regulatory capacity which have their origins in early childhood are common in many psychological disorders and strengthening self-regulation skills is widely recognised as an important goal in many psychological therapies and is a fundamental goal in preventive interventions. Attainment of enhanced self-regulation skills enables individuals to gain a greater sense of personal control and mastery over their life. This paper illustrates how the application of self-regulatory principles can be applied to parenting and family based interventions for children and young people. The Triple P—Positive Parenting Program, which uses a self-regulatory model of intervention, is used as an example to illustrate the robustness and versatility of the self-regulation approach to all phases on the parent consultation process.

Chapter 6 - Self-regulation is assumed to be achieved through both conscious and nonconscious processes. It has recently been argued (Dorris, 2009; Baumeister, Masicampo, & Vohs, 2011) that consciousness plays only an indirect role in self-regulation in that it selects a behaviour to be executed and, from that selection, a series of integrated downstream behavioural processes are set in motion so that the execution of the selected behaviour is carried out nonconsciously. It is argued here, that this refined notion of consciousness is most clearly demonstrated in self-regulatory persistence and that the act of persistence amounts to the same thing as the conscious process described by Dorris (2009) and Baumeister et al. (2011). It is argued, that such a conflation bolsters the notion that consciousness is simply a selector in that it allows us to see selection as a more effortful and, therefore, more organising process.

Chapter 7 - Self-regulation is an important factor affecting the learning process and achievement in education. Although there is ample empirical evidence on the effects of self-regulation on learning in the general education literature, related research in the context of physical education is limited. The present study used a cross-sectional survey-based design to investigate the motivational antecedents and affective consequences of self-regulated learning in physical education lessons. Participants were 345 high school students attending the 8th and 9th grades of typical co-educational secondary schools in Greece. The survey included measures of achievement goals, motivational climate, basic psychological needs, motivational regulation, self-regulation, as well as enjoyment and boredom. Linear regression analysis was used, and showed that approach achievement goals, perceptions of learning motivational climate and satisfaction of basic psychological needs were positive predictors of self-regulated learning in physical education. Also, self-regulated learning positively predicted enjoyment, but had a negative predictive effect on boredom. The findings of the present study highlight the role of motivational variables in self-regulated learning strategies and on student's affective responses within the context of physical education lessons.

Chapter 8 - Several theories have been proposed to explain delinquency; some include environmental factors and others consider personal variables. Personal, cognitive, and emotional deficits have been associated to delinquent or antisocial behavior. It has been argued that low self control is an internal system that manages antisocial behavior; self control is also understood as a tendency to pursue instant gratification. Besides, self-regulation has been related to violent behavior. Self regulation is conceptualized as the capacity to modulate emotions, attention and behavior; this concept has also been linked to emotional control. Effortful control is another term used for emotional regulation, which is associated to modulation of emotional reactivity and behaviors. Control or regulation of emotions and cognitions are the factors related to delinquent behavior. The aim of this chapter is to test a model including self-control and self-regulation as predictors of antisocial behavior. The sample was integrated by 164 participants, 58 were juvenile delinquents internalized in an institution and 106 were selected from the general community in a northern Mexican city. All of them reported some kind of antisocial behavior. Scales investigating impulsivity, risk, self-regulation and antisocial behavior were administered to the participants. The data were analyzed using structural equation modeling. Two factors were constructed: *self –control*, with impulsivity, sensation seeking, and risk indicators, and *self –regulation*, with indicators of emotional volatility, emotional intensity and activity regulation. Both factors exhibited a negative effect on antisocial behavior. The authors conclude that self-control is an important factor in the prediction of antisocial behavior; however there are additional variables that should be included in explanatory models of juvenile delinquency in prospective studies.

Chapter 9 - In hypnosis, suggested behaviours are characteristically accompanied by a diminished sense of effort and personal agency while suggested experiences, which strongly contradict objective reality, appear to be accepted without conflict. Dissociated control theory is a cognitive neuroscience account of hypnosis that emphasises functional disconnections (dissociations) within the predominantly anterior brain networks, which implement cognitive control. Profound alterations in the ongoing experience of the self outside the hypnotic context (labelled by Tellegen as absorption) are a key predictor of a person's ability to experience suggested distortions of reality. Tellegen (1981) defined the trait of absorption as arising from the interplay of two mutually inhibitory mental sets, the instrumental and the experiential mental sets. The capacity to set aside an instrumental set finds a clear counterpart in current neuroimaging and EEG studies of dissociated control in hypnosis. The consequent ability to adopt an experiential set has a clear counterpart in the recent discovery of a characteristic brain network during quiescent mental activity. Neuroimaging studies of suggestions used to induce hypnotic analgesia show strongly overlapping activations with the loci of this network which generates core aspects of internally focused self experience. Tellegen pointed to distinctive roles for the instrumental and experiential mental sets in psychophysiological self-regulation in order to explain the importance of the trait absorption in mediating the mixed pattern of results in earlier biofeedback studies. This account finds further support in recent studies on the roles of these mutually inhibitory neural networks in differing patterns of regulation of peripheral physiology. These findings provide an important foundation from which to understand the unique contributions of absorption and hypnosis in effective practices of self-regulation.

In: Psychology of Self-Regulation
Editor: Vassilis Barkoukis

ISBN: 978-1-61470-380-8
© 2012 Nova Science Publishers, Inc.

Chapter 1

ADAPTIVE METACOGNITIVE SELF-REGULATION AND FUNCTIONAL RESILIENCE-RELATED ASSETS IN THE MIDST OF CHALLENGING TASKS: A QUALITATIVE ANALYSIS

Nils Beer[*1 2] *and Giovanni B. Moneta*[1]
[1]London Metropolitan University, London, UK
[2]The University of Westminster, London, UK

1. EXECUTIVE SUMMARY

This study attempts to derive adaptive metacognitive self-regulatory processes by extending Wells and Matthews' (1994, 1996) and Wells' (2000) metacognitive model of psychological and emotional disorders and blending it with adaptive assets within a positive psychology framework. The assumption of this study is that adaptive self-regulation, specifically in the light of challenge, unpredictability or ambiguity, should contribute to emotional equilibrium, psychological well-being and – in the long term – to life satisfaction and other facets of quality of life. The current economic crisis with increased job insecurity necessitates even more pronounced adaptations to challenge and change.

Thirteen interviewees were recruited by purposive sampling based on their assumed positive metacognitions and adaptive assets. The participants were high profile executives and known to the researcher due to work-related contacts. A semi-structured interview schedule using positive metacognitive priming techniques was applied to elicit interviewees' recall of functional self-regulatory processes and also their accounts of adaptive personality factors (assets) when facing mid- to long-term challenging tasks or projects. The verbatim interview transcripts were analyzed by employing Hayes' (1997) Theory-led Thematic Analysis with focus on 'keyness' rather than prevalence of themes or categories. In an attempt to discover novel themes, potentially emerging above and beyond the framework of the interview schedule, the Theory-led Thematic Analysis was blended with Glaser and Strauss' (1967) Grounded Theory approach. Results showed that the majority of participants used adaptive metacognitive modes of information processing (Wells & Matthews, 1994, 1996) preventing potentially maladaptive metacognitive processing.

Beyond Wells and Matthews' framework participants also accounted for adaptive meta-emotional processes, e.g. mindfulness, frustration tolerance and refraining from inappropriate overreaction. In terms of personality assets, resilience (Masten & Reed, 2005) emerged as a key factor or theme with the two subordinate themes of agency and communion (Wiggins & Broughton, 1985). A plethora of additional more specific adaptive constructs were identified, e.g. persistence, optimism, and the ability to experience positive emotions in the midst of high challenge (Folkman & Moscowitz, 2000).

The study's overall results supported challenge models of resilience. With regard to the duration of the challenge scenarios the following distinction resulted: Very long-term challenge scenarios required a higher degree of resilience-related factors, whereas metacognitive and meta-emotional self-regulation was crucial when challenge was of short- to mid-term nature. Results can potentially inform intervention programs to effectively cope with and functionally adapt to challenge and unpredictability in occupational and other life domains.

The study provided the framework for the recently developed and validated Positive Metacognitions and Positive Meta-Emotions Questionnaire (*PMCEQ*, Beer & Moneta, 2010). The utlization of the PMCEQ in turn provided empirical evidence in quantitative follow-up studies that functional metacognitions and adaptive meta-emotions prevent maladaptive coping, foster adaptive coping and decrease stress perception, anxiety and depression (Beer & Moneta, 2011).

Keywords: Adaptation to challenge; Agency; Communion; Metacognitive self-regulation; Persistence; Resilience; Stress reduction

2. INTRODUCTION

Metacognition(s) can be conceptualized as knowledge and beliefs about one's own cognitive processes (Flavell,1979) and the individual's ability to deconstruct and understand their own cognitive processes involving reflection and awareness of various types of problem-solving (Milne, 2003). The concept of metacognition has been applied to educational settings with positive connotation, e.g. in Wang's (1992) metacognitive competence as the ability to reflect and exhibit advantageous self-regulation (self-regulated learners) and Sternberg's (1984) link between metacognition and adaptive behavior. In psychopathology the focus has

* Correspondence should be addressed to Nils Beer / Giovanni B. Moneta, London Metropolitan University, School of Psychology, Calcutta House, Old Castle Street, London E1 7NT, United Kingdom, Tel. +44 (0)20 7320-3408 / +44 (0)20 7320-2360, fax +44 (0)20 7320-1236, e-mail n.beer@londonmet.ac.uk / g.moneta@londonmet.ac.uk.

been on maladaptive metacognition. In extending schema theory, which predominantly emphasizes content rather than explaining mechanisms, Wells and Matthews' (1994, 1996) Self-Regulatory Executive Function (S-REF) Model has been a valuable and novel attempt to uncover the underlying cognitive processes in psychological disorders. Wells and Matthews' potential explanation of dysfunctional metacognitive processes provided the basis for amending, i.e. partially reversing, this model to derive and test a theoretical framework for core processes with respect to functional, adaptive metacognition (and meta-emotions) within this study.

Yet, two limitations of existing metacognitive models in the realm of psychopathology can be inferred: (1) focus on exclusively cognitive constructs and processes which lacks investigation of the social environment, and (2) not accounting for personality-related factors, specifically for adaptive assets. Research of assets has recently been conducted within positive psychology in order to counterbalance the disorder-focused view in psychopathology and psychiatry (Seligman, Steen, Park & Peterson 2005; Cloninger, 2006). Similarly, work and organizational psychologists emphasize the need for 'effective application of positive traits, states, and behaviors of employees in organizations' (Bakker & Schaufeli, 2008, p. 147).

This study attempts to derive and test adaptive self-regulatory processes individuals display when coping with challenging tasks and to identify associated self-empowering assets or personal resources 'cultivated' within stressful encounters.

2.1. Adaptive Metacognitive Self-regulation

The construct of positive self-regulatory processes is grounded in Wells and Matthews' (1994) S-REF Model and Wells' (2000) metacognitive model of emotional disorders by investigating core mechanisms within psychologically stable individuals. In accordance with Flavell (1979), Wells (2000) posits that metacognition refers to beliefs, psychological structure and cognitive processes implied in the control, interpretation and potential modification of thinking itself. However, in Wells' (2000) model metacognitions have by nature predominantly negative connotations because of their role in emotional and other psychological disorders.

Three metacognitive constructs are relevant for understanding psychological disorders, e.g. major depressive disorder (MDD), generalized anxiety disorder (GAD) and obsessive-compulsive disorder (OCD):

(a) Metacognitive knowledge (beliefs) referring to individuals' information about their own cognition and about task factors and learning strategies affecting this knowledge;

(b) Metacognitive experiences conceptualized as core appraisals of meanings of mental events, i.e. interpretations of cognitive experiences (thoughts) at a conscious level;

(c) Metacognitive control and regulation comprising a plethora of cognitive functions, e.g. allocation of attention, monitoring, checking and planning (Brown, Bansford, Campione & Ferrara, 1983). In emotional disorders metacognitive control and regulation is prolonged and negatively biased, manifested for example by excessive self-focused monitoring and threat monitoring by means of sustained attention to internal and external cues for threat (Wells & Matthews, 1994; Wells, 1995, 2000).[1]

The tenets of the S-REF Model as an information processing model for a range of psychopathological disorders are perseverative and ruminative negative thinking, dysfunctional attentional strategies filtering negative appraisals and subsequent maladaptive behaviors (Wells, 2000). The emphasis on processes, rather than merely content, of negative thoughts and attributions is an attempt to extend the content focus of Beck's (1967, 1976) influential schema theory.

The S-REF Model comprises three distinct but interrelated levels of cognitive operations (Wells, 2000):

(a) The schema-level which stores self-beliefs and knowledge in long-term memory;
(b) The core online-controlled processing level at which metacognitive self-regulation takes place by appraising events and utilizing metacognitive control strategies; this level comprises the core S-REF with a bidirectional relationship to the self-belief or schema level: the S-REF accesses self-beliefs (monitoring) and self-beliefs in turn inform the S-REF by selecting generic plans (control);
(c) The stimuli-driven lower level which is regarded as automatic, predominantly unconscious and requiring minimal attentional demands.

Online-controlled processing is the core metacognitive control strategy, taking place at the conscious level and hence being fundamental for the individual's self-awareness. Maladaptive attentional styles such as dysfunctional cognitive filtering (e.g., threat monitoring, monitoring for somatic cues and negative thoughts) are associated with negative affect and detrimental perseverative strategies (active worry and rumination). More importantly, such a perseverative S-REF disrupts and/or prevents engagement in functional cognitive processes required for goal achievement (Wells, 2000).

It can be concluded from the outlined metacognitive architecture and its underlying processes that Wells' (2000) metacognitive model of emotional disorders proposes that prolonged, rigid and negatively biased control (perseverative S-REF) results in negative affective states and, subsequently, in maladaptive, inflexible and passive (maladaptive) coping strategies and behaviour, thus preventing belief change, utilisation of more adaptive and agentic coping strategies and consequently undermining goal achievement. Bouts of prolonged S-REF activity, which are typical of emotionally volatile individuals, specifically when they encounter challenging or difficult situations, are linked to the object mode of processing; in object mode distressing thoughts are regarded as (threatening) facts. Psychologically stable individuals, when encountering difficulty or challenge, by contrast display a high proportion of the functional metacognitive mode; in metacognitive mode distressing thoughts are not regarded as facts but as cues which require subsequent evaluation in terms of potentially threatening impacts.

---

[1] The majority of researchers favor a central role of awareness in metacognition (metacognitive awareness). Others (e.g. Kentridge & Heywood, 2000), however, include unconscious knowledge, beliefs and processes as aspects of implicit or background information assuming that (some) metacognitive processes not necessarily evoke awareness/consciousness.

Wells and Matthews (1994) and Wells (2000) emphasize the aforementioned crucial distinction between metacognitive and object mode. The metacognitive mode is adaptive and impacts positively on belief elaboration by functionally informing the schema level; in contrast the object is dysfunctional and triggers prolonged bouts of S-REF activity. The object mode is only advantageous in genuinely threatening situations as opposed to mere threat perception, with the latter often displayed by individuals with vulnerability to psychological disorders.

An inherent confusion might occur since metacognitions in the context of psychological disorders have negative and dysfunctional connotations, whereas the characterized metacognitive mode reflects adaptive and functional self-regulation – as opposed to the maladaptive and dysfunctional object mode. This study's focus will be on the derivation of adaptive and functional S-REF predictions which are hypothesized to be inverse to maladaptive and dysfunctional S-REF predictions in Wells' psychopathological model.

Table 1 (first column) shows the core maladaptive self-regulatory processes of the S-REF model and their implications with regard to alternative adaptive self-regulation. Adaptive self-regulation (Table 1, second column) and subsequently reviewed assets (Table 2) provided the theoretical frameworks for this study

2.2. Functional Resilience-related Assets

Despite Wells and Matthews' (1994, 1996) and Wells' (2000) novel and evidence-based contributions to explaining underlying processes in the onset and maintenance of psychopathological disorders three possible limitations can be identified:

(a) The nearly exclusive focus on cognitive processes and the debatable tenet that negative emotions are exclusively resulting from biased, dysfunctional cognitive processing and appraisal;
(b) Not accounting for the role of social components and processes on psychological functioning and well-being[2];
(c) Not explicitly addressing positive personality-related factors or assets (e.g. resilience and persistence), which might intervene in (mediate) or moderate the relationship between challenging situations and (more adaptive) psychological functioning.

Masten and Reed (2005) conceptualize assets as measurable personality-related characteristics which predict positive future outcomes in terms of an outcome criterion – protective factors predict such positive outcomes in situations of risk or adversity. Diverse outcome criteria have been used in resilience research, e.g. psychological well-being or stability and academic, professional and social achievements. This study utilizes Masten and Reed's (2005) hierarchical approach with resilience as the highest-ranking asset: They emphasize that assets, protective factors, external resources and corresponding processes have been investigated in attempts to explain resilience.

---

[2] The neglect of social factors is somewhat surprising in the light of the well-established diathesis stress model of emotional disorders and empirical evidence of the buffering effects of social support (e.g. Cohen & Wills, 1985).

Table 1. Maladaptive versus adaptive self regulatory processes in taxing and challenging situations

Maladaptive cognitive self-regulation and strategies: S-REF Model (Wells & Matthews, 1994, 1996; Wells, 2000)	Adaptive self-regulation and strategies: Derived implications of the S-REF Model
Perseverative S-REF activity, i.e. chronic state of S-REF readiness with active worry, excessive self-focused attention, threat monitoring and rumination which conjointly constitute a cognitive attentional syndrome (*CAS*; Wells; 2000). In extreme cases of emotional disorders (e.g. MDD, GAD and OCD) the S-REF is in a state of nearly permanent readiness.	Short S-REF activity resulting in self-regulatory goal achievements. Such adaptive S-REF routines allow goal achievement when dealing with stress/challenge by: • Task-focused and flexible coping • Coping flexibility • Modification of beliefs (in cases where the envisaged goal cannot be objectively achieved due to current environmental limitations).
Predominant object mode of processing (thoughts are depicted as reality) with the following maladaptive outcomes: • Strengthening of maladaptive self-knowledge • Increasing occurrences and scope of negative automatic thoughts (NAT) • In turn further fostering negative self-schemata.	Prevalence of metacognitive processing mode (thoughts are seen as 'events' or cues which have to be evaluated) resulting in executing functional metacognitive control strategies (suspension of worry and redirection of attention) with the following adaptive outcomes: • Restructuring of knowledge by means of cognitive restructuring and reappraisal • Agentic goal setting (including attainable sub-goals) • Development of alternative plans • Coping flexibility for pursuing (alternative) goals.
Situations where external demands prevent goal achievement trigger activation of perseverative S-REF activity (worry and rumination) instead of (adaptive) coping flexibility.	In situations where external demands (temporarily) prevent the envisaged goal achievement individuals display goal and coping flexibility. Hence, S-REF activity can be moderated by abandoning or modifying not (instantly) achievable goals and developing achievable sub-goals.
Inflexibility: Holding rigid and inflexible beliefs, goals and, moreover impairments in the flexibility of coping and control of processes.	Flexibility in terms of both goal-setting and coping strategies (with the aforementioned ability to formulate achievable sub-goals).
Setting unrealistic (not achievable) goals which are prone to activate repeated instances of S-REF activity, as a failure to meet goals repeatedly activates S-REF processing aimed at (unsuccessful) discrepancy reduction. In addition inability to substitute unrealistic goals by achievable sub-goals (see above).	Setting realistic (achievable) goals or implementing goal correction: • Ability to break goals down into 'economic' and achievable sub-goals. • Flexible corrections in case of unachievable goal formulation.

Emotions are interpreted as reliable indicators how close an individual is to problem-solving or achieving important personal goals.	Emotions or 'feeling states' are appropriately interpreted or appraised as short emotional states and not as potential indicators of goal achievement 'stage'.
Effects of the 'locked-into states' (active worry, threat monitoring and rumination) block cognitive restructuring and functional cognitive reappraisal. Perseveration of S-REF activity blocks the adaptive restructuring of (self-) beliefs and results in corresponding decrease of (cognitive) resources.	Even within challenging encounters two core abilities are more adaptive routines for dealing with (perceived) threat: • Cognitive restructuring (resulting in freeing up resources) • Positive reappraisal (Focusing on the good what is happening and discovering opportunities for growth).
Low tolerance for negative emotions.	Healthy tolerance levels for negative emotions.
Patients diagnosed with an emotional disorder frequently report dissociations between intellectual ('cold') and emotional ('hot') beliefs in the sense that he/she rationally knows that the belief is false but still has the 'feeling state' that it is correct.	Predominant absence or only very briefly experienced episodes of dissociations between cognitive and emotional beliefs.
Albeit not specifically addressed by Wells and Matthew: Holding irrational beliefs in the sense of Ellis' (1962) 'musts', 'oughts' and 'shoulds'.	Absence of irrational beliefs in the sense of Ellis' (1962) conceptualization.
Activating events or environmental stimuli that (temporarily) block realistic desires are regarded and describes as 'awful, horrible, and terrible' (Ellis, 1987) → Low frustration tolerance.	Activating events or environmental stimuli that (temporarily) block realistic desires are merely regarded and describes as 'unfortunate and unfavorable' (Ellis, 1987) → Healthy level of frustration tolerance.

The link between (adaptive) self-regulation and resilience can be based on Luthar, Cicchetti and Becker's (2000) findings that resilience is a dynamic and complex process of displaying positive behavioral adaptation during encounters of risk, adversity or even trauma. Within these lines Masten and Reed (2005, p. 75) conceptualize resilience as 'a class of phenomena characterized by patterns of positive adaptation in the context of significant adversity or risk'; similarly Luthans (2002, p. 702) conceptualizes resilience as the 'capacity to rebound … from adversity, uncertainty, conflict, failure or even positive change.' Beneficial implications of low to moderate levels of risk exposure – in this study challenging tasks and projects – are suggested by Challenge Models of Resilience since moderate challenge levels might induce steeling effects, provide opportunities for mobilizing resources and practicing problem-solving skills (Rutter, 1987; Masten, Hubbard, Gest, Tellegen, Garmezy and Ramierez, 1999).

Werner (1995) and Werner & Smith (2001) provided empirical evidence from their high-risk children studies for the following six core components in resilience-forming processes:

(a) Distancing from unsupportive or even detrimental relationships (healthy defense mechanism) and finding other supportive individuals;

   (b) Developing functional and adaptive coping styles as a balanced combination of autonomy (agency) and support seeking (communion);

   (c) Developing competence in activities (occupational and leisure-related) resulting in a sense of pride;

   (d) Tendency to attribute positive meaning to crucial events (cognitive restructuring and positive reappraisal);

   (e) Ability to generate and use positive emotions (especially in the light of challenge) as positive emotions fuel resilience (Tugade & Fredrickson, 2000);

   (f) Creativity (implying flexibility in goal-setting, problem-solving and coping).

In addition to direct adaptation-enhancing effects of resilience, there is empirical evidence from the aforementioned research that exhibiting resilience is associated with a plethora of other protective factors or assets residing within individuals, e.g. optimism, self-efficacy, self-determination and positive affect.

Further core assets being investigated in this study are agency and communion (Bakan, 1966; Wiggins & Broughton, 1985) which can be subsumed under resilience since findings support the hypothesis that resilient individuals tend to be more active (agentic) and socially more responsive (communal) compared to those exhibiting less resilient coping patterns (Werner & Smith, 1982). The core view taken here is that these assets, despite residing within the individual, are not purely predetermined, trait-like dispositions but constructs that can be cultivated within adaptation processes: 'People can learn to flourish and to be more self-directed by becoming more calm, accepting their limitations and letting go of their fears and conflicts' and 'People can learn to be more cooperative by increasing in mindfulness and working in the service of others' (Cloninger, 2006, p. 71). This approach emphasizes the relevance of a balance between self-directedness (agency) and cooperativeness (communion).

The terms agency and communion were coined by Wiggins & Broughton (1985) based on their findings that dominance is strongly associated with instrumentality, and nurturance is correlated with expressivity, and they renamed these as agency and communion, respectively. Agency can be conceptualized as dissatisfaction with the environment (cause), tension reduction (goal) and modification of the environment in order to reduce its dissatisfactory properties; communion is seen as liking, i.e. acceptance or love, of the environment (cause), union (goal) achieved predominantly by establishing interpersonal relationships.

Beyond such adaptive constructs residing within the individual (health assets) potentially stabilizing or buffering effects of factors external to the individual (resources), specifically social support networks, have to be taken into account. Social support, the ongoing availability of supportive relationships, refers to the comfort, caring and esteem one individual receives from others (Wallston, Alagna, DeVellis & DeVellis, 1983; Cobb, 1976). Social support exerts either direct (main) effects, i.e. beneficial effects on psychological and physical well-being regardless of the existence of stressors, or stress-buffering (indirect) effects. The latter effects only unfold in the presence of high stress (challenge) and are attributed to emotionally-induced beneficial effects on the cardiovascular, endocrine and immune system (Cohen & Wills, 1985). Sarason & Sarason (1985) also provided evidence for the positive impact of social networks and embeddedness on individuals' physical and mental well-being.

Table 2. Resilience-related assets

Asset ⇨ Related constructs	Conceptualization & Associated Assets
Resilience ⇨ Agency ⇨ Communion ⇨ Hardiness	'Patterns of positive adaptation in the context of significant adversity or risk' (Masten & Reed, 2005, p. 75). Rutter's (1987) challenge model proposes that moderate levels of risk exposure or challenge imply beneficial steeling effects providing chances to develop problem-solving skills and resource mobilization.
Agency/ **Metacognition of** **agency** ⇨ Persistence ⇨ Need for achievement	Feeling that we are agents who intentionally can make things happen by means of our own actions; foundational to our understanding of ourselves and thus metacognitive in nature (Metcalfe & Greene, 2007). Attributes: Autonomous, self-confident and resilient; not giving up easily which implies persistence (Wiggins & Broughton, 1985).
Communion ⇨ Need for affiliation ⇨ Emotional intelligence	Expressivity and fellowship referring to relatedness and reflecting the need for interpersonal relationships with being empathetic and rich in emotions as core attributes (Wiggins & Broughton, 1985).
Persistence	Striving against opposition and obstacles; adaptive behavior continuing in times when the initiating stimulus is no longer present (Reber & Reber, 2001).
Need for achievement ⇨ Goal setting ⇨ Intrinsic motivation	Refers to a desire to accomplish tasks and attain standards of excellence (McClelland, Atkins, Clerk & Lowell, 1953, McClelland, 1985). Elliot & Church (1997) distinguish mastery goals reflecting intrinsic motivation and performance goals involving social comparison and competitiveness.
Need for affiliation	The counterpart to achievement motivation referring to rewarding intimate and social relationships regarded as essential for well-being (Reis & Gable, 2003).
Self-determination	Internally controlling one's behavior and acting on the basis of personal beliefs and values rather than on the basis of social norms and group pressure (Reber & Reber, 2001). Related to self-efficacy (Bandura, 1977, 1997; Maddux, 1999), internal locus of control (Rotter, 1966) and sense of personal control (Peterson, 1999).
Emotional intelligence	Ability to perceive, appraise and express one's and others' emotions accurately; ability to access and evoke emotions when they facilitate cognition (Solvey & Meyer, 1990).
Mindfulness/ **Psychological** **acceptance**	Mindfulness refers to acceptance of one's strengths and limitations, to accepting undesirable thoughts and still pursuing set goals (Bond & Bunce, 2000).
Optimism	Expectation that things (at least in the long run) will turn out well. According to Carver & Scheier (2005) optimists display a habitual tendency to experience life's difficulties with less distress.
Coping flexibility	Cheng & Cheung's (2005) differentiation and integration in stressful situations – relatively more monitoring in controllable situations.
Confidence and ability to generate positive emotions in the midst of stress	Predominantly achieved by means of positive reappraisal as a cognitive process by which people focus on the good of what is happening, resulting in personal growth (Folkman & Moskowitz, 2000). Positive emotions fuel resilience (Tugade & Fredrickson, 2002) and result in increased flexibility and creativity.

Core resilience-related assets which, alongside metacognitive and meta-emotional self-regulation, provided the second categorical framework for analyzing the interview transcripts by means of Theory-led Thematic Analysis are shown in Table 2.

2.3. Aims of the Study

This study attempts to expand and augment self-regulatory explanations of Wells and Matthews' (1994, 1996) S-REF Model by deriving and investigating functional and adaptive metacognitive and meta-emotional processes. In addition psychological constructs (assets and resources) that potentially enhance such positive self-regulation will be investigated. In cases of partially dysfunctional or labile cognitive and emotional self-regulation such assets might counterbalance detrimental impacts of dysfunctional self-regulation – in analogy to Fredrickson and Joiner's (2002) undoing hypothesis, which suggests that positive emotions contribute to regaining an equilibrium after the impact of negative emotions.

This study has three core aims. The first aim is to utilize the S-REF Model in order to investigate adaptive metacognitive self-regulation and its impact on psychological functioning. Furthermore, the additional adaptive role of personality-related assets will be examined by utilizing the resilience-focused framework. The final aim comprises the examination of potential interactions between functional self-regulation and self-empowering assets as adaptive constructs in the light of challenge (potentially negative change).

Rather than taking a purely cognitive approach, this study tries to use a more holistic conceptualization comprising cognitive, emotional and behavioral factors and mechanisms. The applied systemic approach requires a social-cognitive rather than a purely cognitive perspective which has been the underlying rationale for taking communion-related personality factors, specifically affiliation and emotional intelligence, into account within the semi-structured interviews.

A genuinely holistic approach would also examine potentially underlying biological factors of positive metacognitive and meta-emotional regulation, which is beyond the scope of this study. It should, however, be mentioned that there is recent research evidence that advanced and complex frontal lobe functions play a core role in purposeful and adaptive self-regulation (Goldberg, 2001). Hemispheric shifts in prefrontal brain activity have also been linked to mindfulness which in turn is regarded as a powerful means to self-regulate negative emotions (Davidson, Kabat-Zinn, Schumacher, Rosenkranz, Muller, Santorelli, Urbanowsky, Harrington, Bonus & Sheridan, 2003).

3. METHOD

A purely qualitative method was utilized in order to gain in-depth and rich accounts. Semi-structured interviews were conducted using a modified version of Matthew and Wells' (1994) metacognitive profiling template. Participants were asked to give narrative outlines of challenging projects or major tasks that started with profound difficulties but worked out well. The questions were aimed at priming participants to provide reflective accounts of how they mastered challenge or even risk and adversity in cognitive, emotional and behavioral respects.

3.1. Participants

Thirteen participants (five males and eight females) were recruited using a purposive sampling method – all of them were high profile professionals living in the Greater London area. Participants, known to the researcher within occupational contexts, were selected on the assumption that they would display functional and adaptive metacognitive self-regulation and hold adaptive personality assets. With 13 out of 14 participants agreed to take part in the study the response rate was high (93%).

The Ethical Guidelines of the British Psychological Society were strictly adhered to particularly with regards to informed consent, assurance of confidentiality and the right to withdraw at any time from the study. Prior to the interview participants received a short written briefing; after completion of the interview, participants were fully debriefed by means of face-to-face discussions.

Core demographic properties and brief descriptions of the individual challenge scenarios of the 13 interviewees are shown in Table 3. Interviews 1 to 6 were subjected to detailed qualitative analysis and will be presented in a case study format in the Results section with reference to their corresponding Case number in Table 3.

Table 3. Interviewee demographics and problem scenarios

PS (I)	Core Interviewee Demographics (M =Male; F = Female)	Theme or Topic (Challenge Scenario) (Order in accordance to reportage in Results)
1	F, Mid 30s, Psychology Teaching Assistant and PhD student.	First seminar teaching session in Psychology. **Case 1**
2	M, late 40s, PhD, Lecturer and Researcher in Psychology.	Undertaking his PhD (accounting for the process – rather than 'doing' a PhD). **Case 2**
3	M, mid 50s, Professor, Lecturer & Researcher in Psychology.	Conducting and coordinating a large-scale research project in the biomedical sciences on motion sickness lasting ten years. **Case 3**
4	F, mid 40s, Psychologist, Training on the 'MSc in CBT'.	Ongoing struggle to get her planning permission for converting a bought barn into a family home. **Case 4**
5	F, early 30s, BSc, MSc Psychology and PhD student.	Training and preparation for a London marathon as a charity run. **Case 5**
6	F, early 30s, Conversion Diploma in Psychology part-time student.	Adjustment to severe impacts resulting from major surgery at the age of twelve because of severe spinal scoliosis. **Case 6**
7	F, late 20s, Psychologist, Postgraduate training on the 'MSc in CBT'.	Negotiating reduction in working hours in order to conduct her one-year 'MSc in CBT' studies.

Table 3. (Continued)

8	M, early 60s, PhD, Psychology Lecturer	Application process for university recognition of a 'Research Centre'.
9*	M, 60s, Researcher and retired Professor of Psychology.	Chairing a charity (for sickle cell disease).
10*	F, mid 30s, PhD, Lecturer in Psychology.	Undertaking her PhD.
11	F, mid 30s, PhD, Postgraduate training on the 'MSc in CBT'.	Smoking cessation (after year-long contemplation).
12	M, early 50s, PhD, Lecturer and Researcher in Psychology.	Setting up and coordinating the CLaSS project (Cognitive Learning Strategies for Students).
13*	F, early 40s, BSc Psychology, Visiting Lecturer & Researcher in Psychology.	Reassuring a distressed student in her seminar group who violated ethical guidelines.

*Excluded from reportage in Results section.

3.2. Interviews and Interview Design

Applying a tailored metacognitive profiling/priming template to successful mastery of mid through longer term challenge scenarios, participants were asked to recall and give their narrative accounts of their mid- to long-term tasks or projects which started with profound difficulties but which they eventually managed to resolve. Interviewees were primed to recall their predominant thoughts, emotions and subsequent behavior when dealing with their challenging encounters. Asking them to account for stages and possible identification of the turning point were attempts to get an insight into underlying metacognitive and meta-emotional processes as well as the potential role of applied strengths (assets) and available resources.

The interviews took place within two university settings in London and lasted between 25 and 40 minutes. The recorded interviews were transcribed verbatim within a day of each interview and the audiotapes (files) were deleted after transcription.

The utilized interview schedule was based on a metacognitive priming template which was developed and tailored for this study with the primary focus on eliciting and capturing adaptive metacognitions as well as associated functional assets. The semi-structured interview schedule comprised the initial question in terms of a brief description of the nature of the challenging task or project. The subsequent questions, which attempt to elicit participants' recall of both functional self-regulation and adaptive personality constructs, were:

1. Can you recall your predominant thoughts and feelings when you first sensed the taxing or challenging nature of this task?
2. Did you think you could do something actively – intentionally make things happen by your self-directed actions when you first sensed the challenging nature of the task?

3. Did you also choose a more contemplative, listening approach? For example did you seek support or approval from other people involved in the task?
4. In addition to acting independently and/or relying on others: Did you try to step back in the sense of 'listening to yourself', trying to increase your self-awareness and thus 'relying on yourself'?

   Please try now to think about the 'turning point' and the impacts of your thoughts, emotions and actions:

5. When and how did you realize that you coped successfully or at least came closer to achieving your goals?
6. In hindsight, to what extent do you feel that the successful outcome was due to external factors and to internal factors, i.e. your thoughts, determination, and emotions?
7. Can you give an account of the importance of the following motives:
   a. Need for achievement and/or the need of power?
   b. Need for affiliation and/or reassurance?
   c. A combination of both. If yes, how did you find the balance?

3.3. Data Analysis

Data were analyzed by utilizing an integrative qualitative approach blending Hayes' (1991) Theory-led Thematic Analysis Hayes' with Glaser and Strauss' (1967) Grounded Theory. The latter technique was used in order to accommodate novel (non-category bound) findings emerging from the data.

Following Braun & Clark's (2006) framework, this study utilized the following specification of a Theory-led Thematic Analysis:

(a) Emphasis on relevance or 'keyness' rather than prevalence of themes;
(b) Preference for a rich description of the whole data set (comprising the 13 verbatim interview transcripts) rather than providing a detailed account of one particular aspect;
(c) Deductive approach since the structured interview schedule and the analyses were widely theory-driven;
(d) Focus on manifest (semantic) themes – however, partial analysis of latent themes to identify possible implicit metacognitions.

Adaptive self-regulatory processes (Table 1) and resilience-related assets (Table 2) provided the core background categories, in which primary coding was grounded. Secondary coding focused on more detailed accounts of potential subcategories. Importantly, rather than prevalence of themes the focus was on crucial themes capturing 'keyness' (Braun & Clarke, 2006) following Hayes' (2000) argument that prevalence or frequency of mentioned themes does not necessarily convey its relevance.

In order to account for non-category-led, unexpected findings emerging from the data, the second phase of the analysis utilized a Grounded Theory (inductive) approach beyond the scope to the thematic categories

4. RESULTS AND DISCUSSION

The section will provide an initial summarizing account of shared findings or commonalities in terms of both resilience-related factors and adaptive self-regulation which interviewees reported with reference to their challenge scenarios. Subsequently the analyses results of six cases will be reported and discussed in depth. Derived from the overall analysis of the individual interviews an integrative metacognitive framework of adaptive self-regulation in times of challenge, ambiguity and unpredictability shall be presented. The section finally addresses a reflexive outline of the study's inherent limitations.

4.1. Summary of Crude Commonalities

All 13 interviewees (I) were able to provide detailed and substantial recollections of their challenging mid- to long-term tasks or projects. With the exception of I 2 all had read and reflected upon the briefing sheet, which they had received at least two days prior to the interview. However, I 2 was orally briefed within the interview session and could, after a very brief reflection, identify 'Conducting his PhD' as a suitable and his most recent long-term challenge scenario.

It is noteworthy that participants were given free choice with regard to the challenge scenario they wanted to focus on; five (out of 13) referred to a task or an obstacle within their private life, the remaining eight interviewees all discussed occupational or academic challenge.

All interviewees displayed high levels of agency, self-determination and persistence and the majority were able to successfully achieve the envisaged result or overcome the obstacle. When task (project) completion or overcoming the obstacle was not (yet) achievable the majority of interviewees replaced unrealistic task-focused coping with adaptive belief alteration and/or plan modifications. Participants predominantly displayed functional metacognitive rather than dysfunctional object mode of cognitive processing. In addition, overall analysis revealed that the majority of participants had a strong sense of meaning and purpose.

Accounts with regard to question 2 (agency) and question 7a (need for achievement) corresponded for each interviewee in the sense that both psychological constructs were interlinked. There was analogous consistency between interviewees' 'ratings' in terms of questions 3 (communion) and 7b (need for affiliation). Investigating pair-wise correspondences between the related questions was a means of triangulation with the finding that intra-interviewee consistency was high.

Analysis of I 9 showed that his, albeit long-term, task did not incorporate profound challenge. His challenge perception of the task at hand was rather low, not necessitating demanding self-regulation or adaptive resilience-related assets: *I can't think of an instance where there was a major problem or a major setback which would have clearly required me to sit and think 'How do we handle this?'* I 9 was thus excluded from analysis because his accounts could not contribute to the research questions under investigation. On similar grounds I 10 and I 13, reporting merely very low levels of challenge, unpredictability or risk perception, were also excluded from in-depth analysis and reportage.

The remaining ten interviewees recalled moderate to severe challenge (perception) necessitating substantial self-regulatory processes and utilization of adaptive resilience related constructs in order to maintain psychological stability and to achieve the envisaged goal.

Despite the briefing, asking interviewees to account for a task or project of fairly long duration, a minority of interviewees accounted for a short-term task, e.g. I 1 (facing her first ever teaching session). A common discriminant pattern in terms of the challenge duration could be identified:

(a) The long-term scenarios (cases 2, 3, 4 and 6) required by their nature a higher degree of resilience-related factors, e.g. persistence, determination and frustration tolerance – compared to metacognitive and meta-emotional self-regulation;

(b) The short- and mid-term scenarios (cases 1 and 5) accounted for utilization of several metacognitive and meta-emotional self-regulatory processes – to a higher extent than relying on personality assets.

Core findings of the six most substantial and in-depth interviews will subsequently be reported in a case study format since both self-regulation and resilience factors were investigated as context-bound processes; nature and context of each single case scenario will be briefly summarized before reporting the main individual findings and providing concise conclusions for each analyzed case.

4.2. Case Results

Reportage, analysis and discussion of each of the six interview cases are structured in equal fashion: a) Case Summary, b) Case Results and Discussion and c) Case Conclusions. Verbatim interview citations are presented in italics.

4.2.1. Case 1: First Teaching Session – Adaptive Self-regulation

a) Case Summary

I 1, a female PhD student and psychology teaching assistant in her mid-thirties, provided substantial and insightfully reflected narrative accounts of her first ever teaching session (Research Methods workshop for Psychology undergraduates). She appeared to be extraordinarily well prepared for the interview on the basis of the briefing sheet. She emphasized that she perceived her first delivered seminar session as a challenge because she herself had just completed her MSc degree and had some doubts whether or not she would sufficiently qualified to deliver seminar sessions: *But I think in the back of my head I had the thing 'I am a bit like a fraud' ... I had just finished the course, I had no teaching experience.* Her second concern was speaking in public because her prior jobs in theatre production and for a literature agent required predominantly one-to-one communication. She emphasized having invested a lot of time and effort to be optimally prepared for her first and subsequent teaching session(s).

b) Case Results and Discussion

The participant reported negative feelings (not being qualified enough, fear of failure and specifically 'disclosure to students') just before entering the classroom for her teaching and public speaking debut. Remarkably, she could within seconds suppress bouts of active worry, excessive self-focused attention and threat mentoring. Rapidly ruling out the (costly) alternative of not facing the challenge by quickly and consciously rationalizing her fear reflected a core self-regulatory strategy for merely short S-REF activity and quick transition from object to adaptive metacognitive mode of processing:

The most vivid memory I've got was standing outside the classroom and hearing the voices of the students inside and actually having stood by the door prior to walking in ... I thought 'I can't do this, really can't do this – this is silly I am not going to do it – I am going to tell R. [module leader of the course] I am sorry [laughs], I made a mistake'.

I mean it wasn't a long thing, these things happen in four, five seconds although it feels like a lifetime – and I just stood there and you think: 'What's worse facing the class that I was scared standing in front of or facing the person who has employed me to doing the task and going downstairs and saying: 'Not only can I not do it but I have given you no notice that I cannot do it?'' So actually I was more scared of that than of the class and I walked in.

Her metacognitive awareness and instant and conscious shift from threat-focused object to task-focused metacognitive S-REF mode, which resulted in positive mood or even a flow-like state, is further underpinned:

So that was the kind of negative feelings; and I suppose the first time I walked in there was probably that kind of butterfly feeling. And then I think you go into performance mode and kind of the adrenaline kicks in and you give the session. And like I said at the end of the first session there were some really nice comments and I remember feeling on a real high after it, probably because I was so tensed up beforehand and I remember of walking out with a kind of big grin on my face 'Yes! I got through that - that was ok! I didn't get found out [laughs]'. So, yeah, I remember having been on a real high that evening.

The interviewee then addressed the reinforcing effect of her first successful session on follow-up sessions with regard to self-efficacy and motivation. There appeared to be a bidirectional link between agency, achievement and intrinsic motivation on one hand and functional self-regulation on the other hand. She reported prudent preparation for the first session (and subsequent sessions), thoroughly reflecting on lecturers she had perceived as good and poor as a student (modeling), and also taking notice of verbal and non-verbal feedback from students (e.g. fidgeting when bored). Such inherent agentic skills, preparedness and modeling might have contributed to displaying the adaptive metacognitive self-regulation, specifically prior to and within her first teaching session.

By addressing less successful or enjoyable teaching sessions the subsequent excerpt reflects her functional and discriminant monitoring, adaptive (external) attributionary style and, in parts, detached mindfulness:

I think you do know when you have performed well and when you have performed badly and everybody has times when they think 'I wasn't really in form today, I wasn't really in the mood and I wasn't as good as I could have been'. And there are times and you know that you have done ... And it can go both ways, you can give an average performance, and you can have good outcomes because the group happens to be kind of positive and engaged and they experience this [performance] as good.

And other times you can think that you have put in loads of effort, you have done lots of preparation, you really know your stuff, you have been keen and enthusiastic and this drippy group keeps on [inaudible] and you think 'That was about them [the students], it wasn't about me'.

c) Case Conclusions

The interviewee's in-depth and rich account supported the inverse metacognitive prediction derived from Wells' S-REF model that adaptive online processing, i.e. predominance of metacognitive over object mode, implies mood stabilizing or even uplifting effects. Above and beyond Wells' metacognitive prediction adaptive online processing here also fostered subsequent goal-setting and goal achievement.

4.2.2. Case 2: Process of Undertaking a PhD – Adaptive Self-regulation and Personality Factors

a) Case Summary

I 2 was the only participant who had not read the briefing sheet prior to the interview but at the beginning of the interview session he could 'instantly' identify his PhD as his most recent, long-term challenging task. Within the subsequently analyzed account he emphasized that undertaking a PhD was a process as opposed to 'doing a PhD': *It's a process – you cannot do a PhD.* Interestingly, although referring to a long-term (six-year lasting) project both adaptive self-regulatory processes and resilience-related assets were found, and interdependencies between functional self-regulation and assets could be identified.

b) Case Results and Discussion

At the very beginning of the interview I 2 stressed his crucial perception of the PhD as a process *... not a thing that can be done ... it certainly is a process. So thinking of it that way just made it like a hurdle of an enormous magnitude because you are thinking of it as a PhD rather than a series of step.*

His corresponding approach or strategy comprised adaptive self-regulation by means of breaking the huge PhD goal down into a set of smaller and achievable sub-goals (as opposed to unrealistic ones with the inherent risk of activating maladaptive S-REF prevalence). This strategy also resulted in high self-efficacy, motivation, self-determination and perception of agency and optimism in terms of goal-striving, regardless of the coexisting negative perception of the *'hurdle of enormous magnitude'* of the complex nature of pursuing PhD research. The following core links between metacognitive self-regulation and stability enhancing personality factors could be identified:

Contemplation – all the time, but there is a couple of tactics, I mean I used to get over that idea of the magnitude of the task: One lesson I learned from the army ...'when you have to climb a mountain, if you go up a steep hill, you take smaller steps'. ... Take smaller steps because it saves energy, all you have to do is take them because it takes you wherever you are going. That's why I had never any doubt that I would complete my PhD. ... I mean whenever you are faced with a task that's long, complicated and involved or in any other way challenging – in order to start it you have to have some belief that you can complete it, otherwise you wouldn't start it!

I 2 also utilized a second crucial element of functional metacognitive self-regulation by allocating activities and energy to controllable domains and not trying to control those beyond effective control. Applying Wells' (2000) model this can be interpreted as the conscious attempt to prevent bouts of S-REF activity/worry, i.e. predominance of adaptive metacognitive over maladaptive object mode. In this context I 2 reflected highly functional self-beliefs and metacognitive awareness in terms of different degrees of controllability and adaptive, functional online processing:

Yes, there are a huge number of things that we do, the outcomes of which or the acceptability of the outcomes is not for us to say. So for example as what I tell third-year project students who, once they've posted their project, continue to worry about – but it's out of their control and subsequent thought is taking up resources they could better spend on other things. But the idea of acknowledging and thinking about it and clearly defining the element that is not in your control is basically saving effort because once you've defined it you can close it off – ignore that. If you can't control it and you intend to do so, it's a waste of effort, better spent on things you can control.

This cognitive and behavioral pattern was consistent with Cheng and Cheung's (2005) concept of coping flexibility with greater monitoring in controllable and less monitoring in uncontrollable situations.

Referring to the anticipation of his Viva Voce and the corresponding involvements of his examiners, I 2 also identified this as being largely out of his control: *The only remaining grey area was whether or not what had been completed other people would find acceptable.* In this context he also showed impressive authenticity and agency reflecting his intrinsic motivation with regard to his PhD research area: *In any science, just because you are being assessed, do you present what your research shows or do you present what you think the assessors want to see? You got to be a scientist; you present what you find and not what you think what somebody else wants to read.* His self-determination, outstanding need for authenticity and honest self-reflection is even stronger underpinned: *But I wouldn't let the idea of being assessed determine what would have to be explained because I had only the results to go by.*

c) Case Conclusions

I 2 displayed highly functional self-regulatory metacognitive strategies combined with resilience-related stabilizing personality attributes. His apparent striving for authenticity combined with his strong intrinsic motivation promoted the underlying psychological needs for autonomy and competences in the sense of Ryan and Deci's (2000) self-determination theory. His outstanding confidence and self-efficacy is accounted by: *After the trouble I had with 'How to do a PhD' I never had a problem with thinking 'Can I do it?' It never occurred to me that I couldn't.*

4.2.3. Case 3: Conducting and Coordinating a Large-scale and Long-term Biomedical Research Project - Persistence

a) Case Summary

I 3 provided an interesting account of his longest ever research project which lasted approximately ten years, required his coordination of several involved researchers and the difficult access to appropriate apparatuses (long tracks for accelerating participants in order to conduct the research of motion sickness). He emphasized the extraordinary length of his project several times within the interview. In addition to their outstanding duration the experimental trials were complex and required a high degree of persistence: *It was probably the longest term experiment I have ever done, I had to sustain it over many years in different contexts and different laboratories.* Subsequently reported results show pronounced predominance of interwoven adaptive personality factors, e.g. agency, intrinsic motivation, persistence, self-determination but also communion, over and beyond adaptive self-regulatory mechanisms. The self-explanatory argument lies in the extraordinary duration of ten years which required resilience-related factors (specifically persistence). The very long nature of the trials might have implied slightly biased recall in the sense of overemphasizing the relevance of personality constructs in comparison to adaptive short-tem self-regulatory processes.

b) Case Results and Discussion

In the light of the extremely long duration and complexity of the novel experiment, persistence and high intrinsic motivation appeared to have been the crucial psychological constructs of I 3, which in turn had positive effects on successful goal setting. He expressed awareness and distinction between short- and long-term tasks: *Because the thing ... is to sustain your attention for a number of years. It's very different from setting short-term goals.* Persistence and formulation of flexible and attainable goals were specifically required because he reported frequent obstacles in terms of accessing the required apparatuses and getting the full cooperation of scientific staff involved in the lengthy trials:

I could see it was feasible, albeit difficult, and I could sense that my motivation went up and down but eventually I pushed it through! I meant there were gaps when I just did other things when there was no more progress to be made. In that sense I suppose the self-awareness is that you maintain the long-term goal in the back of your mind and when you see different possibilities you identify opportunities.

Continuously keeping the long-term goal in mind can in self-regulatory terms be interpreted as implicit metacognition in the sense of – from the very beginning – anticipating a successful outcome and the corresponding emotion of elevation: *I think the self-awareness almost came toward the end in the sense of pleasure and completion, the feeling that you have actually accomplished something that has lasted for many years.*

Optimism – the expectation that things in the long run will turn out well (Carver & Scheier, 2005) and hope with explicit agency and pathway thinking (Snyder, Rand & Sigmond, 1995) could clearly be identified. I 3 also supported Chang and Bridgewell's (1998) findings that optimists show fairly high frustration thresholds: *On the negative side I suppose was the frustration of not being able to get the equipment to work or sometimes not being able to get access to facilities.*

In addition to agency and other autonomy-related factors the interviewee also accounted frequently for communion and its associated positive affect: *The affiliation, the enjoyment of working in teams which is actually good fun, working in teams – is also important.* In the light of the fact that I 3 was the leader of the complete research project, he also reflected a healthy balance between agency and communion which is underpinned by his remark: *I think the core positive emotion is that research is often a shared activity, although you do quite a lot of contemplation and thinking things through yourself and trying to work on new ideas.*

c) Case Conclusions

I 3 displayed fundamental characteristics of persistence, agency and communion enabling him to maintain focus and successfully complete his complex and novel experimental research which lasted literally a decade. His outlined personality-related factors moderated the potentially detrimental impacts of experienced negative emotions. In addition it can cautiously be inferred that potentially implicit metacognitive awareness played a role with respect to anticipating a successful completion from the very start of his novel project.

Adaptive personality assets to a higher degree than functional metacognition appeared to have stabilizing and smoothing effects on fluctuating perceptions of challenge and also enabled frustration tolerance: *It's very difficult, you go through peaks and lows and it's a question of long-term goal setting and sticking to it.*

4.2.4. Case 4: Years-long Attempt to Get a Crucial Planning Permission – Functional Self-regulation and Adaptive Personality Factors

a) Case Summary

Ten years ago I 4 and her husband bought a huge piece of land (2.5 acres with a barn) with no planning permission on it, intending to convert the barn into a family house. They had sold their family property in order to fund the land purchase and moved into a caravan, which had been supposed to serve only as temporary accommodation. Receiving the necessary planning permission became a troublesome (still ongoing) 'battle' with the planning authorities, which have been continuously demanding adjustments to plans for the envisaged family home. The family (interviewee, her husband and two children) are still living in their caravan as interim accommodation! *We are still in the caravan. It's now ten years but we are on the way to finishing the project.*

This case was distinct from all the others because of its potentially devastating financial impact since not receiving the planning permission would have left the family with an effectively worthless piece of land. In terms of duration the case is identical to Case 3 (around 10 years) – however, with the core difference that the goal, i.e. receiving the all important planning permission, has not been achieved yet.

b) Case Results and Discussion

After her first attempt to get the – what was expected to be easily obtainable – planning permission I 4 experienced several months of unsuccessful negotiations with the planning authority, who repeatedly demanded successive submissions of modified plans and drawings. She then realized both the unanticipated and unpredictable reluctance of the planning authority *(there wouldn't be a sense of acknowledgement that we were working toward a goal)* and the implied and severe financial threat: *So I went from being very enthusiastic and excited, not being aware of any difficulties, to be really overcome with a sense of 'This is potentially disastrous'!*

She reported the onset of feeling helpless and overwhelmed but she could fairly quickly overcome her severely depressed mood by displaying personal agency and corresponding problem-focused coping. She could prevent the S-REF from becoming perseverative by what appeared to be linked to a protective personality characteristic in the sense of not suppressing anger and worry and additionally seeking agency-enhancing feedback: *And I think one of my basic characteristics is that I don't bottle things up. I talk about this with people in general actually, so I get feedback.* The concise statement also provides evidence that seeking support and the general social context potentially play a role in adaptive self-regulation. The subsequent quotation reflects this overlap of self-regulatory shift form object to metacognitive processing and her functional personal agency:

I was very, very depressed. And at that point then, I have a tendency, a sort of family motto which is 'There are no problems, there are only solutions'. And I sort of switched off into that and I said 'Right, how do we get out of this?' So I started then looking at understanding a lot of planning law. ... I could then actually start asking for meetings [with the planning commission] to address particular issues.

Interestingly, despite being depressed and anxious in light of the (objective) threat imposed by the dilemma, she only displayed a short bout of Wells' object mode of processing and apparently had pronounced metacognitive awareness of her capability to voluntary 'switch off', i.e. to engage in productive metacognitive mode of online processing.

In another meeting where she was joined by her husband the relationship with the planning officer deteriorated from what I 4 described as *negotiating mode into confrontational mode.* Her reaction to what she perceived as a *personal rather than professional challenge* was requesting a meeting with the head of the planning department. After familiarizing herself with the planning legislation at that time she prepared a document comprising counterarguments to the planning officer's standpoint: *I knew I had to give him [head of planning department] something.* Rather than overreacting by severe confrontation with the planning officer, i.e. refraining from acting impulsively, I 4 displayed the capability to originate and direct problem-focused actions for the given purpose; a reflection of personal agency (Zimmerman & Cleary, 2006).

I 4 also accounted for communion or need for affiliation expressed by seeking emotional support from her mother and having a mutually supportive relationship with her husband: *My husband and I generally are a very united front.* However, she did not overly rely on support or communion *(that was purely for emotional support because there was no other way how she [mother] could have helped us).* Rather than becoming highly sociotropic (McBride, Bacchiochi & Bagdy, 2006) her motives for healthy affiliation were to obtain positive stimulation and receive emotional support (Hill, 1987), thus not undermining her above outlined personal agency and functional instrumentality.

In addition early social learning processes (Bandura, 1977a, 1977b, 1997) had apparent stabilizing effects: I 4 referred to her mother as an agentic role model, having observed her adaptive coping styles in challenging situations: *But I think I also have a bit of a family motto in that my mother is a very proactive person, so I have got that sort of model. ... And I saw her take charge of a difficult family situation when I was still a child. ... So I think I had a model of actually being quite active, so that was helpful.*

A further resilience reflecting and enhancing characteristic was her ability to generate positive emotions in the midst of challenge by means of positive reappraisal (Folkman & Moskowitz, 2000): *Very consciously I made the decision to turn it into a positive experience rather than a negative.* Importantly, 'consciously' making the decision reflected her adaptive and pronounced metacognitive awareness in terms of voluntarily making this decision.

The subsequent quotation reflects detached mindfulness or psychological acceptance as a metacognitive concept operating above the level of immediate experience (Donaldson, 2003) and according to Roger, Jarvis and Najarian (1993) being more adaptive than avoidance and emotional coping:

Being mindful? Only in the sense that I had to question some about my assumptions of a regular lifestyle. I was aware that, in order to achieve this, the ultimate goal obviously was to have the family house, not to get it through the planning permission process. And it was really looking whether I was prepared to living in a caravan with my children in order to achieve it.

c) Case Conclusions

In analogy to Case 2 this case showed several interdependencies between adaptive self-regulation and protective personality-related factors. With regards to the latter I 4 showed a psychologically healthy and stable balance between agency and communion with no tendencies of becoming overly instrumental or sociotropic.

In terms of self-regulation this case revealed the ability to reduce perseverative and ruminative S-REF activities to brief episodes (to exert effective control) and subsequent successful implementation of adaptive metacognitive mode.

The unobservable metacognitive mode could be derived from the interviewee's reflective and rich narrative accounts; moreover, her adaptive processing was manifested in agentic actions and communal seeking for support – reflecting the interplay between self-regulation and adaptive personality assts.

4.2.5. Case 5: Preparing for a Charity Marathon Run – Functional Self-regulation and Anticipation of Beneficial Impacts on other Life Domains

a) Case Summary

I 5 – a female PhD student in her early thirties – provided an in depth account of the cognitive, emotional and behavioral strategies she applied to optimize her preparation for a London marathon. She reported two prior participations in marathons but emphasized the challenging nature of this one because it was a charity run: *... on this third one I was actually running for a charity – so there was a lot at stake.* She accounted for both motivation-enhancing self-regulation and functional personality factors. The distinctiveness of this case was that she anticipated beneficial effects from the training and ultimately from successful completion of the crucial marathon above and beyond the inherent physical and psychological benefits in terms of other life domains.

b) Case Results and Discussion

I 5 expressed high motivation and dedication to raise money for the charity but also showed clear awareness of the challenging nature of her goal (completing the marathon within the given time limit), which would require rigor, discipline and strategy as means for efficient preparation. She reported self-motivation and *keeping the charity in mind* as core initial strategies at the beginning of her 16 weeks' training schedule.

However, she also experienced feelings of anxiety not managing the required marathon preparation because of other commitments in her life at that time: *And then that really made me anxious and I kind of got self-absorbed in those feelings and it got to a point where as soon as I was thinking about running for a charity, I had to get up and think about this more sensibly. So I had been thinking in terms of my nutrition, in terms of my potential and how I could get through this.* Within her constructive contemplation she identified *thinking more positively in terms of what I can achieve, in terms of what is more realistic* as effective means for goal achievement.

Still at the beginning of the interview she also reported *feelings about just loosing self-confidence,* which she tried to control and rationalize be seeking support from her more experienced fellow runners.

In terms of her attempts to seek adequate social support two features are noteworthy: (1) similar to I 4 she did not overly rely on this support, and (2) she looked for informational support in terms of a guideline for 'normal' experiences of other runners: *Just to find out what experiences are normal and what I should normally be thinking. ... So by knowing what is normal and what is not normal kind of helped me to focus a lot more.* Within Wells and Matthews' (1994, 1996) metacognitive model her seeking for 'normality feedback' could be interpreted as an adaptive cognitive strategy for optimal resource allocation – facilitating the required preparation by focusing on the training schedule rather than worrying about possibly not meeting the required time limit in the final run. This was supported by her subsequent remark: *Yes, the motivation to see just how much I can go and just using strategies like maybe putting relaxing music on while I am running and focusing on that.*

When asked whether she could clearly identify a turning point, which gave her the confidence to meet the time limit in the charity run, she pointed to serendipity; toward one of her final training runs she got lost and then realized that she had actually run an additional three miles, 22 miles rather than the 19 miles she meant to run – but within the set time limit for the envisaged 19 miles. She expressed that this experience resulted in an enormous confidence boost: *Even though I was very angry with myself of getting lost, at that point I actually realized 'If I can do 22 [miles] than I can definitely do the extra 4 [miles]'.*

I 5 could also give a rich account of a reciprocal interplay between self-regulation and personality-related assets in terms of maintaining her training commitments: anticipated future transfer, instrumentality and expressivity. The following extract provides evidence for her corresponding metacognitive awareness:

All these aspects made me realize I could probably transfer this into other areas – just individual things like maybe that I kept motivated, that I kept focused on the particular task at hand, that I had people around me who were able to support me, as long as I kept relaxed and not make it the main, not to dominate my life.

She also expressed clear metacognitive awareness in terms of a psychologically adaptive balance between agency (instrumentality) and communion (expressivity): *This kind of using those aspects like this support from friends and the family, knowing that I can actually push myself to a further level of ability, just being aware of those things and that this can easily be transferred to other areas in my life.*

The anticipated transfer of increased self-efficacy into other life domains expressed highly functional flexibility, in turn potentially facilitating successful coping with and adjusting to future challenges in different situations and encounters. This transfer – reflecting adaptive online processing and high metacognitive awareness – informed (and was informed by) her belief system; in Wells & Matthews' (1994, 1996) S-REF model this was manifestation of the reciprocal link between online processing and schema level. The following quotation provides evidence that her corresponding and increasing metacognitive awareness built up in a process like fashion:

Initially I thought the most important point was crossing the line and that I was actually going to raise money for the charity, but in fact it was an overall belief that, if I am capable to put my mind to something, keep motivated and keep self-conscious about a period of that time, that I then could probably transfer this kind of focus to other areas of my life that are not particular physical.

The anticipated synergy effects – transfer of focus into distinctively different life domains – reflected her flexibility: *I might use these aspects in other areas – maybe my studies or going for a new job or maybe when I have got doubts whether I can do something or not. Then I might actually use these experiences I have learned through a physical process for other processes.*

c) Case Conclusions

I 5 – who completed the marathon well under the required time limit – showed an adaptive balance between agency and communion. She also had functional metacognitive awareness which she could even increase in the light of the challenge perception. She appeared to have a high sense of personal control but, moreover, this personal control as conceptualized by Peterson (1999) had effects on increasing emotional, motivational, psychological and behavioral vigor.

She provided narrative evidence for metacognitive awareness, functional metacognitive processing and a plethora of resilience-related assets, e.g. achievement and intrinsic motivation, persistence and clearly hardiness comprising commitment to different domains, personal control and perceiving changes as challenges (Maddi & Kobasa, 1984; Maddi 1998).

4.2.6. Case 6: Coping with Severe Spinal Scoliosis – Ongoing Adaptations and Thriving in the Light of Early Experienced Health Adversity

a) Case Summary

The female interviewee in her early 30s addressed a major health-related challenge or even adversity. Currently in employment and also a part-time Psychology student she had been diagnosed with spinal scoliosis at the age of 12 and had to undergo a series of major surgeries over a two-year period. The short-term implications of the operations were that she had to live in a body brace during this two-year period. Her narrative account starts with her difficult decision-making process in terms of whether to undergo or not to undergo the potentially risky operation. Interestingly her parents tried to encourage her to consciously make this decision herself at that young age. She then provided insight into the continuous adjustments – specifically emotionally – to her condition.

Among all cases this was the most severe with a plethora of ongoing adjustments I 6 had to and still has to make. It was a case of severe health adversity requiring resilience as conceptualized by Luthar, Cicchetti and Becker (2000) as a dynamic process of positive adaptation exhibited by individuals when they are confronted with significant adversity or trauma. The personality-related strengths (assets) she mobilized in order to cope with her illness-implied handicaps – and her capability to even thrive amid this adversity – are outlined and discussed in the following section.

b) Case Results and Discussion

I 6 had to make her most daunting decision when she was diagnosed with severe spinal scoliosis at the young age of twelve. She accounted for having been honestly informed about her options by the consulting surgeon: not undergoing the operation would have incorporated the inherent risk of ending up in a wheel-chair; the operation, however, implied some risk. She recalled vividly at this stage not feeling in control because of her limited understanding of the condition, feeling different from her healthy peers and also due to her anxiety with regard to a possible HIV infection because the operation necessitated blood transfusions.

The surgeon suggested a time frame of one month for her to weigh up pros and cons and her supportive parents showed her more the advantages of undergoing the operations but, yet, did let her make this crucial decision: *But surprisingly they [her parents] didn't dictate what I have to do – they did allow me the choice!*

This can be interpreted as an insightful guidance by her parents who at the same time gave her some feeling of autonomy and control. Due to her young age and the severity of both the illness and the decision-making process she was heavily relying on her family's support: *I feel that I didn't have a healthy inner voice because I was going through a big crisis and so I was heavily dependent on my family.* She experienced the crucial emotional support and crisis support (Cohen & Wills, 1985; Brown, Andrews, Adler & Bridge, 1986) but – as later accounts showed – this did not result in over-dependency or sociotrophy.

In the process of having to cope with the diagnosis and making this all important difficult decision I 6 displayed an impressive ability to generate positive emotions in the midst of high stress or even distress (Folkman & Moskowitz, 2000) by means of positive reappraisal or, more specifically here, by a sense of early maturation and character development: *Although it was daunting, I think a positive sense was that it made me aware and grow up very quickly.*

She then reported that an additional source of distress and crisis was that her parents were breaking up (about three years after the successfully carried out operation). Again, her ability to generate positive emotions amid the simultaneously experienced distress could be derived by her reflection on all the positive focus and emotional support she had been receiving from her parents: *I mean it could have been the other way, they [her parents] could have been negative, and then I think I would have followed that through.*

She identified the subsequently received support from her friends and peers, the feeling of belonging and having been fully accepted as a person, and not having been stigmatized as the crucial turning point:

I think having really loving friends ... I was very fortunate of at school having really loving friends and I was always in the popular group. So I was really fortunate to have that support from my friends: They would come to the hospital in their lunch break, you know, even though I was away from school for a year, they would come and visit me, so my peers were wonderful, they didn't see me, they wouldn't class me as being disabled, or being different or wouldn't treat me differently. I was 'A' [initial changed] who had gone through the operation and they wanted to support me. Yeah, they were real friends and that was the turning point and that motivated me and I really wanted to go back to school. ... So I had a really good turning point in that my friends hadn't abandoned me.

In terms of her friends' support she also said: *I think that really helped me to rehabilitate and really take control* which suggests that meeting her need for affiliation served at the same time as a catalyst for gaining agency and instrumentality. This was supported by her accounts at the end of the interview when having been asked how relevant she rated the need for achievement and she emphasised that achievement alongside with affiliation played a very big role in her life.

When talking about achievement she also addressed impressive resilience in terms of overcoming insecurities – reflecting the steeling effects her experienced health-related adversity have until now:

I still have insecurities in achieving – I always doubt myself. But that helps me as a driving force to proof myself 'Actually you can do it'. ... And it's something I am kind of learning to deal with, kind of the belief 'You have achieved a lot, look, now you're doing your second degree'. ... There is probably still the insecurity as a child within me – even though I am 33 years now. But I think probably one of the drives is: 'Everything I have been through as a young child is a motivator for me, I can get through this - I can do this'.

c) Case Conclusions

Case 6 was distinct from all other cases in three respects. First, the interviewee reported the most severe challenge of the group, close to health-related adversity. Moreover, she provided a life-span account from childhood through adolescence and early adulthood of her required and ongoing adaptations. Finally, for her, provision of not over-protective but, yet very committed, support from family, friends and peers appears to have fuelled agency, commitment and 'drive'.

The last aspect supported the hypothesis that people can thrive and flourish even in the light of adversity. In addition her narratives reflected character development, which according to Cloninger (2006) results in greater self-awareness leading in turn to greater happiness. She clearly expressed remarkable self-awareness with respect to her maturation process: *Although it was daunting, I think a positive sense was that it made me aware and grow up very quickly.*

4.3. Discussion of the Resulting Integrative Metacognitive Framework of Adaptive Self-regulation in Times of Challenge, Ambiguity and Unpredictability

Three cornerstones of functional self-regulation in the light of severe challenge emerged from the interview data; the corresponding constructs and processes were found to be interlinked. In addition to resilience-related factors the analysis focused predominantly on functional metacognitions. Extending Wells' purely cognitive approach the study furthermore took meta-emotions into account. Wells and Matthews' (1994, 1996) and Wells' (2000) metacognitive model of emotional disorders predicts that vulnerable individuals display perseverative thoughts and rumination which in turn prevent effective mind-setting for problem-solving and subsequent goal achievement. Such dysfunctional cognitive, emotional and behavioral patterns are specifically triggered by ambiguous and unpredictable situations and by both short-term and long-term challenges.[3]

In contrast, emotionally stable individuals, when confronted with severe challenge, perceive confidence in rapidly getting out of worrying perseveration and depressive rumination and furthermore confidence in their abilities to refrain from impulsive overreactions. Thus they have the capability to rationally assess their emotional cues. Adaptive metacognitions and meta-emotions of this kind facilitate subsequent functional cognitive and behavioral responses comprising mind-setting for problem-solving, achievable goal formulation and confidence in final goal achievement. More specifically stable individuals display the capability of setting flexible and attainable hierarchies of goals being particularly relevant when obstacles and unpredictable events require adjustments of sub-goals or when tasks are perceived as overwhelmingly huge.

4.3.1. Confidence in Extinguishing Perseverative Thoughts and Emotions

Severe challenge potentially incorporates overly taxing appraisals with possible onset of cognitive dissonance and ruminative negative thinking cycles, as conceptualized by Wells and Matthews' (1994, 1996) perseverative S-REF. In turn these dysfunctions might result in even more pronounced filtering of negative appraisals with rigid attentional focus on threat and danger rather than surmountable challenge. Maladaptive self-regulatory processes of this nature inhibit or at least significantly delay problem-solving and subsequent goal achievement.

In contrast the psychological stable participants in this study accounted for their confidence in rapidly extinguishing perseverative thoughts and emotions. Interestingly, however, the interviewees reported that their experienced challenge scenarios frequently triggered brief cyclical negative thinking patterns. However, rather than getting into spirals of rumination and perseveration they could effectively dipose of these. Successful cessation of rigid and passive perseveration provided adaptive attentional, cognitive and emotional resources resulting in confidence and persistence amid challenge. Resilience and a sense of persistence played by nature a more important role in long-term challenge scenarios than in challenges of short duration. Interviewees frequently also accounted for associated positive emotions such as pride, integrity or just relief due to dissolution of cognitive dissonance. In conjunction with reported problem-solving strategies and behavioral flexibility our findings suggest that confidence in the extinction of perseveration and rumination leads to positive emotions which in turn enhance persistent and flexible goal striving. The outlined adaptive self-regulatory processes can be explained in the light of Fredrickson and Joiner's (2002)

---

[3] Several studies have provided empirical evidence that (maladaptive) metacognitions mediate the relationship between stress/challenge and psychological disorder (Spada and Wells, 2005; Spada, M., Nikcevic, A., Moneta, G.B. and Ireson, J., 2006; Spada, M., Nikcevic, A.V., Moneta, G.B. and Wells, A. 2007). These studies measured metacognitions with Wells and Cartwright-Hatton's (2004) Meta-Cognitions Questionnaire 30 (MCQ-30) comprising five factors: Positive beliefs about worry, negative beliefs about worry regarding uncontrollability and danger, low cognitive confidence, need to control thoughts and cognitive self-consciousness.

broaden-and-build theory of positive emotions. The core tenet of the broaden-and-build approach is the proposition that experiences of positive emotions empower momentary thought-action repertoires.

In terms of the time required for successful extinction or suppression of negative and potentially perseverative thoughts and emotions interviewees reported different timeframes depending on the duration and severity of perceived challenge and furthermore apparent individual differences. Interviewee 1 was confronted with nervousness and doubts when standing outside the classroom to deliver her debut university teaching session and could literally within seconds prevent the onset of negative and inhibitory thinking allowing her to confidently enter the seminar room and facing the challenge by delivering the teaching session: ... *these things [rationalization of fear] happen within four, five seconds*. Interviewee 4 had to master 10-year long bureaucratic obstacles in getting a financially crucial planning permission. Continuously changing requirements of the planning authority and provocative behavior of the planning officer in charge necessitated frequent conscious efforts to prevent ruminative perseveration and to refrain herself from overreactions in order to focus on distinct and flexible actions to persistently pursue her primary goal.

Interviewee 7 (not reported as individual case study), who had to negotiate with her employer her request to take time off work in order to undertake her envisaged one-year MSc course, experienced intermediate bouts of rumination and depression (perseverative S-REF activity). After her employer's initial 'no' she reported active worry and perseveration over one week. Interestingly, her worry and subsequent anger became the catalysts for gaining self-awareness of her cognitive dissonance induced by her employer's instant refusal of a possible compromise. A week later she insisted on a meeting and discussion with her employer and achieved her envisaged part-exemption in order to pursue her MSc course. In her case the negative emotions of frustration, worry, rumination and depression resulted in constructive anger, empowering her to seek the determined and challenging negotiation with her employer: *Initially I just accepted the 'no' and I was feeling quite angry, upset and depressed ... I got angry because they just said 'no'*. She expressed her feelings of relief and liberation when challenging her employer: *Maybe it was also liberating to become active for myself and to make the decision*. Her determination in turn was reflected by: *Then I thought, I have a choice here, and I think I was probably taking my feelings more seriously*. This was a convincing example of constructive and clarifying interpretation of emotional cues which is further discussed in the following section.

In conclusion, interviewees provided evidence for their confidence and ability to prevent getting stuck in negative loops of preservation and rumination when facing difficult situations, but of varying time horizons. Although in the case of interviewee 7 the potentially negative emotion of anger was reported, it was a constructive emotional cue for subsequently challenging her employer; moreover, she did this without reacting overly impulsive. The ability to refrain from impulsive and potentially detrimental overreactions is further discussed in the following section.[4]

---

[4] It is argued here that Wells and Matthews (1994, 1996) and Wells (2000, 2009) do not take into account that such intermittent bouts of S-REF activity can exert potentially constructive and functional effects on problem solving and goal achievement as shown by the interviewees in this study.

4.3.2. Confidence in Interpreting Own Emotions as Cues, Restraining from Immediate Reaction and Mind-Setting for Problem-Solving

Above and beyond their confidence in controlling negative thoughts, psychologically stable individuals have an adaptive and distinctive style how they attend to and deal with emotions. Goleman (1986) posits that such self-awareness results in some sophistication and clarity about their emotional lives. With emphasis on emotions rather than merely cognitions Goleman argues that such mindfulness protects against perseveration and rumination when experiencing brief episodes of low mood, thus contributing to the ability of getting out of the bad mood sooner. Wells' (2000) refers to the functional awareness in terms of emotions being merely transient states rather than accurate reflections of reality. This awareness or clarity of one's own emotions is at the heart of meta-emotions and has the additional functional effect of preventing potential overreactions: 'Self-awareness is not an attention that gets carried away by emotions, overreacting and amplifying what is perceived. Rather it is a neutral mode that maintains self-reflectiveness even amidst turbulent emotions' (Goleman, 1996, p. 47).

The aforementioned Interviewee 7 got angry but rather than resulting in impulsive overreaction her anger brought clarity and determination to seek discussion and negotiation with her employer. Her case highlights functional effects of affect recognition which Vaillant (2000) conceptualizes as an adaptive mental health mechanism – reducing potential conflict and cognitive dissonance in the midst of unpredictable or unanticipated change. Vaillant regards these mental health mechanisms as crucial for restoring psychological homeostasis. Interestingly, however, in the case of Interviewee 7 her intermediate episode of worry and rumination (the active S-REF in Wells' terminology) appeared to have been a catalyst for her subsequent goal-directed negations.

Another vivid account for frequently required restraint from immediate reaction provided interviewee 8 (not reported as individual case study). An anticipated straightforward university application for the recognition as a Research Centre adversely progressed into an 18 months long administrative struggle. He reported increasing frustration specifically because *in obtaining centre status there were no resource implications for the university*. The interviewee's self-awareness or mindfulness with subsequent mind-setting for problem-solving is clearly reflected by his statement: *I suppose listening to oneself was part of this, deciding not to react adversely in terms of the frustration with the bureaucracy* and even more pronounced: *On reflection I think the strategy that I started to take was 'Don't overreact to the system, feel your way through, explore the possibilities and work toward the solution'*. This quotation reflects a high degree of frustration tolerance and, moreover, his underlying confidence in maintaining emotional and behavioural self-control (Gleitman, Fridlund & Reisberg, 2004), thus fostering subsequent problem focus.

4.3.3. Confidence in Setting Flexible and Feasible Hierarchies of Goals

Theories of self-regulation propose an inherent link with goal setting and subsequent goal attainment. Zimmerman (2000) even conceptualizes self-regulation as systematic efforts to direct cognitions, emotions and behavior toward one's goal achievement. He posits that goals empower self-regulation by exerting positive effects on motivation, self-efficacy and satisfaction. Goal formulation facilitates selection and application of efficient strategies and also enhances monitoring of goal progress (Schunk, 1995). The outlined positive effects imply adaptive synergy effects on psychological well-being and are more pronounced if individuals try to attain specific, proximal and self-set goals.

Schunk (1995) emphasizes that potential difficulties occur when single goals are attainable in isolation but together are subject to conflict. Interviewee 7 accounted for the case of conflicting goals which she resolved by setting clear priorities, in her case favoring the envisaged MSc even at the expense of not getting the required work reduction and taking the inherent risk of job loss into account. Her previously reported anger and the resulting clarification of her emotions were the prerequisites for her determination to negotiate with her employer. Setting the two-fold hierarchy by weighing the MSc pursuit higher than maintaining her job can be interpreted as the final determinant in the outlined process of positive self-regulation and goal attainment. Her employer accepted her required job reduction; thus she achieved both of the two potentially conflicting goals simultaneously. It can be argued that a lack of confidence in extinguishing her initial, albeit one week long, rumination and worry could have easily resulted in overreaction to her employer with the likely outcome of not getting the requested job reduction.

The accounts of interviewee 4 (reported as individual case study) clearly identified various obstacles within her attempts over ten years to get the crucial planning permission. Regardless of her experienced frustration and short depressive episodes she could then sustainably focus on her overall goal and, more importantly, could identify adaptive and flexible strategies to achieve necessary sub-goals. These sub-goals comprised acquisition of competence by gaining substantial knowledge of planning permission law, not losing emotional control in the light of ever changing demands by the planning officer and eventually seeking crucial support from the head of the planning authority. It can be concluded that continuously keeping her long-term goal in mind required implicit metacognitions of anticipating goal achievement from the very beginning. Her mindset *I have a tendency ... which is: There are no problems, only solutions* provided the confidence and agency for her goal directed and persistent actions.

Interviewee 2 (reported as individual case study) perceived his PhD, which he pursued when being in full-time employment, as *a hurdle of an enormous magnitude* and conceptualized his PhD research as a process which had to be broken down into attainable steps or sub-goals: *When you have to climb a mountain, if you are going up a steep hill, you take smaller steps.* At the same time he had impressive confidence in his capability: *I never had a problem in thinking: Can I do it? It never occurred to me.* Moreover, he reported not having heavily relied on meetings with and feedback from his supervisor but utilizing a genuinely scientific and prudent approach to his PhD research. This reflected a high degree of intrinsic motivation for a self-set goal which significantly enhanced functional self-regulation as aforementioned.

In conclusion for the majority of interviewees there appeared to be a self-regulatory sequence of related processes consisting of initial, but not necessarily immediate, extinction of worry, perseveration and rumination resulting in emotional control over frustration with restraint from overreactions. This was followed by subsequent problem focus and further fostering of flexible and hierarchical goal setting and adjustments of sub-goals when necessary. As shown, the processes partially overlapped and did not necessarily follow strictly linear transitions. Interestingly brief bouts of frustration, depression and anger resulting from external obstacles are not necessarily counterproductive but might in fact serve as motivation increasing stimuli. This, however, requires metacognitive and meta-emotional competence in the sense of refraining from impulsiveness and at the same time flexible goal pursuit in the midst of challenge or even adversity.

4.4. Reflexivity and Inherent Limitations

The systemic qualitative study approach tried to investigate participants' cognitive, emotional and behavioral mechanisms by means of interviewees' retrospect narrative accounts. Apart from possible response bias and researcher expectations one has to anticipate slightly decreased validity due to potentially somewhat vague recall. However, the utilized positive metacognitive priming technique and the nature of the challenge scenario – mid- to long-term with successful outcome – should imply only minimal recall problems due to the personal significance of the challenge scenarios. Interviewee 2 (reported as individual case study), who did not read the briefing prior to the interview, provided some evidence for the instant recall of such individually highly significant scenarios.

There is research evidence from several studies suggesting that resilience, the main asset under investigation, is potentially domain-specific. In this context interviewee 5 (reported as individual case study) provided an interesting account of her ability to transfer positive assets from the experienced (physical) domain into other anticipated life domains.

5. CONCLUSIONS AND APPLICATIONS

To date hardly any research has been conducted on reversing evidence-based psychopathological models within a positive psychology approach and their applications in terms of to psychological functioning, stability and well-being.

The in-depth study provided evidence that psychologically stable individuals display adaptation-enhancing metacognitive processes when confronted with challenging tasks. Results supported Wells and Matthews' (1994, 1996) and Wells' (2000) inverse metacognitive predictions.

Results also supported Challenge Models of Resilience with more pronounced utilization of resilience-related assets and sub-assets (agency, self-determination, persistence and communion) in times of challenge, perceived unpredictability or even adversity. In addition to the (perceived) degree, the length of challenge (adversity or unpredictability) impacted on the necessary adaptation. As discussed above, in long-term challenge scenarios assets and resources appear to be more relevant than self-regulatory processes. Yet, Interviewee 3 (reported as individual case study) with his ten year major research project expressed some awareness of the long-term nature and appeared to have been anticipating the long-term nature from the very beginning. His remarkable persistence and ongoing goal-focus could have been attributable to 'metacognitions of time-frameworks' – a worthwhile area for future research. This appears to be an example where metacognitive processes not necessarily evoke full awareness in the sense of Kentridge and Heywood's (2000) unconscious meta-cognitions.

Interestingly, a certain degree of challenge also appears to be required to elicit awareness of adaptive self-regulatory processes. This could be established by comparing the 'high challenge' with the 'low challenge' scenarios/participants. The latter group was excluded from in-depth analyses because they did not report consciousness of self-regulatory processes or necessity of stabilizing personality factors.

The interviews also reflected the core role of awareness of volitional control in terms of both positive self-regulation and adaptive personality assets. Awareness of voluntary control appears to be a prerequisite for efficient use or 'cultivation' of agency and communion as argued by Vaillant (2000), who postulates that seeking social support (communion) and cognitive strategies (agency) are both under volitional control with huge self-empowering implications.

In line with Matthew and Wells' (1994, 1996) and Wells' (2000, 2009) (inverse) predictions, metacognitive awareness facilitated interviewees' adaptive self-regulation and emotional and psychological well-being. The interviews also supported the view that increased metacognitive awareness potentially contributes to preventing or overcoming maladaptive self-beliefs (schemas). This is in line with Cloninger's (2006) argument that human consciousness is characterized by capacity for self-awareness and free choices not being completely determined by past experience.

Fostering and increasing mindfulness has recently been integrated in Cognitive Behavioral Therapies. Moreover, psychological acceptance in Bond and Bune's (2000) conceptualization, as the ability to accept negative emotions and still pursue aims, implies agency in the form of goal focus – reflecting synergy effects between self-regulation and assets.

Finally the interviews supported the study's core hypothesis that beyond Matthews and Wells' (1994, 1996) and Wells' (2000, 2009) purely cognitive perspective, social interactions play a crucial role in adaptive self-regulation. Cases 4 and 6 (reported as individual case studies) clearly showed that severe challenge and adversity also necessitate taking the social environment into account: Interviewee 4 provided evidence for the relevance of social learning and modeling processes. Interviewee 6 accounted for core crisis support from significant others (parents, friends and even peers); the experiences of social and crisis support appeared to be crucial for persistent self-regulation and adaptation to the obstacles resulting from her illness.

On these grounds future investigations of positive metacognitions, resulting adaptive self-regulation and health assets for psychological stability should take into account people's embeddedness in their social contexts (Seligman & Csikszentmihalyi, 2000). This study explicitly took the social component into account by investigating the relevance of communion, but the social environment might have distinct impacts on metacognitive self-regulation that were not captured in the present investigation.

In its entirety, this qualitative in-depth study provided first tentative evidence that psychologically stable individuals display adaptation-enhancing metacognitive processes when confronted with challenging tasks. Results supported Wells and Matthews' (1994, 1996) and Wells' (2000, 2009) inverse metacognitive predictions in terms of the confidence construct 'Confidence in Extinguishing Perseverative Thoughts and Emotions'. Above and beyond Wells and Matthews' scope two additional and new (inverse) confidence domains emerged from this qualitative study – 'Confidence in Interpreting Own Emotions as Cues, Refraining from Immediate Reaction and Mind-Setting for Problem-Solving' and subsequent 'Confidence in Setting Flexible and Feasible Hierarchies of Goals'. The three positive confidences constructs underlying functional metacognitions and meta-emotions have provided the basis of item wording of Beer and Moneta's (2010) developed and validated Positive Metacognitions and Positive Meta-Emotions Questionnaire (PMCEQ). Utilizing two validation samples, comprising 313 and 475 participants, first empirical evidence for the validity and good internal consistency of the 18 items comprising novel PMCEQ has been provided.

REFERENCES

Bakan, D. (1966). *The duality of human existence*. Chicago: Rand McNally.

Bakker, A. B., & Schaufeli, W. B. (2008). Positive organizational behavior: Engaged employees in flourishing organizations. *Journal of Organizational Behavior, 29*, 147-154.

Bandura, A.A. (1997). *Self-efficacy: The exercise of control*. New York: W.H. Freeman.

Bandura, A. (1977a). *Social Learning Theory*. Eaglewood Cliffs, New York: Prentice Hall.

Bandura, A. (1977b). Self-efficacy: Toward a unifying theory of behavioral change. *Psychological Review, 84*, 191-225.

Beck, A.T. (1976). *Cognitive Therapies and Emotional Disorders*. New York: International University Press.

Beck, A. T. (1967). *Depression: Clinical, Experimental and Theoretical Aspects*. New York: Hoeber.

Beer, N. (2011). *Effects of Positive Metacognitions and Meta-Emotions on Coping, Stress Perception and Emotions*. PhD thesis, submitted June, 2011, London Metropolitan University. UK: London.

Beer, N., & Moneta, G.B (2010). Coping and perceived stress as a function of positive metacognitions and positive meta-emotions. *Individual Differences Research*, accepted 09-05-2011.

Beer, N., & Moneta, G.B (2010). Construct and Concurrent Validity of the Positive Metacognitions and Positive Meta-Emotions Questionnaire. *Personality and Individual Differences, 49*, 977-982.

Bond, F.W., & Bunce, D. (2000). Mediators of change in emotion-focused and problem-focused worksite stress management interventions. *Journal of Occupational Health Psychology, 5*, 156-163.

Braun, V., & Clarke, V. (2006). Using thematic analysis in psychology. *Qualitative Research in Psychology, 3*, 77-101.

Brown, A.L, Bansford, J.D., Campione, J.C., & Ferrara, R.A. (1983). Learning, Remembering and Understanding. In: J. Flavell and E. Markman (Eds.), *Handbook of Child Psychology, Vol. 3: Cognitive Development*. New York: Wiley.

Carver, C.S., & Scheier, M.F. (2005). Optimism. In: C.R. Snyder and S.J. Lopez, *Handbook of Positive Psychology* (pp. 231-243). New York: Open University Press.

Chang, E.C., & Bridgewell, W.B. (1998). Irrational beliefs, optimism, pessimism, and psychological stress: A preliminary examination of different effects in a college population. *Journal of Clinical Psychology, 54*, 137-142.

Cheng, C., & Cheung, M. (2005). Cognitive Processes Underlying Coping Flexibility: Differentiation and Integration. *Journal of Personality, 73*, 859-886.

Cloninger, C.R. (2006). The science of well-being: an integrative approach to mental health and its disorders. *World of Psychiatry*, *5*, 71-76.

Cobb, S. (1976). Social support as a moderator of life stress. *Psychosomatic Medicine*, *38*, 300-314.

Cohen, S., & Wills, T.A. (1985). Stress, Social Support and the Buffering Hypothesis. *Psychological Bulletin*, *98*, 310-357.

Davidson, R.J., Kabat-Zinn, J, Schumacher, J. Rosenkranz, M., Muller, D., Santorelli, S.F., Urbanowsky, F., Harrington, A., Bonus, K., & Sheridan, J.F. (2003). Alterations in the brain and immune function produced by mindfulness meditation. *Psychosomatic Medicine*, *65*, 567-570.

Donaldson, E. (2003). Psychological Acceptance: And why every OH/HR practitioner should know about it. *Occupational Health Review*, *101*, 31-33.

Ellis, A. (1987). The impossibility of achieving consistently good mental health. *American Psychologist, 42*, 364-375

Elliot, A.J., & Church, M.A. (1997). A Hierarchical Model of Approach and Avoidance Achievement Motivation, *Journal of Personality and Social Psychology, 72*, 218-232.

Flavell, J.H. (1979). Metacognition and metacognitive monitoring: A new area of cognitive-developmental inquiry. *American Psychologist, 34*, 906-911.

Folkman, S., & Moskowitz, T. (2000). Positive Affect and the other Side of Coping. *American Psychologist*, *55*, 647-654.

Fredrickson, B., & Joiner, T. (2002). Positive emotions trigger upward spirals toward emotional wellbeing. *Psychological Science, 13*, 172-175.

Glaser, B.G., & Strauss, A.L. (1967). *The Discovery of Grounded Theory*. Chicago: Aldine.

Gleitman, H., Fridlund, A.J., & Reisberg, D. (2004). *Psychology*, 6th Ed., New York: Norton.

Goldberg, E. (2001). *The executive brain. Frontal lobes and the civilized mind.* New York: Oxford University Press.

Goleman, D. (1996). *Emotional Intelligence.* London: Bloomsbury.

Hayes, N. (1997). Theory-led thematic analysis: Social identification in small companies. In: N. Hayes (Ed.), *Doing qualitative research in psychology*. Hove: Psychology Press.

Hill, C.A. (1987). Affiliation Motivation: People who need people - but in different ways, *Journal of Personality and Social Psychology, 52*, 1008-1018.

Kentridge, R., & Heywood, C.A. (2000). Metacognition and awareness. *Consciousness and Cognition*, *9*, 308-312.

Luthans, F. (2002). Positive organizational behavior: Developing and managing psychological strengths. *Academy of Management Executive, 16*, 57-72.

Luthar, S.S., Cicchetti, D., & Becker, B. (2000). The construct of resilience: A critical evaluation and guidelines for future work. *Child Development*, *71*, 543-562.

Maddi, S. R. (1998). Dispositional hardiness in health and effectiveness. In H.S. Friedman (Ed.), *Encyclopedia of mental health*. San Diego, CA: Academic Press.

Maddi, S.R., & Kobasa, S.C. (1984). *The hardy executive: Health under stress*. Homewood, IL: Dow Jones-Irwin.

Maddux, J.E. (1999). Expectancies and the social-cognitive perspective: Basic principles, processes and variables. In: I. Kirsch (Ed.) *How expectancies shape behavior* (pp. 17-40). Washington, D.C.: American Psychological Society.

Masten A.S., Hubbard J.J., Gest S.D., Tellegan A., Garmezy N., & Ramierez M. (1999). Competence in the context of adversity: Pathways to resilience and maladaptation from childhood to late adolescence. *Developmental Psychology, 11*, 143-169.

Masten, A.S., & Reed, M.G. (2005). Resilience in development. In S.R. Snyder and S.J. Lopez (Eds.). *Handbook of Positive Psychology*. Oxford; Oxford University Press.

McBride, C., Bacchiochi, J., & Bagdy, M. (2006). Gender differences in the manifestation of sociotropy and autonomy personality traits. *Personality and Individual Differences, 38*, 129-136.

McClelland, D.C. (1985), *Human Motivation*, Glenview, IL: Scott & Forseman.

McClelland, D.C., Atkinson, J.W., Clark, R.W., & Lowell, E.L. (1953). *The achievement motive*. New York: Appleton-Century-Crofts.

Metcalfe, J., & Greene, M.J. (2007). Metacognition of Agency. *Journal of Experimental Psychology: General, 136*, 184-199.

Milne, A. (2003). *Counselling*. London: Hodder.

Peterson, C. (1999). Personal control and well-being. In: D. Kahneman, D. Diener & N. Schwarz (Eds.). *Well-being: The foundations of hedonic psychology* (pp. 288-301). New York: Russel Sage Foundation.

Reber, A., & Reber, S. (2001). *Dictionary of Psychology* (3rd Ed). London: Penguin Books.

Reis, H.T., & Gable, L.S. (2003). Toward a positive psychology of relationships. In: C.L. Keyes and J. Heidt (Eds.). *Flourishing: The positive person and the good life*. Washington, D.C.: American Psychological Society.

Roger, D., Jarvis, G. and Najarian, B. (1993). Detachment and coping: The construction and validation of a new scale for measuring coping strategies. *Personality and Individual Differences, 15*, 619-626.

Rotter, J.B. (1966). Generalised expectancies for internal versus external control reinforcement. *Psychological Monographs, 80*, 1-28.

Rutter, M. (1987). Psychological resilience and protective mechanisms. *American Journal of Orthopsychiatry, 57*, 316-331.

Ryan, R.M., & Deci, E.L. (2000). Self-determination theory and the facilitation of intrinsic motivation, social development and well-being. *American Psychologist, 55*, 68-78.

Sarason, I.G., & Sarason, B.R. (1985). *Social support: Theory, research and applications*. Boston: Martinus Nijhoff.

Schunk, D.H. (1995). Self-efficacy and education and instruction. In: J.E. Maddux (Ed.), *Self-efficacy, adaptation and adjustment: Theory, research and application* (pp. 281-303). New York: Plenum Press.

Seligman, M.E.P., & Csikszentmihalyi, M. (2000). Positive Psychology: An Introduction. *American Psychologist, 55*, 5-14.

Seligman, M.E.P., Steen, T.A., Park, N., & Peterson C. (2005). Positive Psychology in Progress: Empirical validation of interventions. *American Psychologist*, 410-421.

Solvey, P., & Mayer, J.D. (1990). Emotional Intelligence. *Imagination, Cognition and Personality, 9*, 185-211

Spada, M., Nikcevic, A., Moneta, G.B., & Ireson, J. (2006). Metacognitions as a mediator of the effect of test anxiety on a surface approach to studying. *Educational Psychology, 26 (5)*, 615-625.

Spada, M., Nikcevic, A., Moneta, G.B., & Wells, A. (2007). Metacognitions as a mediator between emotion and smoking dependence. *Addictive Behaviours, 32*, 2120-2129.

Spada, M., & Wells, A. (2005). Metacognitions, emotions and alcohol use. *Clinical Psychology and Psychotherapy, 12 (2)*, 150-155.

Sternberg, R.J. (1984). *The Triarchic Mind: A New Theory of Human Intelligence*. New York: Penguin Books.

Tugade, M., & Fredrickson, B.L. (2000). Resilient individuals use positive emotions to bounce back from negative emotions, *Journal of Personality and Social Psychology, 86*, 320-333.

Vaillant, G.E. (2000). Adaptive Mental Mechanisms: Their Role in a Positive Psychology, *American Psychologist, 55*, 89-98.

Wang, M.C. (1992). *Adaptive educational strategies: Building on diversity*. Baltimore, MD: Brookes.

Wallston, B. S., Alagna, S. W., DeVellis, B. M., & DeVellis, R. F. (1983). Social support and health. *Health Psychology, 2*, 367-391.

Wells, A. (2000). *Emotional Disorders and Metacognition: Innovative Cognitive Therapy*. Chichester, UK: Wiley.

Wells, A. (1995). Metacognition and Worry: A cognitive model of generalised anxiety disorder. *Behavioural and Cognitive Psychotherapy, 32*, 301-320.

Wells, A., & Cartwright-Hatton, S. (2004). A short form of the metacognitions questionnaire: properties of the MCQ-30. *Behavior Therapy, 42*, 385-396.

Wells, A., & Matthews, G. (1996). Modelling cognition in emotional disorder: The S-REF model. *Behaviour Research and Therapy, 34*, 881-888.

Wells, A., & Matthews, G. (1994). *Attention and Emotion. A Clinical Perspective*. Hove: Erlbaum.

Werner, E.S. (1995). Resilience in Development. *Current Direction in Psychological Sciences, 4*, 81-85.

Werner, E.S., & Smith, R.S. (2001). *Journeys from childhood to midlife: Risk, resilience and recovery*. Ithaca, New York: Cornell University Press.

Werner, E.S., & Smith, R.S. (1982). *Vulnerable but invincible: A study of resilient children*. New York: McGraw-Hill.

Wiggins, J.S., & Broughton, R. (1985). The interpersonal circle: A structural model for the integration of personality research. In: R. Hogan & W.H. Jones (Eds.), *Perspectives in Personality*, (Vol. 1, pp. 1-47). Greenwich, CT: JAU Press.

Zimmerman, B.J. (2000). Attaining self-regulation: A social cognitive perspective. In M. Boekaerts, P.R. Pintrich & M. Zeidner (Eds.). *Handbook of self-regulation* (pp. 13-39). New York: Guilford Press.

Zimmerman, B.J., & Cleary, T.J. (2006). Adolescents' development of personal agency: The role of self-efficacy beliefs and self-regulatory skill. In: F. Pajares and T. Urdan (Eds.). *Self-efficacy beliefs of adolescents*, (pp. 45-69). Greenwich, CT: Information Age Publishing

In: Psychology of Self-Regulation
Editor: Vassilis Barkoukis

ISBN: 978-1-61470-380-8
© 2012 Nova Science Publishers, Inc.

Chapter 2

MONITORING, CONTROL AND THE ILLUSION OF CONTROL

Magda Osman[*]
University of London, UK

ABSTRACT

Adaptive control in the face of uncertainty involves making online predictions about events in order to plan actions to reliably achieve desirable outcomes. However, we often face situations in which the effects of our actions are probabilistic (e.g., returns on our investments), and the environment itself is dynamic, - it can change irrespective of any action we decide to take, and in a relatively stable or unstable way (e.g., economic climate). Therefore, the problem of control concerns learning to isolate the effects that are generated directly by our actions, from those that occur independently of them. We face this problem in a host of uncertain dynamic environments: ecological (using fertilizers to increase crop yield), economic (investing in real estate), industrial (operating nuclear power plants), mechanical (driving cars) and medical (stemming outbreaks of disease). The aim of this review is to bring together empirical research from disparate disciplines spanning Social and Cognitive Psychology as well as Neuroscience all of which are concerned with adaptive control. In order to achieve this, this chapter presents a general framework (Monitoring and control- MC framework) which is used to integrate two central ideas (agency, uncertainty) that have important ramifications for understanding self regulatory processes and their relationship to control processes. In sum, the chapter proposes that control processes involve self-regulatory mechanisms (Task Monitoring and Self Monitoring) that enable us to make subjective estimates of success, which help to anchor our interpretation of uncertain events to expected ones. In addition, these estimates are integrated with estimations of rates of change of the events in the environment which helps us track the outcomes we aim to control. The chapter ends with a discussion on the illusion of control and the possible mechanisms that give rise to it.

---

[*] Correspondence to: M.Osman@qmul.ac.uk. Biological and Experimental Psychology Centre, School of Biological and Chemical Sciences, Queen Mary University of London, Mile End Road, London, E1 4NS, UK, +44 (0) 20 7882 5903

MONITORING, CONTROL AND THE ILLUSION OF CONTROL

The chapter's main focus will be on the role that monitoring processes play in complex decision making and learning environments. The types of environments that are complex range from operating nuclear power plants, managing a large company, planning a drug treatment intervention for an infected patient, maintaining a fragile ecology, to learning to drive a car. In all of these contexts there are unknown factors that influence changes in events in the task environment, and our job is to develop the best plan of decisions and actions that will maintain specific changes in the environment in line with a desirable goal.

To achieve this we need Monitoring and Control processes. Monitoring processes tend to go hand in hand with control processes; this is because monitoring is a process that enables the evaluation of actions and their outcomes with respect to a goal, and control is a process that enables the execution of actions with respect to a goal. So, a good place to start in this chapter is to clarify the psychological phenomena associated with the terms monitoring and control. In addition, this section asks "why is task-monitoring and self-monitoring important while interacting with complex decision making environments?" Answering this question focuses on critical properties that enable the evaluation of the success of our decisions and actions in uncertain environments, namely goals and judgments of self-efficacy. From this the next section will then present a detailed discussion of a framework that integrates monitoring and control processes in such a way as to explain dynamic decision making and learning in complex domains. Final the discussion draws to a close by focusing on the phenomenon commonly referred to as the "illusion of control". The illusion is used to illustrate the powerful role that self-monitoring has on the way in which we perceive and are biased to attribute outcomes to our actions based on the goals we are operating with at the time.

1. MONITORING (SELF-MONITORING, TASK-MONITORING) AND CONTROL

The original impetus for studies of complex decision making and learning that were developed in the early 70's was to examine the relationship between monitoring and control processes. Broadbent's (1977), Dörner's (1975), and Toda's (1962) studies investigated the way in which people planned and evaluated their decisions to act in situations that were dynamic, complex, and that generated a high degree of uncertainty. Their attempts to simulate the same types of conditions in laboratory settings were designed to uncover the mechanisms that enable us to adapt to problematic everyday situations. And so, by designing complex decision making and learning tasks to simulate real world dynamic environments (i.e., uncertain worlds) the objective was to answer the following question: How do we learn to isolate the effects we are generating in the world from the effects that would occur regardless of our actions? Finding answers to this question bears on all aspects of our everyday decision making, and still remains an important research question.

Clearly then, early research on complex decision making and learning tasks addressed a question that succinctly captured the most critical aspects of decision making in real world context. In so doing research on decision making and learning in complex domains took the route of focusing on how people reduce uncertainty by investigating the type of goal-directed behaviors that guide the way we interact with dynamic environments (i.e. control), and how we assess what we have usefully gained in knowledge from our actions (i.e. monitoring). Since then, research in the cognitive and social psychology domain has investigated the properties that contribute to isolating the effects of actions from those occurring independently of them. Critical to identifying the effects of our actions on the world from those that occur independently of them is establishing goals. Goals are able to guide decision making and learning processes involved in managing an uncertain environment (control), but also goals guide processes involved in assessing how the environment is operating (task-monitoring), and finally goals guide processes that enable us to track and evaluate the success of our actions in the environment (self-monitoring).

1.1. Control Processes and their Role in Managing Uncertainty

In social and cognitive psychology domains control is taken to refer to the generation and implementation of goal-directed actions (e.g., Lerch & Harter, 2001; Locke & Latham, 2002; Rossano, 2003; Sweller, 1988; VanLehn, 1996; Vollmeyer et al., 1996). That is, an individual takes actions that are likely to have immediate effects on a environment that relate to an active local goal, as well as contributing to reaching a more general global goal state that can be attained in the long term (Sweller, 1988; Vollmeyer et al., 1996). Short term goals may enable people that have little expertise in the task environment (e.g., trainee managers of a company, trainee nuclear power plant operators) to develop rudimentary knowledge of an uncertain complex environment, whereas with expertise long term achievable goals are set because deeper knowledge of the environment has been acquired.

Control behaviors serve an important function in helping to reduce our experience of uncertainty in the environment by improving the predictability of outcomes through goals. When people are engaged in tasks in which they are required to develop a plan of actions in order to reach a particular outcome, people are usually able to quickly develop expectations of likely outcomes from observed events. Moreover, they are able to do this from relatively little experience of the conditional relationship between the two (Bandura 1989). In particular, close temporal proximity between self-initiated actions and outcomes in the world helps to bind these events to form causal representations (Lagnado & Sloman, 2004). The very fact that control behaviors are purposive actions means that they require some anticipation of likely consequences from our actions. So, the more experiences we have in which we make choices in our environment, the more likely it is that the corresponding outcomes that we observe happening in close conjunction to our actions will contribute to our sense of agency (Bandura, 2001; Pacherie, 2008).

1.2. Task-Monitoring Processes and their Role in Managing Uncertainty

To successfully manage a complex dynamic environment, and to therefore reliably reproduce actions that will generate desirable outcomes, people must identify relevant information from the immediate environment they are in, but also draw from relevant prior experiences (Osman, 2010a, 2010b). In order to develop an accurate representation of a complex dynamic environment we need to form causal representations of the relations between the variables we can manipulate (i.e. cues) and the events we observe that we aim to manage (i.e. outcomes), but also causal knowledge based on the relations between actions taken and effects generated in the environment (Osman, 2010a). Therefore task monitoring involves processing information that is the current focus of attention that is judged to be useful in estimating the changes in effects observed. For instance we can do this in one of three ways, 1) we may encode salient task features (e.g., lights flashing on screen every time a button is pressed), 2) we may selectively attend to salient features (e.g., only focusing on the green light because it signals that an event has been initiated), 3) we may process familiar features of the task based on prior knowledge (e.g., recognizing that blue lights flash every time a sequence of buttons is pressed in sequence). At least for 2 and 3 task monitoring can be internally driven (Corbetta, Patel, & Shulman, 2008). That is, activities which draw from memory such as pattern matching, and inferential processes (e.g., decision making, hypothesis testing, and hypothetical thinking) can be recruited in order to make sense of the environment we find ourselves in. For example, developing knowledge of the structural features of the task necessarily involves rule-based knowledge, which is acquired either through hypothesis testing (predicting and evaluating the prediction) (Osman, 2008a, 2008b, 2008c), or hypothetical thinking – that is, simulating various outcomes and testing this against the actual outcomes (Klein, 1993; Papadelis, Kourtidou-Papadeli, Bamidis, & Albani, 2007). Like control processes, task-monitoring enables the individual to regulate their understanding of the task based on assessing the reliability of their expectations of the outcomes that their actions will produce. This is because task-monitoring belongs to a category of goal directed processes; their function is to continually update and integrate information frequently, in order to reduce uncertainty. When faced with environments in which the events are continually changing, we need to track the changes as they occur, and to do that we need to generate rules/causal representations which we can test in order to increase the accuracy of our knowledge of the environment, and to reduce our experiences of uncertainty when interacting with it.

1.3. Self-Monitoring Processes and their Role in Managing Uncertainty

The way in which we assess the effects of our actions on outcomes in the world, in other words our sense of agency, strongly influences our ability to accurately extract the causal structure of the environment. This is because it influences which features of the environment we choose to attend to (Osman, 2010a, 2010b). Making poor estimates of our ability to impact on the environment, or misjudging the locus of the outcome can have severe consequences in the real world (e.g., disasters in aviation [1996 Charkhi Dadri mid-air collision], nuclear power systems [i.e. Chernobyl disaster] and rail [China Railway train disaster T195], as well as more commonly in context of automated driving systems (Degani, 2004)). As compelling is evidence showing that increasing people's belief in their sense of agency or self efficacy can help to radically improve their problem solving skills because it increases their efforts to seek out relevant information to solve the task (e.g., Bouffard-bouchard, 1990; Osman, 2008a). For example, Huber (1985) conducted an experiment in which a computer program simulated the experience of being in a maze, and people were asked to solve mazes of varying difficulty, and with goals of varying specificity (i.e. start from the middle and reach the exit in the fewest number of moves, vs. do you best and find your way out). Success in solving the mazes was not mediated by people's general problem solving ability, but rather the effort and commitment to solving the task was based on their estimation of their probability in successfully solving it. When told that the maze or goal was "difficult "this influenced people's behavior far more than any objective determinants of the actual difficulty of the maze or goal. Their performance dropped, and the effort in solving the task reduced. Also, feedback from their ongoing performance was negatively viewed, leading to dysfunctional problem solving strategies. Similar findings have since been reported in a variety of contexts including simulated organizational problem solving tasks (Maynard & Hakel, 1997), financial decision making task (Endres, 2006), and group decision making tasks (Crown & Rosse, 1995; Mesch, Farh, & Podsakoff, 1994).

Along with control and task-monitoring, we also seem to need a mechanism that helps us to track our own actions and adapt our behavior in light of changes that are being experienced in the environment (Goldsmith, Koriat & Pansky, 2005; Smith, Shields, & Washburn, 2003). This is a necessary function for humans and animals (Kornell, Son, & Terrace, 2007) and, although controversial, this implies that animals as well as humans have the capacity for metacognition (for a discussion see Smith et al., 2003). Therefore, self-monitoring behaviors offer an adaptive advantage for coping with uncertainty by enabling us to track our ability to successfully manage the environment we are in. This involves assessing what we have usefully gained in knowledge of the task based on the effects we have generated. Moreover, self-monitoring influences how we interpret immediate action-outcomes associations as well as delayed action-outcomes associations, which in turn affects how we learn about and control our environment (Osman, 2008a, 2008b). Thus, Self-monitoring constrains uncertainty by focusing cognitive resources for tracking self-generated changes to outcomes observed in a complex dynamic environment.

1.4. A Little Illustration

At this point it is useful to provide an illustration of the three different processes just discussed, and for this Nelson (1996) gives an elegant example that elucidates the phenomenal experience of control, and task-monitoring and self-monitoring. Moreover, his example hints at the nature of the relationship between monitoring and control processes that will be described later in this chapter when introducing the Monitoring and Control Framework.

Nelson (1996) asks us to consider the following sentence: "THISS SENTENCE CONTAINS THREEE ERRORS." *What are the control processes?* The content of the sentence offers clues as to how to read it, and so the goal focuses our attention in a particular way in order to expect a particular outcome. Our actions are the way in which we read the sentence with respect to the goal that we have in mind. *What are the task-monitoring processes?* As we read the sentence we may mentally note that the first word has an extra "S," and then as we continue we also note the extra "E" in the word three. In this instance we use the goal to evaluate the features of the task that are relevant for us to pursue it. *What are the self-monitoring processes?* While processing the sentence we may experience the conflict between the meaning of the sentence and the two perceptual errors we observed. The mismatch between the current status (i.e having only detected two errors) and the desired goal (i.e. finding all three) may have caused doubt in our ability to accurately detect the errors.

This in turn may lead us to re-evaluate the goal of the task because we have only detected two errors. Or else, we may be prompted to reread the sentence to check where the third mistake might be. Depending on the goal pursued the detection of the meta-level error, that of the proposition that there are three errors in the sentence rather than two, can either be seen as a fulfillment of the target goal in which case we stop processing the sentence at this stage. Or else, it may prompt us to further evaluation the sentence and so we continue to processes it by alternating between control and monitoring processes. The shift from self-monitoring behaviors, back to Control behaviors and Task Monitoring behaviors is a response to re-evaluating performance outcomes with respect to a specific goal. Thus, the behaviors that are involved in achieving a goal will change at various stages because of changes to the goals that are set at any one time. By extension, the interplay between these different processes is experienced in complex decision making domains in which the events we observe are constantly changing.

1.5. Why Is Task-monitoring and Self-monitoring Important in Managing Uncertainty?

In a general sense, monitoring processes (Self-monitoring and Task-monitoring) are the starting point to approaching any task in which 1) there is little performance history to guide the way in which it should be tackled, or in which 2) the task demands change in such a way as to present new challenges to the individual (Bandura, 2001; Karoly, 1993; Vancouver, 2000, 2005). Therefore, in essence, monitoring behaviors are the method by which we estimate the success of our actions with respect to a goal, and the method by which we evaluate the success of our actions with respect to a goal. Without these activities we would be unable to disentangle the effects of our actions on the world from those that are externally determined, and more to the point we would be unable to learn about our environment and how it operates

Our estimations of the success of self-initiated behaviors in the environment help to organize the actions that should be taken in that environment. The actual effects generated by these actions are either directly felt or else observed. In either case, the outcomes of our actions are described as being 'fedback' to the individual as part of a complex dynamic interactive process between self-assessment of behaviors in terms of the impact that the behaviors can have on the world (i.e. agency) and the behavior itself. This type of feedback mechanism has been referred to as negative for the reason that it indicate the stage in the goal seeking process that the individual is at, and prompts the individual to try and reduce the error between desired and achieved outcomes. Negative here refers to the discrepancy between what should have been achieved and what was achieved. Bandura and Locke (2003) have gone as far as to suggest that this alone is not enough, and that the feedback mechanism works in concert with a feedforward mechanism that incrementally increases the challenges of the desired goals. In this sense this is positive because the mechanism continues to extend the potential achievements of the individual by motivating the individual to exceed their initial expectations. In actual fact, Bandura and Locke propose that we have two sorts of systems of regulatory processes and that they interact with each other: 1) a monitoring process that operates at a super-ordinate level in which there is a dynamic feedback relationship between human/organism actions and the environment, and 2) a monitoring process that operates at a sub-ordinate level in which there is a dynamic feedback relationship between perceptions of self and outcomes of actions. The complex interplay between both types of monitoring help to explain the positive and well as negative behaviors that people display when interacting with certain as well as uncertain complex task domains.

1.5.1. The Importance of Goals

Studies examining the mediating effects of different set goals on monitoring processes have revealed that difficult specific goals (SGs), that is goals that state explicitly what the outcome to be reached should be, lead to increases in cognitive, physical, and motivational effort, which in turn can lead to increases in performance compared to "do your best" instructions (Huber, 1985; Locke, Shaw, Saari & Latham, 1981; Mento Steel, & Karren, 1987; Wood and Locke, 1987). In complex management decision making tasks in which the environment is a dynamic one, and there is no obvious dominant strategy for controlling the outcome, SGs have been shown to impair performance compared to non-specific goals such as "do your best" (NSGs) (Chesney & Locke, 1991; Earley, et al, 1989). In complex decision making tasks, introducing difficult SGs in the early stages of the task can impair people's ability in successfully controlling the outcome, but when introduced later it can actually facilitate performance (Kanfer & Ackerman, 1989). Moreover, feedback about how successful the outcome is with respect to the target (i.e. outcome feedback) is sought out more often in SG training conditions than NSG conditions (Huber, 1985). Also, when varying goal specificity and outcome feedback, the more difficult the task and the more specific the goal, process feedback (i.e. information about the success of implemented strategies) increases performance compared to outcome feedback (Earley, et al, 1990; Neubert, 1998). The same findings have been reported in studies examining decision making in organizational and job setting contexts (Vigoda-Gadot & Angert, 2007).

1.5.2. The Importance of Self-efficacy

There are cognitive factors such as judgments of self-efficacy that influence the success of our actions in the world. Locke (2000) described self-efficacy as a cognitive factor that contributes to the ways in which control processes are executed. This is because Locke took self efficacy to refer to the conviction that an individual has in performing a certain skill to a certain level. From this point of view, self-efficacy engages evaluative thinking because the individual performs a self-assessment of their capability in achieving the goal-directed behavior. Bandura (1977), the main proponent of self-efficacy, presents an alternative description of this construct. Rather than describing cognitive factors are separate influences on actions to those of motivation, as Locke (2000) proposes, Bandura suggests that motivation is primarily concerned with activation and persistence of behaviour, but is based in part in cognitive activities that include expectancies of outcomes, the capacity to represent future consequences of actions, and self-evaluation and goal-setting. Representing future outcomes provides the incentive to carry out the action because given the expectancy estimate and the reliability of making an accurate prediction, the individual will then either act or not. Similarly, self-rewarding goal-directed behaviours are conditional on achieving a certain standard of behaviour and this is what motivates action. This conditional self-inducement propels individuals towards maintaining their efforts until their performance matches the standards/goals they had set themselves to begin with. The complement to this is perceived negative discrepancies between performance and standards/goals, and this can lead to the creation of a state of dissatisfaction. This in turn will motivate the search for corrective behaviours that can be directed towards attaining the desired goal.

Bandura (1977, 1989, 2001) proposes that all psychological processes are designed to increase and strengthen self efficacy, and this is because it is the method by which we act and control our environment. Therefore self-efficacy is concerned with the estimation of how successfully one can execute a course of action designed to deal with a prospective situation, and for this reason it precedes outcome expectances. People can estimate that an outcome will occur given a set of actions, but if estimations of self-efficacy are low because the individual doubts their ability in executing the actions in a particular fashion, then there will be little motivation to carry out the actions. Alternatively, there are conditions in which estimations of self-efficacy misalign with the actual outcomes produced by actions in such a way so that self-efficacy is high, and the estimation of the outcome occurring is too low, but with the same effect on motivation and eventual lack of action. The main idea is that estimations of self-efficacy and outcomes will change because our internal judgments of our capabilities will change, and also because the environment in which the actions are executed is uncertain and changes.

Alternatively, Vancouver, More, and Yoder (2008) and Olson, Roese and Zanna (1996) describe self-efficacy as a type of expectancy related to an individual's belief that they can execute actions necessary for achieve a goal. In addition, other related social domains such as Organizational psychological and Management research that examines the impact of the work environment on behaviour have adopted a similar perspective of self-efficacy. For instance, Gist and Mitchell (1992) refer to self-efficacy as an individual's estimate of their capacity to co-ordinate performance on a specific task, and Jones (1986) describes self-efficacy as influencing people's expectations about their abilities to perform successfully in new situations. In general then, expectations about self-efficacy are directly related to people's perceptions of their success in dealing with past situations and their expectancy for future successful outcomes.

In sum, in the social and cognitive domain there is much evidence to suggest that estimations of self-efficacy are a reliable and superior predictor of behaviour compared with estimations of outcomes of behavior. For example, empirical studies have reported that judged self-efficacy predicts affective processes (e.g., Bandura & Cervone, 1986; Elliot & Dweck, 1988; Spering, Wagener, & Funke, 2005), decisional processes (e.g., DeShon & Alexander, 1996; Earley, Connolly, & Ekegren, 1989; Kanfer et al., 1994; Tversky & Kahneman, 1974) and problem solving ability (Bandura & Wood, 1989; Bouffard-Bouchard, 1990; Hogarth et al., 1991; Wood & Bandura, 1989). Clearly, self-efficacy is an important component of all Social and related domains because it signals what behavioral change will occur, and when. Moreover, some are explicit about connecting self-efficacy to regulatory processes (Azjen, 1991), whereas others suggest that self-efficacy is simply a reflection of judged causal agency (Bandura, 2001) - or, as some call it, personal causation in the world (DeCharms, 1979). Common to all references of self-efficacy is the claim that the relationship between perceived expectations of self generated goal directed behaviors is continually weighed against the changing demands of the environment. In other words, we are constantly updating and adjusting our judgments of self efficacy because we have to continurally monitor and respond to the changes we face in our decision making environment.

2. MONITORING AND CONTROL FRAMEWORK

The aim of introducing the MC framework here is that it serves to connect the various different discussions concerning monitoring processes and control processes. Moreover, to date there have been few attempts to drawn together the disparate literatures in the psychology domain that have investigated these processes. So, to this end, the MC framework (Osman, 2010a, 2010b) provides a basis for integrating the findings on monitoring and control from the social and cognitive domain, as well as those generated outside of that (e.g., engineering, cybernetics, human factors, machine learning).

In principle the MC framework proposes that our experiences of uncertainty mediates monitoring and control processes. There has been considerable work examining the relationship between uncertainty and control task behavior (Dörner, 1975; Kersholt, 1996; Sterman, 1989; Toda, 1962), particularly research distinguishing between experts and novices behavior in skilled complex decision making domains (Klein, 1993; Lipshitz & Strauss, 2006). However, the present framework differs somewhat from previous work because it uses the concept of uncertainty as a way of unifying the different domains of research on complex decision making and learning. It achieves this by proposing that all complex decision making and learning domains generate experiences of uncertainty. Also, individuals differ in the degree of uncertainty that they experience, and their experiences of uncertainty will change over time. . The reason for the change in judgments of uncertainty is because complex decision making environments are often probabilistic and or dynamic and therefore, representations of how uncertain we are about the environment we are in ought to track the fluctuations within it. This view is consistent with recent neuropsychological (e.g., Huettel, Song, & McCarthy, 2005) and behavioral (e.g., Kording, & Wolpert, 2006) work describing the interaction between judgments of our uncertainty about an environment and the events that are experienced and the cognitive processes that are designed to reduce it.

2.1. The Main Tenets of the MC Framework

Predicting and controlling our environment is based on incomplete and or uncertain knowledge, and the success of these activities is based on the way in which uncertainties are represented. Perceived uncertainty, which is essentially determined by the individual; that is, people make subjective judgments of how accurately they are able to predict an action-outcome association, and people make subjective judgments of self-efficacy – their success in achieving a particular action-outcome association (Bandura & Locke, 2003; Bandura & Wood, 1989; Kanfer et al., 1994; Sterman, 1989; Vancouver & Putka, 2000). These are indices of an individual's subjective state of uncertainty while interacting with a complex decision making task (Kersholt, 1996; Klein, 1993; Lipshitz & Strauss, 1997; Sterman, 1989).

High and Low Subjective Judgments of Uncertainty

Those who have little or no experience with complex decision making domain (e.g. diabetes presented with a new blood sugar monitor) are likely to be highly uncertainty about the various associations between the events they observe (e.g., changing readings of sugar levels throughout the day). However, even when individuals have acquired significant experience changes in the system that go undetected (i.e., delayed outcomes) and can suddenly create instability, making the system appear out of control. This can sharply increase uncertainty because the outcomes that are experienced are unpredictable which raises doubts about the accuracy of one's underlying causal representations between actions and effects (for real world examples, see Degani, 2004). Contrasting this, judgments of low uncertainty indicate that the environment is perceived to be predictable and stable. This type of experience is often associated with expertise in which learnt behaviors are highly practiced and the complex decision making and learning task is familiar. But this type of judgment can also be made in simple tasks in which changes to the outcome, and the source of the change are easily detectable (e.g., traffic lights and traffic button presses).

Judgments of high uncertainty may lead to the search for new ways of interacting with a complex decision making and learning tasks, and eventually to a better understanding of how the system operates (Burns & Vollmeyer, 2002; Korbus, Protor, Holste, 2001). But poorly calibrated judgments of uncertainty in which a complex decision making and learning task is judged as highly uncertain can also lead to the abandonment of accurate hypotheses and turn a seemingly controllably system into an impossible one (Osman, 2008a, 2008b). Low assessments of uncertainty mean that causes of observed changes to outcomes are judged to be well-defined and easily controllable. In these cases people's belief in the ability to find a way to reliably generate specific outcomes to an immediate problem, or to successfully achieving a particular goal will increase (e.g., Coury, Boulette, & Smith, 1989; Wood & Bandura, 1989). However, estimating how stable and predictable en environment can encourage the persistence of inappropriate actions. This is because if the environment appears to be a highly familiar one, it is easier to implement well practiced behaviors, but it is harder to monitor unexpected outcomes (e.g, delays in outcomes and anomalies) because they are either overlooked or discounted as spurious (Dörner, 1989).

The Effects of Varying Subjective Judgments of Uncertainty

Given the many interactions an individual will have with a complex decision making task (e.g., navigating through a new city in a rental car), their subjective experience of uncertainty will vary over time, and often can increase. Typically in laboratory based version of complex decision making tasks decision making ability is shown to fluctuate as exposure to the task increases (Sterman, 1989; Yeo & Neal, 2006). As has been discussed previously, task-monitoring, self-monitoring and control behaviors are ways of managing uncertainty, and if subjective experiences of uncertainty change throughout a complex decision making and learning task, then so too will the behaviors designed to reduce it. This is an important aspect of behavior in complex decision making and learning task that has often been overlooked.

2.2. The Relationship between Monitoring and Control Processes

The MC-framework describes the relationship between self-monitoring and control, and the relationship between task-monitoring and control, as interactive and dynamic. Monitoring (self-monitoring, task-monitoring) and control alternate in a cascaded pattern, with the feedback from control actions serving as the input for later monitoring processes, and so on. This type of relationship is particularly usefu because if the environment is dynamic, then the changes to the outcome need to be monitored and control behaviors need to be adapted to respond to the changing demands placed on the decision maker (Koriat, Ma'ayan, & Nussinson, 2006). In the social cognition domain, Bandura (Bandura & Locke, 2003; Bandura & Wood, 1989; Wood & Bandura, 1989) and others (Seijts & Latham, 2001; Tabernero & Wood, 1999) have shown that, when controlling complex systems (e.g., management based scenarios), prior performance influences perceived self-efficacy. Prior experience and famailiarity with similar domains will affect subsequent performance. In support, many of the accounts developed to describe control behaviors in CDC tasks propose an interactive relationship, for which there is considerable supporting evidence in studies in Engineering (Kirlik & Strauss, 2006), Ergonomics (Kaber & Endsley, 2004), Management (Aitkins, Wood, & Rutgers, 2002), Problem solving (Burns & Vollmeyer, 2002), and Social cognition (Chesney & Locke, 1991; Kanfer et al., 1994).

The MC-Framework proposes that subjective judgments of uncertainty underlie task-monitoring and self-monitoring behaviors, on which control behaviors critically depend. Task-monitoring behaviors are responsible for producing and reproducing actions that will generate desirable outcomes. Through interactions with a complex decision making environment, our estimates of our knowledge of the causal relations between our actions and the complex decision making environment are based on: how reliably we can infer one or more of the following: (a) self initiated action-outcome sequences; (b) system initiated action-outcome sequences (c) value of consequences; (d) appropriateness of decisions taken (e) future preferences and actions; (f) one's ability to affect future events. These various sources are used to form our ongoing judgments of how the environment operates and the extent to which we can control it. It is our judgment that mediates task-monitoring behaviors, and therefore, determine the processing effort directed towards learning about, and learning to control a complex decision making task.

Self-monitoring behaviors serve a regulatory function of control behaviors. Through interactions with a complex decision making environment, our estimates of how uncertain a complex decision making and learning environment are based on: one's ability to reliably affect future events, and one's ability to reliably predict future events. These sources of information are used to form our ongoing judgments of the uncertainty of the environment we are in. Self Monitoring enables the individual to judge the relationship between their current status in a task and their desired goal. Subjective judgments of uncertainty mediate self-monitoring behaviors, by determining the extent (i.e. continuous, periodic) to which they are directed towards evaluating and assessing the outcome of control behaviors in complex decision making and learning tasks. Subjective judgments of high uncertainty will lead to greater vigilance in tracking task relevant behavior that could usefully contribute to achieving a target goal. Moreover, the same subjective judgments will prompt regular evaluation of the proximity between the current status in the task and the target goal. Subjective judgments of low uncertainty will lead to less effortful cognitive processing. If the task is a highly familiar one, or is judged to be highly predictable, neither the task nor the individual's actions in it require careful evaluation. This is because the likelihood of achieving a desired goal is easy to assess.

The framework proposes that, by empirically investigating people's subjective experiences of uncertainty and their changing estimates of uncertainty over time, it is also possible to describe the effects this will have on task-monitoring, and the interactive relationship between monitoring (Task-monitoring, Self-monitoring) and control behaviors. For control behaviours, monitoring processes are an essential component to track the effects of behaviour and the success of the actions taken towards achieving a particular goal. Studies in social and cognitive psychology suggest that our internal reflective process is fundamental to directing our behaviours when interacting with a complex decision making environment. Moreover our reflective process is not static, rather, given the goals that we pursue and the various changes that are observed (both from our actions and independent of them) our sense of agency can change quite radically for good reason because we may have little control over the events we see. In addition, even if the environment that we are acting on remains relatively stable our sense of agency can quite radically change, this is usually as a result of a distorted perception of events, and this can led to poor control over the events we see.

2.3. Task Uncertainty

Until now, the chapter has focused primarily on the effects of subjective judgments of uncertainty on monitoring and control processes. However, there are two different types of uncertainty that affect our monitoring and control processes and they are based on psychological uncertainty (e.g., confusion, inattention, stress) and uncertainty from the task itself (Osman, 2010a). That is, the task can generate uncertainty (U) because of: (1) those fluctuations in the system that will occur that are not accurately predicted by the individual, but that are infrequent fluctuations that contribute to the system perceived as having low uncertainty (Low-U); and (2) those fluctuations in the system that will occur that are not accurately predicted by the individual, and are highly erratic fluctuations that contribute to the system perceived as having high uncertainty (High-U). This following discussion proposes that there are common underlying characteristics of complex decision and learning environments that are a source of uncertainty, which can also influence our monitoring and control processes.

2.3.1. Characteristics of Complex Decision Making and Learning Environments

If we consider the essential properties of complex decision making and learning environments, the most obvious common features are that they are probabilistic and dynamic (Osman, 2010a). That is, the two most critical features of a control system are the probabilistic and dynamic relationship between causes initiated by an individual or resulting from actions independent of those made by the individual (i.e., other environmental factors, or internal triggers in the system) and their effects on the state of the control system. The cause–effect relations are ***probabilistic***: the effect may not always occur in the presence of the cause, and/or in the absence of the cause the effect may still be present (Osman, 2010b). The cause–effect relations are ***dynamic***: the internal mechanisms that are the functional relationship between causes and effects in control systems are what make the relationship between causes and effects dynamic. In addition, there are two other aspects of the environment that can contribute overall to uncertainty, and this is ***the stability of the environment*** and the ***rate at which changes are observed***. The greater the flexibility and range of outcomes generated by the control system, the greater its instability, and the greater the demands it places on exerting control on the system. Finally, the objective characteristics of the environment that are most important for the purposes of influencing monitoring and control processes are (1) the rate of changes in the outcome of the system over time that is non-contingent on external interventions (i.e., the changes that occur when we don't act on the system), in combination with (2) the rate of absent changes in the outcome of the system over time that should follow external interventions (i.e., occasions in which nothing changes when in fact we expect a change in the system from our actions). From the perspective of the individual, this can translate into two types of judgment uncertainty: (1) those fluctuations in the system that will occur that are not accurately predicted by the individual, but that are infrequent fluctuations that contribute to the system perceived as having Low-U; and (2) those fluctuations in the system that will occur that are not accurately predicted by the individual, and are highly erratic fluctuations that contribute to the system perceived as having high-U.

2.3.2. Interaction between Task and Monitoring and Control Processes in Order to Reduce Task Uncertainty

The final discussion of this section aims to outline the relationship between monitoring and control processes with respect to task uncertainty by outlining specific claims that follow from the framework.

1. The complex decision making and learning environment that we aim to control is often assumed to be goal directed – that is, we take for granted that the environment is operating with an objective (e.g., each button on a mobile phone has a function which contributes to enabling the device to function as a method of communication) and that we too are interacting with it following our own objective (e.g., push the correct buttons in the correct order to operate the mobile phone to communicate to a friend). As a starting point, to reduce uncertainty about how the system operates we too must interact with the system in a goal directed manner (e.g. call a friend now). By devising a goal, we help to motivate our actions in a specific way, and this forms the basis of our control behaviors (e.g. find and select the correct buttons). In turn, we generate an action that produces an outcome (e.g., the mobile phone is active and starts to dial the number we punched in). From this, we will also generate a discrepancy between the goal [desirable outcome – speak to our friend] and the actual outcome [achieved outcome – dial the right number]. The discrepancy between the goal and the actual outcome is evaluated in two ways [monitoring the control system, monitoring our own behavior].

2. In order to motivate our actions for the purposes of reducing uncertainty, we tend to invoke two methods of evaluation [Task-monitoring- predictability of the environment, Self-monitoring - predictability of our control over it]. The more encounters we have with the complex decision making environment, the more examples we have of the discrepancy between our estimates of the predictability of the environment and the outcomes generated by the system, and between our estimates of the controllability of the environment and the outcome generated in the environment. Combined, these generate an overall judgment of the uncertainty of the control system. The important point to bear is that people differ with respect to their threshold of uncertainty. If the overall judgment of uncertainty exceeds the threshold, then the control system is judged to be High-U. If the overall judgment of uncertainty falls below the threshold, then the control system is judged as Low-U.

3. The way in which we seek out knowledge, and the way in which we implement it in order to reduce our subjective experiences of uncertainty, both depend on the type of

uncertainty in the task environment. High-U will not lead to regular exploitation of the control system [i.e. a systematic application of the same pattern of interactions with the system] after every change to an outcome in the system. Low-U will lead to regular exploration of the control system [i.e. a change in the pattern of interactions with the system designed to seek out additional knowledge about the relationship between self-generated actions and outcomes in the system] after every change to an outcome in the system.

4. Finally, the underlying mechanisms that enable us to track the effects of our actions from those that occur independently of our interventions, involves tracking our actions and evaluating them with respect to our expectations of an outcome and the actual outcome that has occurred. It is likely that the ability to monitor self-generated outcomes and the ability to monitor task-generated outcomes are supported by the same neurological mechanism. Ullsperger, Nittono and von Cramon (2007) provide evidence for this based on examining the patterns of activation in the posterior medial frontal cortex (pMFC) during the execution of a conflict monitoring task. The pMFC has often been associated with performance monitoring behaviors, particularly when compensatory actions are recruited to correct an undesirable outcome. The task simply involved responding as quickly and as accurately as possible to a series of letter e.g., XXXHXXX, the target middle letter (e.g., in this case H). Participants were told that the apparatus that they were using to give their responses was faulty and that on occasion they may respond correctly but the program would not indicate this and that they were to repeat the correct response. The critical point of their study was to examine the corresponding patterns of activation when participants experienced genuine self generated errors, and when they experienced errors that were externally generated by the experimental program. They found that while people could reliably detect when errors were self generated, and also identify conditions in which they were uncertain about the source of errors. Regardless of the actual source of error, the magnitude of pMFC activity corresponded with the amount of time needed to correct for the error. Thus, it seems that while our self-monitoring mechanism enables us to explicitly identify outcomes that deviate from expectancies, and task monitoring can help us to locate the source of the deviation from expectancies, neurological evidence suggests that the pMFC region becomes active on the basis of the deviation from a target or correct response, and not the actual source of error.

3. ILLUSION OF CONTROL

In this final section, the aim is to discuss the effects of being in situations which can appear to be highly ambiguous because of our active monitoring processes. The MC framework raises an important question concerning the expectations we have of the environment that we are monitoring and attempting to control: *Do we expect that we can affect the environment through our actions, and therefore change it in a way that it behaves differently to what it would do without our intervention?* As has been briefly discussed earlier, our judgments of when actions and their effects are a result out our intention, or when they are the result of situational factors may be the result of perceived rather than actually the result of our actions. This implies a serious issue concerning the success of controlling uncertain decision making environments. Our sense of agency (Bandura, 2001) and our causal attributions (Kelley, 1967; Kelley & Michela, 1980) are critical in determining what happens in that environment. But, it appears that we have a fluid understanding of the causal relationship between our actions and what effects they may produce in the environment. In fact, even if the environment may be changing independently of our actions, we aren't always willing to accept that we have no control of the events we observe. Why might this be the case? It seems that we operate with a tacit assumption that our actions in the world have causal efficacy. Moreover, our self-monitoring mechanism appears to be designed to interpret the changing events in favour of self-attribution, particularly when we are faced with noisy, uncertain dynamic environments.

3.1. Studies of the Illusion of Control

Langer's (1975) pivotal study demonstrated that we have a bias towards inflating the probability of successful outcomes to our self generated actions. Since this early finding, there has been considerable supporting evidence suggesting that we prioritize the effects of our actions over chance outcomes (Alloy, & Abramson, 1982; Biner, Johnson, Summer, & Chudzynski, 2008; Burger, 1986; Fast, Cruenfeld, Sivanathan, & Galinsky, 2009, Mirowsky & Ross, 1990; Wenger, 2003; Whitson & Galinsky, 2008). Langer (1975) consistently found illusionary control over positive valence outcomes when selecting playing cards with the higher value while playing either an attractive or unattractive opponent (Experiment 1), selecting vs. being allocated lottery cards (Experiment 2-3, 5-6), and even playing a familiar vs. unfamiliar electric circuit board game (Experiment 4). Thus, in a variety of contexts in which the outcomes are entirely based on chance, factors such as intent, familiarity, choice and competition contribute to heightening our illusion of control. Langer speculated that the illusion of control shows how far we are motivated to perceive the extent of our control of our environment. Viewed from this light, control implies that we are beating the odds. It implies that if we can control adverse outcomes we can in effect reduce them. Finally, control implies that our skilled behavior, or intentional decision making, is directing a change in events that suits our purposes. In our everyday experiences of control, often the ambiguity of the task or its complexity means that skill and chance are interwoven. This is why we struggle to discriminate situations in which the events are truly down to our skill, from those that are simply the result of chance. For instance, gambling scenarios are one of the purest ways of displaying an illusion of control, because it is clear that we cannot influence the outcome of random events, but we often maintain a strong belief that our skill can affect a change in the outcome.

Following on from Langer's (1975) findings was the highly influential study by Alloy and Abramson (1982). Whereas Langer investigated the range of task conditions that generated the illusion of control, Alloy and Abramson examined specific factors associated with susceptibility to the illusion of control. There was two contexts in which control was examined, the first context involved situations in which the contingency between the individual's actions and the outcome was varied. In the contingency condition learning the correct sequence of button presses could temporarily stop an unpleasant noise from being played (Control-noise). In the second condition - the no contingency condition, there was no association between button presses and prevention of the noise, it would switch off randomly and start randomly (No control-noise). A baseline condition was also included in which no noise was played. All participants were then presented with a second task in which they could chose to press a button or not press a button, after which a green light flashed which indicated they had won a small amount of money (25 cent), or no green light flashed which indicated they had lost a small amount of money (25cent). There was no contingency between actions on the button (i.e. press, not press) and the absence or presence of the green light. The interesting effects they reported concerned the experiences in the first task and the facilitation of the illusion of control in the second task. Moreover, they compared students that scored low with those that scored high on Beck's Depression Inventory (BDI). They found that regardless of what experience they had in the first task, depressed individuals did not succumb to the illusion of control. They accurately judged that their button pressing had no effect on the final wins. Similarly, non-depressed individuals in the baseline condition in the first task, also accurately judged the status of their actions in the second task. However, non-depressed individuals that had either experienced the control-noise or no-control-noise condition misattributed positively valenced outcomes to their button presses; though they were as accurate as all other groups in judging their influence over negative valenced outcomes.

The key aspect of the findings from both these early studies is that they show that we general tend to make an attribution in favour of our own hand guiding positive outcomes, but we remain unbiased when experiencing negative outcomes that our not of our making. When it comes to losses that our not generated by our actions, regardless of our underlying state, we accurately perceive that we have no control over them. These findings speak to the issue of whether we behave under self-deception by maintaining an asymmetric attribution of events under our control depending on their valence. In other words, we may tend to view the world such that positive events in general (even if some aren't under our control) are attributed to our skilled actions, and negative events (even if some are under our control) are attributed to chance. Mirowsky and Ross (1990) claim that regardless of valence, non-depressed individuals by and large seem to accurately attribute outcomes to their own actions, and this has overall beneficial effects on people's ability to accurately understand the underlying causal relations in the world. Moreover it helps improve the ability to learn and exploit knowledge of the causal relations in favour of achieving desirable outcomes. Mirowsky and Ross (1990) examined the effects of individuals' judgments of responsibility of good events, and good outcomes, and bad events, as well as bad outcomes. They reported that those with low BDI scores (i.e. non-depressed individuals) also attributed a high degree of control over all possible ranges of events and outcomes. Those with high BDI scores (i.e. depressed individuals) tend to perceive all ranges of events as out of their control. The implications here are that if the locus of control is strongly located internally then it is associated with other aspects of behavior that indicate high levels of motivated, goal-directed thinking (Rotter, 1966). If the locus of control is located externally, in other words personal agency is not attributed to the events that are observed but rather external factors (e.g., luck, fate, chance, powerful others, unpredictable complex mechanisms) learning about actual contingencies in the world becomes vastly impaired. This has since been supported by findings from Stadelhofen, Aufrere, Besson, and Rosser (2009). They examined patients suffering from pathological gambling. Those scoring high in desire for control, a scale that examines the extent to which individuals are motivated to control outcomes in their environment (Burger & Cooper, 1979), tended to make higher attribution judgments of negative as well as positive outcomes, as compared to those scoring low on the scale (Burger & Hemans, 1988). Taken together, these findings support the general idea that the illusion of control generalizes to negative as well as positive outcomes, and is not simply a misattribution based on associating positive valenced outcome to self generated actions.

3.2. Individual Differences and the Illusion of Control

Why might people differ in their perception of their influence of chance events? Burger (1986) proposed that people vary in their desire for control and that this interacts with situations in which the illusion of control is more likely to emerge (e.g., familiarity, type of feedback). Compared to those with a low desire for control, those with a high desire for control tend to greatly distort perceived causality between their actions and the observed events. As with typical illusion of control tasks, participants in Burger's (1986) study played a card game in which they had to bet on winning hands which they were familiar with or unfamiliar (Experiment 1), or predict the outcome of a series of coin tosses (Experiment 2). Overall, individuals that scored high on the desire for control tended to perceive a stronger causal association between their choices (bets, predictions) and the outcomes compared with those scoring low on desire for control. Burger's (1986) coin toss task was a replication of Langer and Ross's (1975) original task, and in both studies the sequence of correct and incorrect predictions was pre-determined; some experienced descending number of correct predictions over 15 trials, and the rest experienced ascending number of correct predictions over 15 trials. Langer and Ross reported that the extent of the illusion of control was strongly influenced by the sequence of correct predictions. Experiencing a high number of correct predictions early in the trial sequence strengthened the illusion of control. In support, Burger found that those experiencing events that were consistent with their predictions early on in the game led to inflated estimates of accuracy of their skill in predicting outcome, whereas those experiencing events consistent with their predictions later in the game judged the accuracy of their own predictions to be much lower. Burger also reported that those scoring high in the desire for control estimated that if they experienced a further 100 trials, they expected a proportion of correct guesses that was in fact higher than the low scoring group. However, when asked to judge how good they were at predicting the outcomes of the coin toss game, estimates did not differ by group but rather by situational factors.

Not only does people's desire for control influence the extent to which they experience an illusion of control, but also their need for a particular change-based outcome [i.e. an outcome that is generated in a dynamic environment – e.g., sporting matches, stock markets] (Biner et al, 2009). In fact there are profound demonstrations in which people's needs bias their perception of random stimuli. For instance individuals in a hungry state were more likely to see food in ambiguous images than those that were fully sated (Biner & Hua, 1995; Levine, Chein, & Murphy, 1942). Biner et al (2009) have shown that as the need for a particular outcome increases in a chance based scenario, so too does the desire to control it. Confidence in achieving the desirable outcome also increases with motivational need to attain the desirable outcome. In addition, when artificially inducing a lack of control, the need to gain in back also leads to misperception of random events, which is biased in the direction of the desirable outcome being generated by the individual (Whitson & Galinsky, 2008). Clearly then, motivation plays a strong role in determining the extent to which we experience an illusion of control.

3.3. Summing up

The strong relationship between monitoring and control process is built on tracking changes in events in our environment in order to control them. Regardless of whether we are faced with complex environments in which many elements change as a result of our actions, or experiencing frequent changes to outcomes that have zero contingency without actions, we seem to perceive a relationship between our actions and the outcomes we observe. This perceived relationship between the effects and our actions is brought about through our highly active monitoring process. Our ability to interpret the causal associations between our actions and the effects in the world does seem to be necessary to controlling outcomes in noisy, uncertain decision making and learning environments. When uncertainty in our decision making and learning environment increases, we seek out ways of reducing it and increase our control over outcomes. Much of the work in the cognitive and social cognition domain has shown that the ability to control complex dynamic environments that generate high degrees of uncertainty is just as much a factor of our perceptions of the environment and our capabilities, as it is the actual characteristics of the environment and our true capabilities. But the ability to reduce uncertainty in this way comes at a price. Our goal directed monitoring and control processes are biased towards strengthening our sense of agency to such a degree that we perceive an association between random events and our own actions.

The illusion of control demonstrates that even in randomly changing environments, we choose to misattribute agency to the outcomes regardless of whether the outcomes are good or bad. This suggests that our self-monitoring mechanism operates with a general bias to attribute outcomes to our actions based on the goals we are operating with at the time (e.g., reduce our hunger, increase our wealth, increase our happiness, reduce our losses). The more motivated we are, the more likely we are to attribute the causes of events that we experience to our own actions, despite the fact that they are random events. The strong influence of motivation on the illusion of control suggests that it too is goal directed much in the same way as monitoring and control processes. The illusion appears to be the product of mechanisms that are designed to reduce our subjective experiences of uncertainty, and increase our sense of agency.

ACKNOWLEDGMENTS

Preparation for this research project was supported by the Engineering and Physical Sciences Research Council, EPSRC grant - EP/F069421/1.

REFERENCES

Alloy, L., & Abramson, L. (1982). Learned helplessness, depression, and the illusion of control. *Journal of Personality and Social Psychology*, *42*, 1114-1126.

Atkins, P., Wood R., & Rutgers, P. (2002). The effects of feedback format on dynamic decision making, *Organizational Behavior and Human Decision processes, 88,* 587–604.

Azjen, I. (1991). The theory of planned behavior. *Organizational Behavior and Human Decision Processes*, *50*, 179-211.

Bandura, A. (1977). Self-efficacy: Towards a unifying theory of behavioral change. *Psychological Review*, *84*, 191-215.

Bandura, A. (1989). Human agency in Social Cognitive Theory. *American Psychologist*, *44*, 1175-1184.

Bandura, A. (2001). Social cognitive theory: An agentic perspective. *Annual Review of Psychology*, *52*, 1-26.

Bandura, A., & Cervone, D. (1986). Differential engagement of self-active influences in cognitive motivation. *Organizational Behavior and Human Decision Processes*, *38*, 92-113.

Bandura, A., & Locke, E. A. (2003). Negative self-efficacy and goal effects revisited. *Journal of Applied Psychology*, *88,* 87-99.

Bandura, A., & Wood, R. E. (1989). Effect of perceived controllability and performance standards on self-regulation of complex decision making. *Journal of Personality and Social Psychology*, *56*, 805-814.

Biner, P., & Hua, D. (1995). Determinants of the magnitude of goal valence: The interactive effects of need, instrumentality, and the difficulty of goal attainment. *Basic and Applied Social Psychology*, *16*, 53-74.

Biner, P., Johnson, B., Summer, A., & Chudzynski, E. (2008). Illusory control as a function of the motivation to avoid randomly determined aversive outcomes. *Motivation and Emotion*, *33*, 32-41.

Bouffard-Bouchard, T. (1990). Influence of self-efficacy on performance in a cognitive task. *Journal of Social Psychology*, *130*, 353-363.

Broadbent, D. E., (1977). Levels, hierarchies and the locus of control. *Quarterly Journal of Experimental Psychology*, *32*, 109–118.

Burger (1986). Desire for control and the illusion of control: The effects of familiarity and sequence of outcomes. *Journal of Research in Personality*, *20*, 66-76.

Burger, J M , & Cooper, H M (1979) The desirability of control *Motivation and Emotion,3,* 381-393.

Burger, J. M., & Hemans, (1988). Desire for control and the attribution process. *Journal of Personality*, *56*, 531-546.

Burns, B. D., & Vollmeyer, R. (2002). Goal specificity effects on hypothesis testing in problem solving. *Quarterly Journal of Experimental Psychology, 55*, 241-261.

Chesney, A., & Locke, E. (1991). An examination of the relationship among goal difficulty, business strategies, and performance on a complex management simulation task. *Academy of Management Journal*, *34*, 400-424.

Corbetta, M., Patel, G., & Shulman, G. (2008). The reorienting system of the human brain: From the environment to theory of mind. *Neuron, 58*, 306-324.

Coury, B. G., Boulette, M. D., & Smith, R. A. (1989). Effect of uncertainty and diagnosticity on classification of multidimensional data with integral and separable displays of system status. *Human Factors, 31*, 551-570.

Crown, D. F., & Rosse, J. G. (1995). Yours, mine and ours – facilitating group productivity through the integration of individual and group goals. *Organizational Behavior and Human Decision Processes, 64*, 138-150.

Degani, A. (2004). *Taming HAL: Designing interfaces beyond 2001*. New York: Palgrave Macmillan.

DeCharms, R. (1979). Personal causation and perceived control. In L. C. Perlmuter, R. A. Monty (Eds), *Choice and Perceived Control*. Hillsdale, NJ: Erlbaum.

DeShon, R. P., & Alexander, R. A.. (1996). Goal setting effects on implicit and explicit learning of complex tasks.*Organizational Behavior and Human Decision Processes, 65*, 18–36.

Dörner, D. (1975). Wie menschen eine welt verbessern wollten und sie dabei zersto¨ rten [How people wanted to improve the world]. Bild der Wissenschaft, Heft 2 (Popula¨ rwissenschaftlicher Aufsatz).

Earley, P. C., Connolly, T., & Ekegren, G. (1989). Goals, strategy development and task performance: Some limits on the efficacy of goal setting. *Journal of Applied Psychology, 74*, 24-33.

Early, P. C., Northcraft, G. B., Lee, C., & Lituchy, T. R. (1990). Impact of process and outcome feedback on the relation of goal setting to task performance. *Academy of Management Journal, 33*, 87-105.

Elliot & Dweck, (1988). Goals: An approach to motivation and achievement. *Journal of personality and social psychology, 54*, 5-12.

Endres, M. L. (2006). The effectiveness of assigned goals in complex financial decision making and the importance of gender. *Theory and Decision, 61*, 129-157.

Fast, N., Cruenfeld, D., Sivanathan, N., & Galinsky, A. (2009). Illusory control; A generative force behind power's far-reaching effects. *Psychological Science, 20,* 502-508.

Goldsmith, M., Koriat, A., & Pansky, A. (2005). Strategic regulation of grain size in memory reporting over time. Journal of Memory and Language, 52, 505–525.

Gist, M. E., & Mitchell, T. R. (1992). Self-efficacy: A theoretical analysis of its determinants and malleability. *Academy of Management Review, 17*, 183-211.

Hogarth, R. M., Gibbs, B. J., McKenzie, C. R. M., & Marquis, M. A. (1991). Learning from feedback: Exactingness and incentives. *Journal of Experimental Psychology: Learning, Memory, and Cognition, 17*, 734-752.

Huber, V. (1985). Effects of task difficulty, goal setting, and strategy on performance of a heursitic task. *Journal of Applied Psychology, 70*, 492-504.

Huettel, S., Song, A., & McCarthy, G. (2005). Decision under uncertainty: Probabilistic context influences activation of prefrontal and parietal cortices. *The Journal of Neuroscience,25,* 3304 –3311.

Jones, G. R. (1986). Socalization tactics, self-efficacy, and newcomers' adjustment to organizations. *The Academy of Management Journal, 29*, 262-279.

Kaber, D, B., & Endsley, M. R. (2004). The effects of level of automation and adaptive automation on human performance, situation awareness and workload in a dynamic control task. *Theoretical Issues in Ergonomics Science, 5*, 113-153.

Kanfer, R., Ackerman, P. L., Murtha, T. C., Dugdale, B., & Nelson, L. (1994). Goals setting, conditions of practice, and task performance: A resource allocation perspective. *Journal of Applied Psychology, 79*, 826-835.

Karoly, P. (1993). Mechanisms of self-regulation: A systems view. *Annual Review of Psychology, 44*, 23-52.

Kelley, H. H. (1967). Attribution theory in social psychology. *Nebraska Symposium on Motivation, 15*, 192-238.

Kelley, H. H., & Mischela, J. L. (1980). Attribution theory and research. *Annual Review of Psychology, 31*, 457-501.

Kersholt, J. H. (1996). The effect of information cost on strategy selection in dynamic tasks. *Acta Psychologia, 94*, 273-290.

Kirlik, A., & Strauss, R. (2006). Situation awareness as judgment I: Statistical modelling and quantitative measurement. *International Journal of Industrial Ergonomics, 36*, 463-474.

Klein, G. (1993). A recognition-primed decision (RPD) model of rapid decision making. In G. A. Klein, J. Orasanu, R. Calderwood, & C. E. Zambok (Eds.). *Decision making in actionL Models and Methods*. Norwood, CT: Ablex.

Kobus, D., Proctor, S., & Holste, S. (2001). Effects of experience and uncertainty during dynamic decision making. *International Journal of Industrial Ergonomics, 28*, 275-290.

Kording, K. P., & Wolpert, D. M. (2006). Bayesian decision theory in sensorimotor control. Trends in Cognitive Sciences, 10, 319-326.

Koriat, A., Ma'ayan, H., & Nussinson, R. (2006). The Intricate Relationships Between Monitoring and Control in Metacognition: Lessons for the Cause-and-Effect Relation Between Subjective Experience and Behavior. *Journal of Experimental Psychology: General, 135*, 36-69.

Kornell N., Son L.K., Terrace H.S. (2007). Transfer of metacognitive skills and hint seeking in monkeys. *Psychological Science, 18*, 64–71

Langer, E. (1975). The illusion of control. *Journal of Personality and Social Psychology, 32*, 311-328.

Langer, E. & Roth, J. (1975). Heads I win, tails it's chance: The illusion of control as a function of the sequence of outcomes in a purely chance task. *Journal of Personality and Social Psychology, 32*, 951-955.

Lagnado, D., & Sloman, S. (2004). The advantage of timely intervention. *Journal of Experimental Psychology: Learning, Memory, and Cognition, 30*, 856-876.

Lerch, F. J., & Harter, D. E. (2001). Cognitive support for real-time dynamic decision making. *Information Systems Research, 12*, 63-82.

Levine, R., Chein, I., & Murphy, J. (1942). The relation of the intensity of a need to the amount of perceptual distortion: A preliminary report. *Journal of Psychology: Interdisciplinary and Applied, 13*, 283–293.

Lipshitz R., & Strauss, O. (1997). Coping with uncertainty : A naturalistic decision-making analysis. *Organizational Behavior and Human Decision Processes, 69*, 149-163.

Locke, E. A. (2000). Motivation, cognition, and action: An analysis of studies of task goals and knowledge. *Applied Psychology: An International Review*, *49*, 408-429.

Locke, E. A., & Latham, G. P. (2002). Building a practically useful theory of goal setting and task motivation. *American Psychologist*, 57, 705-717.

Locke, E. A., Shaw, K., Saari, L., & Latham, G. (1981). Goal setting and task performance: 1968-1980. *Psychological Bulletin*, *90*, 125-152.

Maynard, D., & Hakel, M. (1997). Effects of objective and subjective task complexity on performance. *Human Performance*, *10*, 303-330.

Mento, A. J., Steel, R. P., & Karren, R. J. (1987). A meta-analytic study of the effects of goal setting on task performance: 1966-1984. *Organizational Behavior and Human Decision Processes, 39*, 52-83.

Mesch, D., Farh, J., & Podsakoff, P. (1994). The effects of feedback sign on group goal-setting, strategies, and performance. *Group and Organizational Management*, *19*, 309-333.

Mirowsky, J., & Ross, C. (1990). Control or defense? Depression and the sense of control over good and bad outcomes. *Journal of Health and Social Behavior*, *31*, 71-86.

Nelson, T. O. (1996). Consciousness and Metacognition. *American Psychologist*, *51*, 102-116.

Neubert, M. (1998). The value of feedback and goal setting over goal setting along and potential moderators of this effect: A meta-analysis. *Human Performance*, *11*, 321-335.

Olson, J. M., Roese, N. J., & Zanna, M. P. (1996). Expectancies. In E. T. Higgins & A. W. Kurglanski (Eds). *Social Psychology: Handbook of basic principles* (pp. 211-238). New York: Guildford Press.

Osman, M. (2008a). Evidence for positive transfer and negative transfer/Anti-learning of problem solving skills. *Journal of Experimental Psychology: General*, *137*, 97-115.

Osman, M. (2008b). Observation can be as effective as action in problem solving. *Cognitive Science*, *32*, 162-183.

Osman, M., (2008c). Seeing is as good as doing. *Journal of Problem Solving, 2.1.*

Osman, M. (2010a). Controlling Uncertainty: A Review of Human Behavior in Complex Dynamic Environments. Psychological Bulletin, 136, 65-86.

Osman, M. (2010b). Controlling Uncertainty: Learning and Decision Making in complex worlds. Wiley-Blackwell Publishers, Oxford.

Pacherie, E. (2008). The phenomenology of action: A conceptual framework. *Cognition*, *107*, 179-217.

Papadelis, C., Kourtidou-Papadeli, C., Bamidis, P., & Albani, M. (2007). Effects of imagery training on cognitive performance and use of physiological measures as an assessment tool of mental effort. *Brain and Cognition, 64*, 74-85.

Rossano, M. J. (2003). Expertise and the evolution of consciousness. *Cognition, 89*, 207-236.

Seijts, G. H., & Latham, G. P. (2001). The effect of learning, outcome, and proximal goals on a moderately complex task. *Organizational Behavior and Human Decision Processes*, *46*, 118-134.

Smith, J.D., Shields, W.E., & Washburn, D.A. (2003). The comparative psychology of uncertainty monitoring and metacognition. *Behavioral and Brain Sciences*, *26*, 317–373.

Spering, M., Wagener, D., & Funke, J. (2005). The role of emotions in complex problem solving. *Cognition and Emotion, 19*, 1252-1261.

Stadelhofen, F., Aufrere, L., Besson, J., & Rosser, J. (2009). Somewhere between illusion of control and powerlessness: Trying to situate the pathological gambler's locus of control. *International Journal of Clinical and Health Psychology, 9*, 117-126.

Sterman, J. D. (1989). Misperceptions of feedback in dynamic decision making. *Organizational Behavior & Human Decision Processes, 43*, 301–335.

Sweller, J. (1988). Cognitive load during problem solving: Effects of learning. *Cognitive Science, 12*, 257-285.

Toda, M. (1962) The design of the fungus eater: A model of human behavior in an unsophisticated environment. *Behavioral Science, 7,* 164-183.

Tabernero, C., & Wood, R. E., (1999). Implicit Theories versus the Social Construal of Ability in Self-Regulation and Performance on a Complex Task. *Organizational Behavior and Human Decision Processes, 78*, 104-127.

Tversky, A., & Kahneman, D. (1974). Judgment under uncertainty: Heuristics and biases. *Science, 185*, 1124-1131.

Ullsperger, M., Nittono, H., & von Cramon, D. (2007). When goals are missed: Dealing with self-generated and externally induced failure. *NeuroImage, 35,* 1356-1364.

Vancouver, J. B. (2000). Self-regulation in organizational settings: A tale of two paradigms. *Handbook of Self-Regulation.* Academic Press.

Vancouver, J. B. (2005). The Depth of History and Explanation as Benefit and Bane for Psychological Control Theories. *Journal of Applied Psychology, 90*, 38-52.

Vancouver, J. B., More, K. M., & Yoder, R. J. (2008). Self-efficacy and resource allocation: support for a nonmonotonic discontinuous model. *Journal of Applied Psychology, 93*, 35-47.

Vancouver, J. B., & Putka, D. J. (2000). Analyzing goal-striving processes and a test of the generalizability of perceptual control theory. *Organizational Behavior and Human Decision Processes, 82*, 334-362.

VanLehn, K. (1996). Cognitive skill acquisition. *Annual Review of Psychology, 47*, 513-539.

Vigoda-Gadot, E., & Angert, L. (2007). Goal setting theory, job feedback, and OCB: Lessons from a longitudinal study. *Basic and Applied Social Psychology, 29*, 119-128.

Vollmeyer, R., Burns, B. D., & Holyoak, K. J. (1996). The impact of goal specificity and systematicity of strategies on the acquisition of problem structure. *Cognitive Science, 20*, 75-100.

Wenger, D. (2003). The mind's best trick: how we experience conscious will. *Trends in Cognitive Sciences, 7*, 65-69.

Whitson, J., & Galinsky, A. (2008). Lacking control increases illusory pattern perception. *Science, 322*, 115-117.

Wood, R. E., & Bandura, A. (1989). Impact of conceptions of ability on self-regulatory mechanisms and complex decision making. *Journal of Personality and Social Psychology, 56*, 407-415.

Yeo, G. B., & Neal, A. (2006). An examination of the dynamic relationship between self-efficacy and performance across levels of analysis and levels of specificity. *Journal of Applied Psychology, 91,* 1088 –1101.

In: Psychology of Self-Regulation
Editor: Vassilis Barkoukis

ISBN: 978-1-61470-380-8
© 2012 Nova Science Publishers, Inc.

Chapter 3

LEARNING ABOUT NON-DOGMATIC THINKING

Daniel Favre and Lionel Simonneau[1]

Laboratoire Interdisciplinaire de Recherche sur la Didactique Education
et Formation, (Team Didactique et Socialisation)
Université Montpellier, France

ABSTRACT

Very often, teaching the sciences still tends to set out stabilized knowledge and not the cognitive processes and values which lead to its collective elaboration. Consequently, the epistemic postures which characterize the scientific process and the scientific mind, are not the subject of learning at school or at the university. In this chapter, we try to understand what type of learning, including scientific and epistemological education, should be developed. An epistemo-historical survey will first show the stages which have enabled Western philosophers to work out new epistemic postures to objectify the world. We developed models for these postures, in language and texts, with linguistic indicators to distinguish "dogmatism" from "non-dogmatism" and applied these models to various contexts. We suggest that knowing about these postures should help to self-regulate one's thinking and learning by facilitating the "destabilization/stabilization" cycle of ideas. Indeed, when people become perceptive to the linguistic indicators identifying dogmatic and non-dogmatic modes of thought, and are able to grasp the shifts between these two modes, they also become able to regulate their own thoughts and, consequently, their behaviour. Various experiments on pupils, students and teachers have shown how learning about these postures can modify pupils' behaviour (violence, school learning). They have also shown the difficulties encountered by adults in regular Master's degree learning. As an attempt to explain these data and difficulties, we suggest that learning about the epistemic postures of the scientific process could be an intermediary between Level two and Level three learning as described by Gregory Bateson.

---

[1] Correspondence should be addressed to Daniel Favre / Lionel Simonneau, e-mail favre@univ-montp2.fr / lionel.simonneau@inserm.fr.

INTRODUCTION

In this chapter, we shed light on the self-regulation resources which, by taking other people's thoughts into account, with epistemic postures parallel to those occurring between scientific researchers, could widely improve learning at school and at university by regulating social behaviour and cognitive processes.

In our university of Science and Technology, many teachers complain that their students are not able to think critically. Moreover, like Kolstø in 2001, some authors report the difficulties that students have in understanding the domain of validation of scientific knowledge, due to their lack of epistemological training. Consequently, they do not develop the critical thinking skills that could allow them to take part in the great scientific debates of our times. What most science teachers probably do not realise is that they are actually contributing to these difficulties. Indeed, teachers, as well as students, have in mind an implicit, empirico-realistic representation of scientific knowledge (Hodson, 1985; Collins, 1989; Roberts & Chastko, 1990; Désautels, 1994). As shown by Ryan & Aikenhead in 1992, since university professors are training the future teachers, this conception of science apparently forms a perennial loop from the primary school to university, in a kind of vicious circle. Thus, the image of "ready-made science" is installed in the mind, i.e. the truth exists before it has even been discovered, and words are basically used to describe observations and not to elaborate theories (Sutter, 1996).

Since 1991, in parallel with work by Désautels, Larochelle, Gagné & Ruel (1993), we have been trying to understand the epistemological changes which have gradually emerged over the last twenty six centuries due to scientific thought, in the way knowledge is depicted and, particularly, the relationships that a person may have with his own knowledge. Among the most noticeable difficulties is the "motivation", as a consequence of the "empirico-realistic" concept of science, of giving knowledge a status of certainty, a negative value to error, and the idea that subjectivity does not interfere or only slightly interferes with the observations or the scientific reasoning. Several authors have questioned the roles of objectivity and subjectivity in cognitive scientific explanations (Holton 1975, Morin 1982, Schiff 1992). Everything seems to point to the fact that the scholar, academic teaching and functioning of society are in favour of a positivist and dogmatic way of processing information, leading science students to depend on the stability of their knowledge because they lack an epistemological education. This is often reported by teachers who complain that their students lack critical thinking. Therefore, they feel discomfort when they are shown the temporary and approximate features of scientific knowledge, its statistical nature and the controversial issues emanating within the scientific community as a common means of building the scientific knowledge.

Following our first attempts (Favre, 1991 ; Favre & Rancoule, 1993 ; Bélanger, Rancoule & Favre, 1994 ; Favre, 1995, Berthou-Gueydan & Favre, 1995) to identify the epistemic postures or cognitive attitudes linked to the scientific approach, we designed a test (Favre & Joly, 2001) to characterize the cognitive functioning mode of pupils who presented violent behaviour and/or educational failure. We described two modes of thinking; dogmatic and non-dogmatic. The dogmatic functioning mode leads its users to be addicted to the stability of their knowledge which is prejudicial to interpersonal relationships when points of view diverge, and to learning which requires ideas to go through deconstructive phases.

Conversely, communication training workshops for pupils, 58 % of whom were beyond the level of pathological aggressiveness (set at 95 on a 0 to 100 level scale, Favre and Fortin, 1997) allowed them to develop their inward language by adopting a more open and reflexive way of thinking (Favre, 1998) thus reducing their aggressiveness and all its related variables (anxiety-depression, attention disorders, dogmatic functioning…) by half (Favre and Joly, 2003). In addition to the fact that the youths had developed behaviour which made them less rejected by their communities, their attitude in relation to learning had changed, with a less dogmatic mode of processing information, they felt safer in dealing with uncertainties and their academic results had improved (Favre, 2007). We showed that our learning programmes were only partially successful from the point of view that they worked best if the subject was young and female. Our experience has shown that the training must be longer if the subject is an adult, whether it be with patients suffering from backache (Gatto & Favre, 1997) or with primary or secondary school teachers in teacher-training schools (Favre, 2007).

Conversely to our learning programs, the standard university system for training students (master's degree level), which teaches the theoretical contents of epistemology that characterize the scientific approach, seems to show that these contents are less transferable outside the context of academic tests.

Is our way of training (i.e. making students aware of the way one's thinking shifts between dogmatic and non-dogmatic modes) related to a different style of learning? Is it likely to greatly modify our relationship with the world and others?

The aim of this article is to understand what type of learning is operational, so that a person becomes aware of his own epistemic postures and of the shifting of his thinking activity from being open-minded to narrow-minded, and vice versa.

First of all, in the context of an epistemo-historical survey, we will set out how and through what stages, western philosophers have developed new epistemic postures in their attempt to understand the world more objectively.

Secondly using the psychology of self-regulation, we will describe a model which helps to understand how these epistemic postures, by controlling our thoughts and behaviours in everyday social life, get a grip on our thinking activity by the feedback they induce.

Thirdly, by explaining our various experiments with young pupils and older students, we will show not only how learning these postures, when possible, can modify their behaviour (violence, school learning…) but also what difficulties may be encountered with this type of learning in adults.

In conclusion, as way of explaining these results and difficulties, we will suggest the hypothesis according to which learning epistemic postures with a scientific approach can be situated between learning levels II and III as defined by Gregory Bateson.

1. HUMANITY HAS GRADUALLY INVENTED POSTURES TO *PUT THOUGHT INTO MOVEMENT*

Through a mainly epistemological and historical approach, different ways have been pointed out for preparing one's "body and mind", to receive and process the information captured by our senses during learning (Favre, 1997, pp. 13-38).

The aim of the following epistemological and historical approach is to show how successive criticism of the characteristics of modal thought have made it possible to define scientific thought. Far from locking us in certainties, scientific thought integrates us into a world of ideas in which uncertainty, approximation and provisional situations prevail.

Long before the invention of science and philosophy, human beings had become used to transmitting knowledge to one another. According to the specialists of Antiquity, such as Lloyd (1974), the knowledge of the Egyptians, Mesopotamians and Greeks (before Thales) was based on the encyclopaedic accumulation of juxtaposed notions including, in particular, descriptions of techniques which had been worked out empirically and directly associated with the practice of magic. This encyclopaedic accumulation was passed on from master to student who, in turn, became a master himself . "In Great Antiquity, the understanding of the world was essentially mythical and magical; Man participated directly in the world through his deeds and rites; even highly specialized techniques such as metalwork were accompanied by magico-mystical rites". There was scarcely any distinction between a word and a thing and, in an almost magical relationship, the word was part of Nature as one of its strengths (Pichot, 1991).

Later, the trend of using more and more phonetic writing and language gradually evolved towards abstraction, by imposing a signifier-signified system, and contributed to separating Man from the world, making him more likely to apprehend the world. Words were used to represent the world conceptually or abstractly. "In just under three centuries, the Greek world saw the invention of the phonetic alphabet, currency and democracy. These three events, although they each have their appropriate historical explanation, correspond to the birth of science and philosophy" (Pichot, 1991). Besides, this author claims not to know whether there is any causal link between these two events or whether they emanate from the same current of thought.

For us, it corresponds to the appearance of the *first cognitive attitude or epistemic posture to* allow abstraction, as we know it. It goes from the implicit to the explicit, by definition, distinction and classification. This attitude has no precise origin but is illustrated in the biblical text of Genesis, in which Man was asked to name vegetables, animals, mountains …

The Second Epistemic Posture Concerns the Way of Providing Proof

In agreement with Popper's point of view (1972) [2], we believe that a founder time before Socrates in the Eleatic and Ionian schools must have existed, when Anaximandre (610 - 547?) criticized his master, Thales of Milet, and when the latter encouraged him to continue doing so. By this means, Thales was somehow legitimising such unusual cognitive behaviour. New freedom, together with a new relationship with knowledge and authority were born. After Anaximandre, almost all Milesian disciples criticized their masters.

By finding interest in critical, "de-constructive" speech, Thales broke away from tradition and the value which aimed to preserve knowledge as it stood, like a treasure to be passed on

---

[2] In agreement with Thales de Milet's interest in critical speech, Karl Popper wrote (in 1965 p. 22):
"in order to seek the truth, maybe the best method consists of starting by subjecting our most precious beliefs to criticism. This prospect may seem rather twisted to some, but not for those who want to discover the truth and are not afraid of it. "

"intact" to future generations. "De-constructive" speech allows thought to progress since it attempts to define more precisely the domains of validity of the cognitive objects arising from the different activities of thought. Both philosophy and science find their origin in this valuable change. A new relationship with knowledge - critical knowledge about knowledge - and authority appears, as knowledge is no longer assimilated to the accumulation of the knowledge by a single person.

In western countries, philosophy and science merged together for twenty centuries but their use was not really spread until the Renaissance. In spite of the open-mindedness introduced by Thales, the "high priests" of knowledge established their power by hoarding knowledge and punishing those who dared to question them. For example, the Pythagorean School, with mathematical beliefs within a spiritualistic view of life was extremely authoritarian. Indeed, it is important to notice that, in society's eyes, science was a two-faced Janus: comforting vs threatening; adventurous and off the beaten tracks vs serious and respectable; subversive and critical-minded vs dogmatic and producing certainties.

Bacon (1620) and Descartes (1637) allowed knowledge "to be released". Bacon, by inviting one to harmonize thought and reality in a more pragmatic way and Descartes by inviting one to stand back in relation to one's own thought. Just like Montaigne, Descartes[1] emphasized the application of reason and suggests dissipating prejudices, suspending judgment to give oneself time to think: "I have learned to believe nothing too firmly". According to Descartes and Bacon, the sciences began to develop in the West as this "less firm" thought led to a *third epistemic posture* which consisted of reasoning in terms of hypotheses about the world, of approximate and provisional modelling, rather than in terms of the absolute, unchanging truth. This distance taken from one's own way of thinking makes it possible to develop it. On the other hand, attachment or, rather, "addiction to certainties" (Favre, 2000a), can remove the freedom to learn, leading to blindness, or even fundamentalism and fanaticism.

Later, Kant went on to develop the idea according to which our data about the world are in fact mental constructions; this idea was later to be developed by phenomenology, itself at the origin of existentialism. Husserl (1931) calls the remarkable property of the conscience to be conscious of itself "intentionality". The inclusion of the world in the conscious is not real, like a tree in a park, but intentional, which prevents one from considering the relationship of the conscious to the thing as being like the relationship between the inside to the outside. According to phenomenology, the ego thinks and turns out to be at the origin of sense. This current of thought denounces the error which consists of believing in the existence of a duality represented by pure consciousness confronted with a pure object. Phenomenology thus appears as an antidote for the positivism which had raised objectivity to the rank of ideal and ignored the effects of subjectivity.

The *fourth epistemic posture* allows us to characterize the contemporary scientific approach. It involves taking into account subjectivity, the reflexive activity of the subject who is thinking of his desires and fears as well as of their impact on his own thought (for example, "I notice that the sky is grey, which gives me a feeling of melancholy!"). This approach is contrary to a way of functioning which consists of projecting one's emotions, feelings, and explanatory or theoretical plans on the outside world when subjectivity has not been taken into account by its author (for example if I claim the weather is dull). Nowadays, considering and eliminating subjectivity in science is mostly done by methodological precautions such as blind or double-blind testing medicines and processing statistics in order to establish the reliability and significance of the data obtained. However, we may notice that these attempts are trying to neutralize only the negative aspects of subjectivity.

Now, subjectivity arises at practically all stages of research: in the choice of hypothesis, the theoretical context, the methods, the way of presenting results, and right up to the choice of a journal to publish them (Schiff, 1992). Indeed, the history of science truly shows *a posteriori* that the division between fact and theory is difficult to define and the limits of validity of "scientific fact" correspond more or less to those of the way in which reality is represented and characterize the scientific community at a given period.

Indeed, in his book "The Mismeasure of Man", which carefully analyses the works on human intelligence carried out by eminent American scientists in the XIXème century, Stephen Jay Gould showed that this research was based more on prejudice than scientific rigour. Indeed, the data were compatible with a representation of a social hierarchical organization including the practice of slavery, with white Americans at the top and black Africans or Australian aborigines at the very bottom. In his book, Stephen Jay Gould showed how their data were biased to fit with these social representations.

The border between scientific and non-scientific thought therefore turns out to be quite difficult to identify and its limits are debatable. And yet the contributions of various epistemologists do complement each other. In 1972 Popper emphasized criticism which prevents the formation of closed thought. In 1962 Kuhn[3] demonstrated how the community of researchers had been functioning for four or five centuries. In 1979, Feyerabend[4] described the way in which the invention process is opposed to the order previously established by other researchers. Finally, Morin (1986) denounced the incapability of classical science - which is based on the paradigm of simplification - to grasp a world whose complexity it had partly revealed.

And so, like Bachelard (1938) we come to the temporary conclusion that facts and theories go forwards together. This kind of progress uses what can be understood as "error" only afterwards, and what really connects researchers during this movement is a "scientific

---

[3] The criticism of Popper's thesis by Kuhn. As a historian and sociologist of sciences, he does not observe that the scientists proceed by formulations of hypothesis and refutations, because, according to him, the theories (indeed, the supporters of these theories) resist the facts which refute them. With this approach to science as it stands, Kuhn notices that when one "paradigm" becomes dominant within the scientific community, it is then practically irrefutable, and ongoing research work mostly aims to confirm it. As a paradigm is a set of theories, behaviours, methods and values with strong coherence between them locally, one may notice that, historically, the supporters of an old paradigm have never been sensitive to the experimental proofs refuting it. Very often, it only becomes possible to have a change of paradigm leading to a "scientific revolution" when a significant number of supporters of the former paradigm have died. That way, scientific truth is then accepted by the majority.

[4] Feyerabend's thoughts about the development of science brings to light the fact that this development includes a creative contribution, which is often, as shown in the previous example, a rebellion against customary methods. This shows the potential danger of methodological rules which freeze and standardize thought. For Feyerabend, there are thus no particular methods which lead to scientific discovery, "All ways are good ".
Imagination, combinations of circumstances, dreams like Kekulé's, play an important role in the invention of a new concept and this part of irrationality seems completely necessary. But in addition to this, Kékulé managed to deal with the problem with rigor and constancy. So, from "dreaming about a snake biting its own tail", he was able to imagine the structure of a benzene molecule as a symmetrical six-legged ring of carbon atoms with alternating single and double bonds. However it was only seventeen years later, when he was in a stable university position, that he referred to this dream and the role it had played in the publication which made him famous as a scientist !

state of mind" or "objective intention", according to Gonseth (1975). We must also point out the fact that, for the French Nobel prize-winning biologist Jacques Monod, objectivity in science is defined as a metaphysical postulate (Simonneau, 2010), considering that objectivity must not be mistaken as the mere opposite of subjectivity. Monod (1977) wrote: "Everybody knows that a man of Science is not objective from a subjective point of view".

By trying to characterize this state of mind or intention, we identified and defined four cognitive and epistemic postures for use in the objectivity project characterizing the scientific approach. They concerned:

- the mode of formulation;
- the attitude towards knowledge;
- the way proof is established;
- the attitude towards subjectivity.

By considering these four postures we can situate such and such a term between the limits forming two theoretically opposite mental attitudes, which we call a "dogmatic thinking mode" or "closed-mindedness" and a "non-dogmatic thinking mode" or "open-mindedness". However, there are no fixed limits between these two attitudes, but a continuum containing several intermediate situations. We move between these two ways of thinking, according to circumstances and, depending on which of the four postures we are in (Favre, 2000b). By familiarising ourselves with this model, it should be possible to situate oneself and identify the "epistemological context of our activity of thinking ".

2. FROM DOGMATISM TO A MORE OPEN ATTITUDE: LEARNING TO FEEL WHAT WE ARE THINKING

Here we suggest models which can help us understand the evolution of the epistemic and psychological features on a scale ranging from dogmatic to non-dogmatic postures. These models when put into practice, must be understood as theories, just like Lewin wrote in 1952 when he said : "There is nothing more practical than a good theory".

In our models, dogmatic thought is characterized by four epistemic postures:

- The person turns to the implicit to express himself;
- The statements have a character of absolute truth and definite judgments (verb "to be" in the present indicative form, absence of other modes and other tenses);
- Argumentation only aims to take into account the "facts" which confirm the personal precepts by neglecting all others and leads to improper generalizations;
- The person hides his own emotions and feelings, whilst exteriorising them by unconsciously projecting them on his environment. The most striking feature is the inclination to remove the mark of the enunciator and of his subjectivity (the word "I" disappears and is replaced by "He", "She", "We" or "One").

Non-dogmatic thinking or open-mindedness is expressed by four opposite attitudes or postures. This involves:

- Becoming aware that the self is different from others and that efficient communication with others requires us to clarify our own point of view sufficiently by naming it, distinguishing it, etc.;
- Assigning an approximate and temporary nature to statements (by formulating hypotheses and questioning, using conditional forms and assertions which suspend judgment: "It seems to me that...", "Maybe....");
- Situating and exposing the limits in which the statement finds its domain of validity or area of application (for example, the search for counter-evidence);
- Taking into account the subjectivity of the person who is speaking. This becomes possible when the person is able to identify his needs, feelings (fears and desires frustrated or not) and to situate them in their context. In this way, one is not denying one's feelings, but giving them the right to exist and show through, without any emotional outburst.

Predominant range of expression in "violent" pupils

Predominant range of expression in "non-violent" pupils

Dogmatic thought	Cognitive posture (with possibility of shifts between 2 poles)	Non-dogmatic thought
Range of the implicit	Formulation modes	Explicitation, definition, classification ...
Expressed in the form of unchanging truth or final certainties	Attitude towards knowledge	Expressed in the form of questioning, hypotheses or approximate, provisional-models
Abusive generalization, Only those elements which confirm the statement are retained	Administration modes of proof	Critical search of counter-examples and re-contextualisation of the statements and their domain of validity
Subjectivity is ignored but emotions like personal explanatory plans representations are projected on the world outside	Attitude towards subjectivity	Subjectivity, desires, fears, are taken into account to try to represent reality reflexively
Knowledge Stabilization pole Normal, science[5] and logic for testing in learning	*The scientific approach, like learning, corresponds to movements between these two poles*	Destabilization pole of the knowledge Situation of scientific crisis[6] and logic of regulation in learning

Figure 1. Modelling the epistemic postures associated with the scientific approach.

In Figure 1, four epistemic postures can be visualized together with the "differentials" by which they can be linked to their opposites.

In this figure, two poles with a dialectical relationship can be seen: stabilization and destabilization of knowledge. The cursor on each differential (the four lines with a double arrow) suggests that we can move between these two ways of processing information, depending on the circumstances.

This modelling of epistemic postures can be applied to various contexts such as the appropriation of scientific concepts or the relationship between the teacher and his pupils, and then be used as an explanatory model for various problems such as learning disorders, violence at school or even academic failure.

In the school environment, the logic of testing, which is essential in any society, aims to measure the distance from a set standard so that those individuals with certain skills or knowledge can be easily selected. Error therefore corresponds to failure and contributes to eliminating individuals, to social sorting, and its status is a result of dogmatic thought. The evaluation resulting from it is cumulative and the relevant time of its use is when we consider that learning the expected knowledge and know-how should have finished.

On the other hand, the logic of regulation seems essential, at the time of learning, to cognitive destabilization, because, by attributing a status of "interesting information" to error, and a process of cognition to results, it provides the learner with information so that he may overcome possible difficulties and thus progress towards the acquisition of new skills or knowledge (Favre, 1995).

There are at least two possible uses of this analysis grid (Figure 1).

Moving the cursor along each differential can be used as "external feedback". With a pragmatic analysis of the language used, it becomes possible to pinpoint the predominating epistemological context of the person expressing himself (orally or in writing) (Favre and Joly, 2001).

The subject may also consciously integrate these differentials. With this acquired capacity, he becomes sensitive to his own epistemological context of thought, allowing him, in Descartes terms "to direct his thoughts better".

Feedback[5] is indeed required to put one's thinking to use in this conscious project: stabilizing or destabilizing knowledge (one's own knowledge or that of others) and to adapt it to this aim (Favre, 2000b). A person who thinks with no feedback is likely to be subject to automatic thinking and/or family, cultural, conditioning from the media, etc..., and will neither understand nor accept the self-regulation attitude. Without the epistemological distance allowing us to realize that our way of thinking is becoming dogmatic, we are likely to accumulate all the conditions for self-deception, by masking our needs, even our dependence on stable contents of thought which apparently have the status of Truth. However, although all of us can recognise that our capacity for being open to novelty and variety varies according to circumstances and our emotional state, few studies have been made on modelling the dynamics of thought between these two poles. That is to say that, between closing (our minds) and being incapable of letting our representations be modified on the one hand and, on the other hand, opening (our minds) and being led to a more or less important cognitive and emotional destabilization as the price to pay for encountering the unknown.

Open-mindedness with non-dogmatic thought, combining the cognitive attitudes of the scientific approach, requires awareness and distance. Furthermore, accepting our emotions invites us to stop being purely objective creatures but to remain vigilant by checking whether our "intention to be objective" (to quote to Gonseth, 1975) is really present. It is always

---

[5] This is the case when making a voluntary movement. If we want our muscles to obey us and serve our demands, for example to grab an object with our hand, we require different receptors, or sensors, sensitive to muscle tension and position of our joints. These receptors inform us with successive feedbacks on the progression of a given movement and allow us to adjust it. Likewise, the more sensors a robot has to inform it about the effects of its different activities, then the more reliable, autonomous and adaptable it is. The differentials felt with the shift of our cursors are intended to play this role of sensors.

possible to make mistakes, and that is a good thing because science can only progress by rectifying mistakes (Bachelard, 1938), but it becomes more difficult to mistake oneself than in a dogmatic posture.

The epistemological analysis grid presented here as standard methodology, is suggested as a mental activity procedure for feeling one's thought become stabilized or destabilized. The back and forth movement between these two poles is necessary, on one hand, to enable us to live in community by sharing sufficiently stable contents of thought and, on the other hand, to keep our thoughts moving. The history of scientific thinking illustrates these movements as, in each discipline, periods of "normal science" (with theories being validated i.e. dogmatisation) and periods of crisis (destabilization of theories) alternate (Kuhn, 1962).

The grid also helps us to understand that the maximum amount of objectivity we can pretend to does not reside in the search for unchanging truth, but in our capacity to gradually adapt our representations to the complexity of the universe and ourselves. Are we ready for that? Letting go of what we strongly believe in and venturing into the unknown may give us a feeling of exaltation, but feelings of a very different nature from those, although as exciting, also encourage us to look for certainties (Favre, 2000c).

Meanwhile, by developing the open-minded postures of a scientific approach, humanity has favoured the emergence of postures to allow new ways of learning. Understanding how, and in what conditions, a person can accept or refuse this inward disturbance can give a new insight into learning and academic failure, and will help us to develop educational systems so that this disturbance is taken further into account. This should also help us to better understand how certain teenagers act by adopting violent behaviour and, in so doing, avoid new situations which require them to adapt (Van Caneghem, 1978, p. 236). Indeed, this difficulty in letting their personal ideas be destabilized might also explain why academic failure is so often associated with violence (Fortin and Bigras, 1996). As stated in Figure 1, pupils considered as violent tend to exteriorise dogmatic thought more than pupils who are considered as non violent (Favre and Fortin, 1997).

Violence feeds and grows more easily on dogmatic thought in which the implicit, the systematic, the certainty and the projection are mutually engendered accompanied by the thrill of being right. However, educating pupils towards open-mindedness might be a good antidote, as our experiments with pupils and teachers have already shown.

3. A FEW LEARNING SYSTEMS FOR RECOGNISING EPISTEMOLOGICAL LANDMARKS IN THINKING

In this next section, with a summary for each one, we are going present three kinds of results obtained with high school pupils, middle and primary school teachers and pupils, and also university students at master's degree level where didactics, epistemology and the history of science are taught.

3.1. First Experiments at High School with Non-selected Pupils

From 1991-1992, in high schools in the region of Avignon (Bélanger et al., 1994), we began a study aiming at allowing pupils to develop better relational autonomy in the school environment. This research was meant to carry out an evaluation of the effects of an epistemological "education" for high school students. This education was supposed to develop the linguistic skills of the students correlated with a mode of "non-dogmatic" information-processing (Favre and Rancoule,1993). As previously described, this mode of processing is based on explanations of facts, the formulation of hypotheses, the search for counter-evidences and by taking the enunciator's subjectivity into account (use of the pronoun "I", expressing one's feelings, resorting to the conditional form, better contextualisation, use of definitions,…). Conversely, a person making use of a dogmatic information-processing turns to the register of the implicit in his comments, uses statements as if they were the absolute truth and hides his emotions and feelings.

In our opinion, this education focusing on language should have helped the students to identify their linguistic production, by referring to the two extreme ways of processing information: dogmatic and non-dogmatic. Our hypothesis was that, keeping a distance would allow them to be more autonomous in interpersonal relationships, particularly when these generate strong affective and emotional reactions, which is often the case with frustration, knowing that learning is also a source of frustration.

The teenagers who did this training course of thirty hours showed a significant increase of more reflexive statements, so expressing a non-dogmatic processing of information, and their marks increased by one point out of twenty on average, which we had not planned at first. This increase continued into the following year whereas they were split up into several high school senior classes. Many reports suggest that the students who have done this training course have got better, that they are less submissive and passive at school without being rebellious.

On the other hand, the students in the control groups (i.e. students coming from "any other" high school classrooms) produced more answers expressing passivity, submissiveness and projection attitudes with no improvement of the school results. We thus proposed the hypothesis that the violent behaviour partly originated from reactions of frustration (amplified for some students by family and socio-economic parameters). For lack of an education allowing them "to step back from" unpleasant affects by the use of language, they express these frustrations in the form of violent behaviour.

As regards the academic result improvement of the students having followed the training course, we believed that the progression we had observed and found again in other similar experiments might have resulted from the ability "to step back from" their mental activity and raising their frustration intolerance threshold. All learning includes a longer or shorter period of time when we do not know how to do something and during which time our representations must be destabilized. Learning a less dogmatic cognitive way of functioning had perhaps made it possible to accept the fact of being unsure more easily, and in any case, of not knowing, for a longer period.

3.2. Experiments in Middle School with Pupils Labelled as "Violent" by their Teachers, and with Primary and Middle School Teachers

The following section sums up our research carried out in France, Canada and Switzerland from 1994 to 2005 on the study of links between violence and academic failure. First, a psycho-socio-cognitive portrait of the teenager labelled as "violent" by his teachers will be presented, then the data obtained following a weekly communication workshop (twenty-five 45-minute meetings), and finally the prevention perspectives allowing us to plan specific training for teachers, combining didactics and socialization.

The Teenager Described as Violent
From these previous works it came out that the teenager considered as "violent" by his teachers, in France and in Québec, showed strong aggressiveness[6]: the mean values obtained from psychological and cognitive tests were seven to eight times higher than those of the controls, strictly and significantly correlated ($r= 0.56$) with anxiety and depression syndromes, which were twice as high as those of controls in France and three times higher than those of controls in Canada (Favre & Fortin, 1997).

Studying the way in which pupils considered as "violent" processed information showed us that they "functioned" in a very dogmatic way. This type of functioning was significantly correlated ($r = 0.51$ in Canada, $r = 0.41$ in France) with aggressiveness, and teenagers lived in a logic of immediacy. Most often, they placed the origin of unpleasant events in their lives outside, and were almost incapable of naming and identifying their feelings and emotions and situations of frustration (Favre and Fortin, 1999; Favre and Joly, 2001).

With these results, it is possible to understand why academic failure is so often associated with violence and why negative judgments about these pupils should be avoided, this avoidance being essential if we are to help them efficiently (Fortin and coll., on 1996). Indeed, at school where there are plenty of different learning situations (and therefore, cognitive destabilization), those pupils who depend on the "stability" of their representational world cannot make any progress in their knowledge and, therefore, fail more easily than the others, even if they have an equal IQ. This academic failure causes them to be gradually excluded on a social level, which then produces or maintains anxiety and frustration and, for some of them afterwards, violent impulsive reactions. Unlike a minority whose strong aggressiveness is not associated with dogmatic processing, these pupils are apparently seeking great stability in their representational world upon which they are highly dependent.

---

[6] Distinguishing aggressiveness from violence. Our studies have shown that 1) aggressiveness is a biological function, like hunger, thirst, sexual impulse, which purpose is to protect our physical, psychological and territorial integrity while, 2) violence is defined as "any behaviour requiring, consciously or not, the need to make others weak, helpless or uncomfortable in order for one to feel strong, powerful and comfortable". Violence would be an addiction to endogenous behaviour, an addiction-free drug, working in the same way as motivation for addiction.

Remedying Violence in the School Environment?

During the second phase of this research we were able to confirm that it is not easy to progressively abandon the satisfactions associated with the practice of violence (the pleasant emotions and feelings of power obtained when others are made to feel fear or helplessness). Just like exogenous drug addiction (to a product), it is necessary to wean these pupils and case-pupils often tried to discourage their teacher by communicating to him the feeling that with them, he was doomed to fail. It turned out to be necessary to analyse practices with the teacher-trainer, in the same way as one might work with a "Balint" group[7] (Favre, 2007, part 2). Actually, Michael Balint showed that, within the therapeutic relationship between a physician and his patient, emotional involvement and transfer of affection occurs.

The core of our interventions thus consisted of suggesting to "violent" pupils that they adopt a non-dogmatic way of processing information, which would mean substituting the representations they usually use with new ones. To this purpose, we suggested using language mediation in its function of regulating and self-controlling behaviour in order to develop different cognitive attitudes for situations in which pupils might feel frustrated (Favre, 1998).

There were four main objectives, aiming to helping these teenagers to:

- Abandon the implicit postulate according to which "others have less value than myself", and to make the hypothesis that "others are different from me and have just as good reasons as myself to think what they are thinking, to act as they are acting, to say what they are saying and to feel what they are feeling".

- To abandon the idea that experiencing emotions and feelings is a sign of weakness and vulnerability, even femininity (seen by the males) and to admit that, on the contrary, it is richness, a source of sensations and important information about oneself and the world.

- To replace the belief that expressing one's emotions and feelings makes one vulnerable to the one it makes strong, and consists of daring to fully exist, whereas hiding these emotions and feelings is proof of weakness (like a hermit crab hiding its soft inner belly in a hard shell borrowed from a mollusc).

- To give up the idea that in a situation of confrontation, there cannot be one winner and one loser, one person who is right and one person who is wrong, one who dominates and one who gives in, and to become tolerant and open to other points of view than one's own, to admit that any "truth" is only in a given context and that the knowledge of this context is also important as the truth itself.

We were surprised by the positive results obtained with the same tests done one month after the end of the communication workshop, in spite of the difficulties encountered during our interventions (Favre and Joly, 2003).

1. a very significant decrease in aggressive behaviour of 60 % , making the case-pupil average going below the pathological threshold.
2. a very significant decrease in "social problems", also of 60 %, for these pupils, which confirms the previous result: as these pupils are less aggressive, they interact more

---

[7] The Balint group is a group method of training doctors, teachers or other professionals in the trainer-trainee relationship. This method was developed by Michael Balint and Enid Albu starting in 1945.

positively with their neighbours. We noted too a significant 66 % decrease in attention deficit, a 58 % decrease in the tendency to "withdraw", a 40 % decrease in exteriorised problems, all of these confirming a modification of behaviour involving better adequation with the school context.

3. the average of the variable "anxiety-depression" correlated with the variable "aggressiveness" is also significantly lowered by 50 % in the case-pupils, so placing them widely below the pathological threshold.

4. a very significant 84 % increase in "non-dogmatic answers", another variable correlated with aggressiveness. This is because these pupils acquire the ability to use the appropriate language to express their needs and emotions and have them respected. In addition, they can transfer these skills in different situations, particularly in family relationships.

During this research study it was important to show that violent behaviour could be changed, knowing that it has the reputation of being difficult to modify once installed. However, putting all the "most terrible" case-pupils of a school together in the same group, as here described, does not seem relevant to us with regard to the missions which are pertinent to teachers and their training. We therefore tried to estimate the effects of teacher training aimed at *preventing* violence on the pupils.

Teacher Training Aimed at Preventing Violence and Academic Failure

The aim was to estimate in France, at primary schools situated in priority education areas[8] and in Switzerland at middle school, the impact on the pupils of their teachers' heightened awareness of the shift in their thinking activity between each of the two modes of information processing we have described: dogmatic and non-dogmatic. Several arguments, justifying the necessity to become aware of this problem, were at the origin of this research project.

1. Violence only exists within an interaction, whether the partners are present or not.

2. Up until 2006, nineteen out of twenty teachers did not refer to emotions or personal feelings when they defined what the violence represented to them, and approximately 4/5 of them placed the causes of violence outside themselves.

3. Teachers, whether they like it or not, are adult models for their pupils and their pupils will try to identify with them either positively, by miming their attitudes, or negatively, by rejecting them.

By reminding that violence appears within an interaction, one emphasizes the fact that between the two extremes: "I am 100 % responsible for violence, or 100 % *not* responsible for it", it is likely that the teacher does indeed have some responsibility. Since 1983, the beginning of the Daniel Favre's interventions in teacher training, many situations experienced by teenagers, in which they have been victims of behaviour or words that make them feel weak (in the sense of our previous definition) have been recorded (Favre and Fortin, 1997).

Consequently, we investigated the possibility that the teachers might be able to prevent violence with the help of a different kind of training emphasizing the ability to identify

---

[8] Zones d'Education Prioritaire: an environmentally protected area, targeted for special and priority help in education.

dogmatic and non- dogmatic postures in pupils, and in themselves. By merely becoming immediately aware of the fact that we are working dogmatically we are already being less dogmatic!

The positive effects that we obtained in primary and middle schools (Favre, 2007, part 2) such as the increase of marks in French and especially the significant increase in the capacity for empathy on the behalf of pupils proved the success of transmitting knowledge in a less dogmatic way. Indeed, empathy corresponds to the ability to imagine what others are thinking and feeling, whilst distinguishing what one is thinking and feeling oneself (Favre, Joly, Reynaud and Salvador, 2005; 2009). Thus, coming back to the categories of Figure 1, we cannot be in a "dogmatic projection" and "non-dogmatic reflection" mode at the same time.

However, teacher training has certainly involved working, not only on dogmatic and non-dogmatic epistemological aspects associated with language, but also on the relationship with error, the possible confusion between domination-submission behaviour and authoritarian behaviour, on various modes of self assertion and on the fact that the ways in which knowledge is transmitted and pupils learn might become socialization situations. However, all these areas are strictly linked to each other and to values (Favre, Hasni and Reynaud, 2008).

In order to be developed and accepted by teachers, these training sessions (72 hours over two years) required collective "work" on explaining the values and representations associated with them. Following this reflection, a greater coherence arose between the values most teachers adhere to, i.e. transmitting knowledge, forming autonomous, responsible citizens in a society in which the members show solidarity between each other, and educational practices in everyday life. The values that had to be given up (domination of the weak by the strong, logic of exclusion…) are Man-made, and so it is Man who can modify them. They question our idea of Man, Life, the World and the place of Man within that world. How can we constructively associate the logic of cooperation and the logic of competition? The subject should indeed fear for himself the effects of conflicts between opposite values which are not recognized as such. A sense of citizenship and education towards responsibility involves making a conscious choice between values; once again it is necessary to become aware of them before that choice is made.

3.3. Training Students at Master's Degree Level

In contrast to the teacher training methods (established between 1998 and 2005 in France and Switzerland), in the context of our research, the epistemology learning process of the students in our master's degree classes is very classical and consists of a frontal presentation of the elements explained in the first two parts of this article: examples given in each of the disciplines represented (mathematics, physics and chemistry, biology…), small problems to be solved and a final exam as a means of testing.

For over ten years, this exam has allowed us to check if most of the students memorized without problem both epistemic postures attributed to the scientific approach, that is to say, first, the injunction to name, define and clarify one's way of thinking and secondly the importance of the break introduced by Thales with the critical thought, which makes reasoning evolve whilst giving error an epistemological status different from the one it had before. Because it is actually an epistemological Bachelardian leap which is required of them: to go from intellectual hoarding with the passive and uncritical accumulation of data to capitalization or, even better, cognitive mutualisation in a register of epistemic thought based on self-regulation abilities.

The posture concerning the *situation with regard to knowledge giving scientific contents a status of approximate and temporary wording* mode is retained by half of them.

As if the idea of "thinking less firmly" (to paraphrase Descartes), and remaining in uncertainty, represented something difficult or irrelevant for them.

Finally the last posture, the one concerning the *situation with regard to subjectivity* mode coming from the rupture brought by phenomenology, remains absent from students' writings nine times out of ten.

In the restricted context of academic teaching, so many parameters have been changed to improve students' results: supply of documents, authorization to use documents for the exam, modification of questions, contribution of examples, humour, or no humour... nothing seems to want to change these figures. However, these students were often teachers themselves and not very different from those we had trained in France or Switzerland and who had been able to mobilize the four epistemic postures!

This is why we may make the two following remarks:

1. From a historical viewpoint, we have noticed that the ability to memorize and mobilize these epistemic postures depends on how long ago they appeared in philosophical thought. As the phenomenological approach came last, it re-situates subjectivity within our mode of perception, is opposed to positivism and the empirico-realistic aspects of science, which so many students and teachers seem to share.

2. The experience of those teachers who took part in the training on the prevention of violence and academic failures seems to show that their relationship with the world has changed. They are less afraid of making mistakes, have become more tolerant about their pupils' mistakes, have learned to step back and are less easily manipulated ...

Have the links made with the relationship to error, authority, others, and to values created a different learning context, the one required for this type of learning?

CONCLUSION

Although nowadays developing the critical thinking of our students is, for many academics, a necessity and indeed a shield against closed or rigid forms of thinking produced by any kind of fundamentalism, one might ask how to deal with scientific education. Quessada's thesis (2008) clearly shows that Darwin's theory can only be an efficient shield against the creationism only if pupils have integrated and adopted the epistemic postures of the scientific approach and have understood how science works from the inside. Initiating students to the experimental process ties in with this but is this enough, since it is difficult to experiment with evolution!

The difficulties and the successes we met in "teaching non-dogmatic thought" for the young students and for teachers make us think that such teaching goes beyond simply modifying our ideas, it modifies the person both at a cognitive and emotional level.

Bateson (1977) defined three levels of learning:

1. The individual receives new information and adapts to it.
2. He partly modifies his way of interpreting the world, following this new information.
3. He becomes aware of the way he is learning, the rules which led him to change his conceptions of the world and the possibilities of using again these rules in other circumstances.

From an educational viewpoint, we have noticed that, in their work, teachers often demonstrate the importance of retroactive information in the learning process. This kind of information which has its source outside the learner, allows the latter to adapt his approach to the educational objective set by the teacher. With this kind of learning, which Bateson would qualify as Level 1 learning, the teacher gives back to the learner information or evaluations about his verbal, written or graphic productions.

The capacity to apply one's experience in the same disciplinary field and to self-assess what one has produced seems to testify to the acquisition of internalized indicators replacing the teacher's external feedback. The capacity to mobilize one's know-how in other areas for which direct application is impossible requires the existence of a self-assessment skill on a higher level corresponding the to "learn to learn" ability (Level 2 according to Bateson). This level does not simply require learning an answer to a stimulus, but transferring the information to other contexts. The subject is capable of transposing what he has learnt. This learning is similar to the process of generalization, which we use when we unify apparently different contexts.

According to Bateson, the individual needs to attain learning Level 3 when contradictions, inadequacies, suffering and blockages have been engendered by Level 2 learning. So when Level 2 learning becomes more difficult, and a source of confinement, failure and dissatisfaction, the person must learn to change the habits he has acquired with learning Level 2, in order to re-orientate his behaviour to more appropriate contexts.

In each shift towards a higher level of learning, the subject integrates into his activity stimuli from one contextual stratum which is bigger than the one he was working on before with a broader and broader "glance at himself ".

In the context of learning non-dogmatic thought, the subject becomes able to pick out different ways of receiving and processing the information he is receiving or has already received and to identify his epistemic postures in deferred time or real-time. He thus has conscious access to the context in which learning levels 1 and 2 are made. Bateson wrote: "if Level II learning is about learning the contexts of Level I learning, then Level III learning should be about learning the context of these contexts". Therefore Level III learning must be linked to re-defining one-self and results from a new construction of reality (Bateson, 1977, pp. 253-280).

Developing a critical mind and autonomy is one of the school's missions, but are teachers prepared to spend more time at school and at the university so that their pupils can "feel what they think *and* think what they feel"? Indeed, certain educational practices from our "dogmatic" past which are opposed to acquiring non-dogmatic thought postures and to taking into account the relationship with error, may contribute to creating interpersonal relationships likely to inhibit learning.

The question asked by Désautels and Larochelle (1997) thus remains relevant in the context of teacher training. "How can we help our future teachers to develop the capacity to make critical feedback on the ins and outs of their actions, to make reflexive and critical checks on what they are doing, and what they are making their students do. In short, how can we make them devoted to a form of reflexivity which is both epistemological and social ?"

ACKNOWLEDGMENTS

We thank Claude Caussidier for her help. In addition we thank Teresa Sawyers and Ann Willett, for their collaboration on the English version of this article.

REFERENCES

Bachelard, G. (1938). *La formation de l'esprit scientifique.* Vrin, Paris, 1987.

Bacon, F. (1620). *Nuvum organum,* selon une étude sous la dir. de M. Malherbe & J.M. Pousseur : *Francis Bacon, Science et Méthode.* Paris, Vrin, 1985.

Bateson, G. (1977). *Vers une écologie de l'esprit - tome 1.* Paris, Le Seuil.

Bélanger, R., Rancoule, Y. & Favre, D. (1994). Une éducation épistémologique portant sur le langage peut-elle favoriser les performances scolaires ? In A. Giordan, J.L. Martinand & D. Raichvarg (Eds.), *L'alphabétisation scientifique et technique,* Chamonix, pp. 243-248.

Berthou-Gueydan, G. & Favre, D. (1995). Les attitudes cognitives de la démarche scientifique sont-elles compatibles avec les représentations majoritaires actuelles de la science? In A. Giordan, J.L. Martinand & D. Raichvarg. *Que savons-nous des savoirs scientifiques et techniques ?* Chamonix, pp. 317- 321.

Collins, A. (1989). Assessing biology teachers: understanding the nature of science and its influence on the practice of teaching. In Herget D.E. (Ed.), *The history and philosophy of science in science teaching,* pp. 61-70. Tallahassee, Florida State University.

Désautels, J. & Larochelle, M. (1997). A propos de la posture épistémologique des enseignants et enseignantes de science. In A. Tiberghien, E.L. Jossem, J. Barojas (Eds.), *Des résultats de recherche en didactique de la physique à la formation des maîtres.* International Commission on Physics Education 1997, 1998, section D3. http://www. physics.ohio-state.edu/~jossem/ICPE/TOC.html

Désautels, J. (1994). Le constructivisme en action : des étudiants et des étudiantes se penchent sur leur idée de sciences. *Revue des sciences de l'éducation, 20-1,*135-155.

Désautels, J., Larochelle, M., Gagné, B. & Ruel, F. (1993). La formation à l'enseignement des sciences: le virage épistémologique. *Didasklia, 1*, 49-67.

Descartes, R. (1637). *Discours de la méthode pour bien conduire sa raison et chercher la vérité dans les sciences*. Paris, Granier-Flammarion, 1966.

Favre, D. & Fortin, L. (1997). Étude des aspects socio-cognitifs de la violence chez les adolescents et développement d'attitudes alternatives utilisant le langage. In B. Charlot & J.C Émin (Eds.). *La violence à l'école : état des savoirs*. Paris, Armand Colin, pp. 225-253.

Favre, D. & Fortin, L. (1999). Portrait de l'adolescent désigné comme violent. *Bulletin de Psychologie, 52(3)*, 363-372.

Favre, D. & Joly, J. (2001). Évaluation des postures cognitives et épistémiques associées aux modes de traitement dogmatique et non-dogmatique des informations – application à l'étude de la violence et de l'échec scolaires. *Revue Psychologie et Psychométrie, 22(3-4)*, 115-151.

Favre, D. & Joly, J. (2003). Mode de traitement de l'information, sa relation avec l'adaptation sociale et son évolution consécutive à des ateliers de communication axés sur le langage intérieur. In F. Larose (Ed.). *Difficultés d'adaptation sociale ou scolaire et interventions éducatives*. Canada, Édition du CRP de l'Université de Sherbrooke, pp. 23-40.

Favre, D. & Rancoule, Y. (1993). Peut-on décontextualiser la démarche scientifique ?. *Aster, 16*, 29-46.

Favre, D. (1991). Démarche scientifique et pédagogie. *Transversales Science/Culture, 8,* 12-13.

Favre, D. (1995). Conception de l'erreur et rupture épistémologique: *Revue Française de Pédagogie, 111*, 85-94.

Favre, D. (1997). *Des Neurosciences aux Sciences de l'Éducation : contribution à une épistémologie de la variance*. Thèse de Doctorat en Sciences de l'Éducation, Université Lyon 2. Lille, Presses Universitaires du Septentrion, 1998.

Favre, D. (1998). Le rôle du langage dans la régulation des comportements violents. *Revue Empan, 32*, 41-45.

Favre, D. (2000a). De l'addiction aux certitudes. *Psychologie de la Motivation, 30*, 88-94.

Favre, D. (2000b). Du neurone au différentiel. In G. Jucquois & C. Vielle (Eds.), *Le comparatisme dans les Sciences de l'Homme - approches pluridisciplinaires*. Collection Méthodes en Sciences Humaines. Bruxelles, De Boeck Université, pp. 101-117.

Favre, D. (2000c). Se tromper soi-même : plaisir ou fatalité ? In A. Mouchès (Ed.), *Illusions*. Paris, L'Harmatan, pp. 37-54.

Favre, D. (2007). L'erreur et la faute. In A. Tarpignan, L. Baranski, G. Hervé & B. Mattéi (Eds.), *École : changer de cap, contributions à une éducation humanisante*. Lyon, Chroniques Sociales, pp. 50-59.

Favre, D. (2007). *Transformer la violence des élèves : cerveau, motivations et apprentissage*. Paris, Dunod.

Favre, D., Hasni, A. & Reynaud, C. (2008). *Les valeurs explicites et implicites dans la formation des enseignants*. Bruxelles, De Boeck Université.

Favre, D., Joly J., Reynaud, C. & Salvador, L.L. (2005). Empathie, contagion émotionnelle et coupure émotionnelle - Historique critique de la notion d'empathie. *Enfance, 4,* 363-382.

Favre, D., Joly J., Reynaud, C. & Salvador, L.L. (2007). Empathie, contagion émotionnelle et coupure émotionnelle, Validation d'un test pour repérer et aider les élèves à risque. *European Review of Applied Psychology, 59,* 211–227.

Favre, D., Pithon G., Reynaud, C. & Salvador, L.L. (2004). Pensée non-dogmatique et développement de savoir-faire démocratiques (en famille, à l'école…). In M. Tozzi. (Ed.) *La discussion en éducation et en formation.* Collection « Action et savoir ». Paris, L'Harmathan, pp. 33-52.

Feyerabend P. (1979). *Contre la méthode, esquisse d'une théorie anarchiste de la connaissance.* Paris, Le Seuil.

Fortin, L. & Bigras, M. (1996). *Les facteurs de risque et les programmes de prévention auprès d'enfants en troubles de comportement.* Québec, Béhaviora, Eastman, Paris : Exportlivre.

Gatto, F. & Favre, D. (1997). Utilisation d'indicateurs discursifs pour optimiser les effets de la rééducation auprès de patients lombalgiques. *Santé Publique, 3,* 341-360.

Gonseth F. (1975). *Le référentiel, univers obligé de médiatisation.* Lausanne, L'Âge d'Homme.

Gould S.J. (1981). *The Mismeasure of Man.* New York, W. W. Norton

Hodson, D. (1985). Philosophy of science, science, and science education. *Studies in Science Education. 12,* 25-57.

Holton, G (1975). On the role of Themata in scientific thought. *Science, 188 (4186),* 328-334.

Husserl E. (1931). *Méditations cartésiennes: introduction à la phénoménologie.* Paris, Vrin, 1986.

Kolstø, S. D. (2001). Scientific literacy for citizenship : tools for dealing with the science dimension of controversial socioscientific issues. *Science Education, 85,* 291-310.

Kolstø, S. D. (2001). To trust or not to trust…, pupils' ways of judging information encountered in a socio-scientific issue. *International Journal of Science Education, 23,* 877-901.

Kuhn, T. (1962). *La structure des révolutions scientifiques.* Paris, Flammarion, French translation. 1983.

Lewin K. (1952). *Field theory in social science: selected theoretical papers by Kurt Lewin.* London, Tavistock.

Llyod, G. E. R. (1974). *Les débuts de la science grecque.* Paris, La Découverte, 1990.

Monod, J. (1977). *"Notes de bas de pages", Prospectives et Santé,* n°1, 11-22.

Morin, E. (1982). *Science avec conscience,* Paris, Fayard.

Morin, E. (1986). *La méthode : T.3 La connaissance de la connaissance,* Paris, Le Seuil.

Pichot A. (1991). La naissance de la science T.2. Coll. Folio-essais. Gallimard, Paris.

Popper, K. (1969). Conjectures et réfutations. Paris, Payot, french trad. 1985.

Popper, K. (1972). The myth of the framework, In Colloque de Cerisy. *Karl Popper et la science d'aujourd'hui.* Paris, Aubier, 1989.

Popper, K. (1965). *Conjectures and refutations.* London : Routledge & Kegan Paul,1965. *Conjectures et réfutations.* Paris, Payot, french trad. 1986.

Quessada M.P. (2008). *L'enseignement des origines d'Homo sapiens, hier et aujourd'hui, en France et ailleurs : programmes, manuels scolaires, conceptions des enseignants.* Thèse de Doctorat en Sciences de l'Éducation, Université de Montpellier 2. http://tel.archives-ouvertes.fr/tel-00353971/fr/

Roberts, D.A. & Chastko, A.M. (1990). Absorption, refraction, reflection: An exploration of beginning science teacher thinking. *Science Education, 74(2),* 197-224.

Ryan, A.G. & Aikenhead, G.S. (1992). Students' preconceptions about the epistemology of science. *Science Education, 76(6),* 559-580.

Schiff, M. (1992). *L'homme occulté. Le citoyen face à la science.* Paris, Editions Ouvrières.

Simonneau, L. (2010). L' "autocritique" de Jacques Monod, 40 ans après: La contingence et la contrainte... *Bull. Hist. Epistem. Sci. Vie, 17-2,* 125-145.

Sutton, C. (1996). Beliefs about science and beliefs about language. *International Journal of Science Education,* 18(1), 1-18.

Van Caneghem, D. (1978). *Agressivité et combativité,* Paris, P.U.F.

In: Psychology of Self-Regulation
Editor: Vassilis Barkoukis

ISBN: 978-1-61470-380-8
© 2012 Nova Science Publishers, Inc.

Chapter 4

ABOUT THE FUELS OF SELF-REGULATION: TIME PERSPECTIVE AND DESIRE FOR CONTROL IN ADOLESCENTS SUBSTANCE USE

Nicolas Fieulaine[*1] *and Frédéric Martinez*[2]

[1]Social Psychology Research Group, Institute of Psychology, University of Lyon, Lyon, France
[2]Social Psychology Research Group, Institute of Psychology, University of Lyon, Lyon, France

ABSTRACT

In this chapter, we focus on the role of time perspective (TP) and desire for Control (DC) in self-regulation theory (SRT). Whereas self-control is the muscle of self-regulatory processes, time and control, as distal factors in self-regulation, may be considered as the fuels of this activity. We present results from a study investigating how SRT and TP frameworks can be related empirically, and to evaluate the role played by DC in the context of an extended model of the theory of planned behavior (TPB). The study was designed to explore the intervention of Desire for Control (DC) in the relation of TP to substance use, and to evaluate the contribution of these constructs to the TPB model and SRT. Participants were randomly recruited in high schools (N=690) and the study was prospective in design with an assessment of behaviors one week later. Findings showed the moderating role of DC in the relation of TP to substance use, suggesting the impact of those constructs on cannabis use behaviors, through their impact on proximal predictors. Findings of this research program offer some perspectives to integrate further TP research in the framework of self-regulation, and have some practical implications for promotion-or prevention-focused intervention related to substance use behaviors. They also open perspectives for a more "social" view on self-regulation.

SELF-REGULATION AND SELF-CONTROL

In the last decade, Self-regulation theory (SRT) became one of the most influential and promising theoretical framework to deeper our understanding of how and why people engage in health damaging behaviors, or escape from those behaviors (De Ridder & De Wit, 2006; Hagger, 2010). Grounded in motivation theories, SRT is a deeply dynamical model depicting conscious and nonconscious processes by which people regulate their thoughts, emotions, attention or behaviors and extended research has shown its implications for addictions or substance consumption. A key factor in SRT is the way individuals differ in their basic styles of self-control, which appeared as a crucial predictor of self-regulation capacity (Baumeister, Vohs & Tice, 2007). Self-control relate to the process through which people manage their dispositional tendencies and control their thoughts, feelings, impulses and task performance in order to be consistent with their goals and standards of behaviors, and is a basic element of the capacity to self-regulate (cf. Baumeister, Gailliot, DeWall & Oaten, 2006; Rasmussen, Wrosch, Scheier & Carver, 2006). As various studies evidenced, people with high abilities to self-control are less vulnerable to impulsivity and delay more gratification than people with low self-control (DeRidder & DeWitt, 2006). Therefore, people with low capacities to regulate appeared as more susceptible to engage in substance use, to sustain their consumption et to have difficulties in quitting (Wills, Sandy & Yaeger, 2002 ; Wills & Stoolmiller, 2002 ; Wills, Ainette, Stoolmiller, Gibbons & Shinar, 2008). Beyond its main effect on substance use (Brody & Ge, 2001; Wills, Walker, Mendoza & Ainette, 2006), self-control repeatedly appeared as a buffering agent in the relation of risk factors to substance use behaviors (Wills & al., 2008; Wills, Pokhrel, Morehouse & Fenster, 2011). In these studies, having good (or high) self-control appears to be negatively related to substance use, and to reduce the impact of risk factors on substance use. This buffering effect of self-control on the impact of risk factors to substance use has been extensively acknowledged for different populations, using a variety of methods (see Wills & al., 2008 for a review).

BEYOND THE MUSCLE, THE FUELS OF SELF-REGULATION CAPACITY

Its central functional role in self-regulation processes lead some authors to depict self-control as a "muscle" that allow and sustain self-regulation activity, susceptible to become tired after exertion, and to be increased via exercise (Muraven & Baumeister, 2000; Baumeister & al., 2006). In a recent study, Fieulaine & Martinez (2010) claimed for consideration of another control construct, distinct from self-control, but that can act as a main motivational factor in self-regulation, namely the construct of desire for control (Burger & Cooper, 1979). Desire for control (DC) or motivation to control is a specific and significant construct amongst the various concepts envisaged in the framework of "control" (Skinner, 1996). Specifically, it corresponds to the desire or motivation to maintain control, make one's own decisions, and be in charge of one's activities (Burger & Cooper, 1979). Although need for control is generally taken for granted in psychology, it can manifest itself at various levels or strengths. DC is distinct from other measures related to perceptions or beliefs about control, given that it examines the degree to which control is attractive, desirable and valuable, while other measures generally assess the level to which, and how, control is attained or perceived (cf. Skinner, 1996). Thus, one can attain high control in a given situation, but may wish to relinquish this control over others. Conversely, one may actually desire high control, but perceive his/her effective control as low. DC is presumed to be a source of motivation for control (Burger & Cooper, 1979), varying from situation to situation but resulting in a general and measurable level, and was evidenced as an important dispositional factor within various phenomena, such as achievement, psychological adaptation, stress, or health (Burger, 1992; Gebhardt & Brosschot, 2002). Following Fieulaine & Martinez (2010), "if self-control resembles a muscle in self-regulation processes, then desire for control could function as the oxygen or the fuel of muscular activity" (pp. 799-800), and should be considered as a motivational basis for self-control capacity in self-regulation processes. When considering the energetic role of self-control in self-regulation, one may pay more attention to the motivational basis of self-control, and therefore to its desirability for individuals. Power or strength of self-control, and resources enhancement or depletion in self-regulatory processes could find an antecedent, at least for a part, in the level of motivation or desire for control.

TIME PERSPECTIVE AND SELF-CONTROL

To investigate further how DC can intervene in self-regulation Fieulaine & Martinez (2010) tested its role as a buffering agent in the relation of a dispositional risk factor to substance use and evidenced that desire for control can buffer the link between time perspective (TP) and substance use. There are several strong theoretical reasons why TP deserve particular attention when considering self-regulatory processes and self-control. First, self-control, and self-regulatory capacity in general, are deeply temporally based (Hall & Fong, 2007) and shaped (Wills, Sandy & Yaeger, 2001; Joireman, Balliet, Sprott, Spangenberg & Schultz, 2008). Balancing short term and long term consequences of decisions and behaviors can adequately be considered as the core definition of self-control. Second, among the psychological factors that relate to health behaviors, time perspective has received growing attention and has been identified as one of the most important by numerous studies, based on various approaches and methods, sometimes involving large representative samples (Guthrie, Butler & Ward, 2009; Adams & White, 2009; Crockett, Weinman, Hankins & Marteau, 2009). Third, several studies suggested that TP and self-control are not only intercorrelated, but also interact in their impact on behaviors (Joireman & al., 2008; Barber & al., 2009).

The hypothesis underlying the incorporation of time in this field of research is that health behaviors fundamentally involve temporal dilemmas, creating conflicts between immediate benefits and future costs (in the case of risk-taking behaviors), or between immediate costs and future benefits (in the case of health protective ones). Time preference and time orientation thus appeared as personal variables likely to influence, more or less directly, the decision-making process. While time preference corresponds specifically to the differential value attached to outcomes in relation to temporal location for a particular behavior or event (Fuchs, 1982; Chapman & Coups, 1999; Chapman, Brewer, Coups, Brownlee, Leventhal & Leventhal, 2001; Chapman, 2001), temporal orientation corresponds to the attention paid to the past, present, and future time frames across a broader range of situations (Cottle, 1968; Zaleski, 1994; Finke, 2005). Both have been extensively acknowledged in relation to preventive and risky health behaviors, and from these studies it emerges that future time preference and orientation, (as opposed to present preference and orientation), is associated with less risky and with more preventive behaviors, and this for a variety of health behaviors (e.g. Agnew & Loving, 1998; Björgvinsson & Wilde, 1996; Strathman, Gleicher, Boninger & Edwards, 1994; Chapman & Coups, 1999; Orbell & Kyriakaki, 2008).

In the last decade, a field of research has emerged based specifically on the broader concept of time perspective (TP), originally proposed by Lewin (1942), and recently reactivated by the work of Zimbardo and colleagues (Gonzales & Zimbardo, 1985; Zimbardo & Boyd, 1999; Zimbardo & Boyd, 2008). This construct corresponds to *"the often nonconscious process whereby the continual flow of personal and social experiences are decomposed or allocated into selected temporal categories or frames that help give order, coherence, and meaning to those events"* (Keough, Zimbardo & Boyd, 1999). It describes how one's experiences, feelings, perceptions, or behaviors can be influenced by one's orientation and attitude towards the past, present and future, and appeared to be a strong psychosocial predictor of many behaviors, particularly in the field of health (Boyd & Zimbardo, 2005; Henson, Carey, Carey & Maisto, 2005; Crockett & al. 2009; Guthrie & al., 2009). From the perspective of Zimbardo & Boyd's theory of time, which postulates that TP consists of five factors based on orientation and attitudes towards timeframes (Zimbardo & Boyd, 1999), several studies have shown that present orientation, in a hedonistic and sensation-seeking attitude (Present-hedonistic time perspective – PHTP), and future orientation, in a planning and goal-oriented attitude (Future time perspective – FTP), are the most predictive TP dimensions in health behaviors, and in substance use (Keough & al., 1999; Wills & al., 2001; Apostolidis, Fieulaine, Simonin & Rolland, 2006). While individuals focused on FTP are more likely to engage in health protective behaviors and to avoid risky ones, individuals predominantly possessing a PHTP are more likely to adopt risky behaviors.

Nevertheless, there was claims to deeper our understanding of the two aspects of why or how and when or for whom this relation occurs (Wills & al., 2001; Apostolidis & al., 2006; Apostilidis, Fieulaine & Soulé, 2006; Fieulaine & Martinez, 2010). The first was investigated in relation with different potential mediating variables, whereas testing for moderators or buffering factors explored the second. In relation with self-control, whereas Wills & al. (2001) suggested that TP produce good self-control that in turn impacts exposure to risk factors for substance use, Joireman & al. (2008) and Barber, Munz, Bagsb & Grawitch (2009) relied on the hypothesis of a buffering effect of self-control in the link between TP and problem behaviors (temporal discounting and academic achievement). In a recent study in a general sample, Fieulaine & Martinez (2010) argued for a buffering hypothesis, considering that both TP and DC are distal dispositional constructs, without strong theoretical basis for the hypothesis of a causal order between them. Moreover, in line with a large body of research on the buffering effect of self-control on the impact of risks factors, they investigated how DC can intervene when considering TP as a risk factor of substance use. Despite risk factors are most frequently related to a background of adverse living circumstances, there is reason to consider TP as a risk factor given the consistent findings on its socioeconomically patterning (Agarwal, Tripathi & Srivastava, 1983; Fieulaine, Apostolidis & Olivetto, 2006; Adams & White, 2009; Guthrie & al., 2009), and on its predictive role in substance use (Keough & al., 1999; Wills & al., 2001; Apostolidis & al., 2006; Fieulaine & Martinez, 2010). This buffering hypothesis was also in line with prior studies showing the relation of TP to control components (Ego control; cf. Zimbardo & Boyd, 1999; Health LOC, Sundaramurthy, Bush, Neuwelt & Ward, 2003; Perceived control, Wills & al., 2001; Self-control, Barber & al., 2009), or suggesting that the relation between TP and substance use can be moderated by other constructs (Apostolidis, Fieulaine, Simonin & Rolland, 2006), self-control among others (Barber & al., 2009; Joireman & al., 2008). In a previous study, results strongly suggest the existence of such a buffering effect, showing that Present hedonistic and future time perspective are significantly related to a composite score of substance use only for those who are high in desiring control (Fieulaine & Martinez, 2010). Therefore, PHTP seems to be at risk and FTP appeared as a protective factor only when linked to a high desire for control. These results lead to question the role desire for control may play in the impact of TP as a dispositional risk factor for substance use. To focus on sensation seeking and pleasure in the present, with low concern for future consequences is related to highest substance use only for those who simultaneously are motivated for controlling their life and situation. In the same way, being focused on future issues in a planning and conscientious attitude is linked to lower substance use only when simultaneously related to a high desire to control one's life. More important in a self-regulation perspective, motivation to control has no main effect on substance use but acts only as a buffering agent, enhancing or reducing the impact of TP on substance use. Hence, if DC has to be considered as a fuel in self-regulation processes, this is through its activating or inhibiting role on the impact of a dispositional factor such as time perspective. Therefore, these distal predictors of behavioral edification seem to find their energetic role as a mixture of fuels for the proximal muscular activity of self-regulation.

LIMITATIONS AND DIRECTIONS FOR RESEARCH

While this body of research provides strong theoretical and empirical bases for future studies, it remains limited from various reasons. First, self-regulatory constructs need to be related to well-established prediction models of health behaviours, to evaluate the degree to which broad constructs such as TP and DC can increase the predictive power of these models, or, more interesting in our view, provide new insights on their principal limitations. For instance, the theory of planned behavior (TPB) is one of the most widely used models to predict and change behaviors, particularly in the field of health, but its main limitation is due to the lack of clear and predictable relation between intentions and behaviors (Godin & Kok, 1996; Armitage & Conner, 2001; Sheeran, Conner & Norman, 2001; Webb & Sheeran, 2006). This intentions-behavior gap can fruitfully be investigated using the framework of self-regulation (Conner & Armitage, 1998; Orbell, 2003; Hall & Fong, 2007) and by considering the role of dispositional constructs such as TP or control (Rhodes, Courneya & Jones, 2005; Kovac & Rise, 2007; Armitage, Conner, Loach & Willetts, 1999; Griva, Anagnostopoulos & Madoglou, 2010). A second limitation is the lack of prospective or longitudinal studies to overcome weakness of cross-sectional studies design, particularly on causal statements and measures of behaviours related to TPB components (Armitage & Conner, 2001) or to TP construct (Apostolidis & al. 2006; Adams, 2009). A third limitation is the definition of populations or behaviours under study. While general population samples and composite indicators of health behaviours are useful for providing results in representative sample and for relatively common behaviors, there is the need to complete these studies with more focused designs, precise populations and specific behaviors.

In summary, there was several lack of research we tried to overcome with the study we present in this chapter: Does DC intervene as a buffering agent in the relation of TP to substance use? Can the previous findings be replicated in a study on cannabis use in an adolescent sample? How the main and interaction effects of TP and DC on cannabis use can be observed using a prospective study design? What is the contribution of these variables to an existing model, namely the theory of planned behavior? These few questions are those deserving attention for future research, and present findings are an invitation to pursue these research avenues, and surely not their definitive answers.

METHOD AND PARTICIPANTS

The present study was designed as prospective, with TPB variables assessed at Time 1, in addition with measures of DC, TP, and cannabis perceptions, and behavior was assessed one week later (Time 2). Participants were high school students, recruited in all classes of two high schools located in an metropolitan area in center France. Those high schools are dedicated to general and professional education, and students originate from diversified socioeconomic levels. Data were obtained through a self-report questionnaire administrated to students during normal class hours by trained research staff. The study was presented as "a survey on opinion and lifestyles", and it was stressed that participation was anonymous and on a voluntary basis. Anonymity was stressed by keeping professors away in the classroom, and by inviting participants to depose their filled questionnaire in an opaque ballot box. Participants were asked to provide a code number one the first page of the questionnaire, and to cautiously note it somewhere to be sure to remind it if necessary. Study introduction and data collection was performed by researchers and by trained assistants. 690 students participated at Time 1 (M age=16,7, SD=1,42), 54% were women and 46% were men. At Time 2 (1 week later), 664 filled the questionnaire assessing behavior (M age=16,7; SD=1,41), a response rate of 96,3%. Of these, 53% were women and 47% were men.

MEASURES

Participants completed a self-report questionnaire that included at Time 1 TPB, TP and DC measures together with assessment of substance perceptions, use, and demographics. At time 2, only behaviors were assessed, with several demographics in order to check for the reliability of numerical codes. Scales structures were verified with factor analyses (principal components method with Varimax rotation) followed by internal consistency analyses (Cronbach's alpha). Scales were coded such that higher scores represent positive positioning towards cannabis use for TPB measures, and more of the named attributes for other measures.

TPB Measures

The targeted behavior for TPB was *"to consume cannabis next week"*, and this behavior was directly assessed at Time 2. The proximal determinants of intention and behavior (attitude, subjective norm, perceived behavioral control) were assessed by multi-items measures, following the guidelines proposed by Ajzen (2002). Attitude was assessed using four bipolar items, ranging from 1 (*harmful, pleasant, boring, good*) to 7 (*beneficial, unpleasant, enjoying, bad*). Subjective norm was measured through 4 items each on a 7-point Likert scale ranging from 1 to 7, reflecting descriptive (*most people who are important to me will use cannabis next week, most people whose opinions are important for me will use cannabis next week*) and injonctive (*most people who are important to me think I should/should not use cannabis next week; most people whose opinions are important for me approve/disapprove my using of cannabis*) norms. Perceived behavioral control beliefs were assessed using 4 items, referring to perceived control (*Using cannabis next week depends only on my willing; If I want, I can easily use cannabis next week*) and efficacy (*For me, to use cannabis next week is easy/difficult; For me, using cannabis netx week is possible/impossible*), using a7-point Likert scale (from 1-*not at all* to 7-*very much*). Lastly, intention was assessed with three items (*I plan to; I intent to; I want to – consume cannabis next week*) measured on a 7-point Likert scale ranging from 1 (*not at all*) to 7 (*very much*).

Time Perspective

Time perspective construct was assessed using the Zimbardo Time Perspective Inventory (Zimbardo & Boyd, 1999), in its shorten form (Fieulaine, Apostolidis & Zimbardo, in press). ZTPI measures TP through an inventory of temporally marked propositions concerning the beliefs, values and preferences that individuals associate with their experiences. This 15-item scale contains 5 subscales: "Past-Positive" (PP: nostalgic, positive construction of the past); "Past-Negative" (PN: aversive attitude towards the past); "Present-Fatalistic" (PF: hopeless, nihilistic attitude towards life); "Present -Hedonistic" (PH: orientation towards enjoyment and pleasure in the present) and "Future" (F: planning for and achievement of future goals). Each subscale is composed of three items, assessed on a 5-point Likert scale according to how characteristic each statement is considered to be by the respondent (ranging from 1 [*very uncharacteristic*] to 5 [*very characteristic*]). In previous studies, "Present hedonistic" (PH) and "Future" (F) subscales appeared as the two most predictive TP dimensions for substance use (Keough, Zimbardo & Boyd, 1999; Apostolidis, Fieulaine, Simonin & Rolland, 2006; Fieulaine & Martinez, 2010). Yet, we decided to introduce past subscales, to explore how past TP can impact TPB measures and cannabis use behaviors, following the claim made by Hall & Fong (2007) for the attention past deserve in self-regulatory processes.

Desire for Control

Desire for Control was measured using the scale proposed by Burger & Cooper (1979, Desire for Control Scale – DCS), and recently validated in French (Fieulaine & Martinez, 2010). DCS measures general desire for control over life events in several domains, such as making one's own decisions, taking preventive action to control upcoming situations, controlling others, or avoiding situations in which others have control (cf. Burger & Cooper, 1979). This scale is a 20-item self-report questionnaire, in which participants indicate their degree of agreement with each statement on a seven-point Likert scale (from 1: *strong disagreement* to 7: *strong agreement*). Factor analysis of the scale in different samples has yielded unstable results (see Burger & Cooper, 1979; Burger, 1992; Gebhardt & Brosschot, 2002; Abdullatif & Hamadah, 2005), and DCS is mostly used as an unidimensionnal measure of motivation to control, despite subfactors were observed in the original study (General Desire for control, Decisiveness, Preparation-prevention, Avoidance of dependance) but have been only partially replicated in subsequent studies (Gebhardt & Brosschot, 2002, Fieulaine & Martinez, 2010). General DC as measured by the whole scale has been found to have high internal and test-retest reliabilities; its construct and predictive validities have been rigorously and frequently demonstrated (Burger, 1992; McCutcheon, 2000; Gebhardt & Brosschot, 2002); and it has also demonstrated discriminant validity with measures of social desirability and locus of control (Burger, 1992; Gebhardt & Brosschot, 2002).

Behavior

Cannabis use was self-reported at both waves of the study. Past behavior at Time 1 was measured as lifetime, last 12 months and last month use; Level of use measure was based on the patterns used in surveys conducted by the French Monitoring Centre for Drugs and Addiction (OFDT; cf. Beck & Legleye, 2003) with a response format containing 5 levels of consumption; experimental (*to have smoked cannabis but not during the last 12 months*), occasional (*to have smoked cannabis less than 10 times during the last 12 months*), repeated (*to have smoked cannabis less than 10 times during the last 30 days*), regular (*to have smoked cannabis more than 10 times during the last 30 days*) and daily (*to have smoked cannabis at least once per day*). Proximity and accessibility of substance were measured using two items (having received cannabis offers and having cannabis users as friends). Similar measures were used at Time 2, with a focus on behaviors for the preceding week (offer, use, number of use, level of use).

ANALYSIS

Hierarchical multiple linear regression models were used to explore the role of TP and DC in relation with the TPB model of prediction for subsequent cannabis use. Considering the more distal to the more proximal predictors of behaviors, we tested for a mediation of proximal predictors of intention in the relation of TP and DC to intentions at Time 1, and then tested intention as the more proximal predictor of T2 behavior. Indirect effects were tested following Baron & Kenny (1986) approach for testing mediating effects, and significance of these effects were assessed using the Sobel test (Sobel, 1982). Buffering effect of DC on the relation of TP to cannabis use was tested using hierarchical regression analysis (Holmbeck, 1997; Cohen & Cohen, 1983). Regression models therefore included concurrent main effects terms for DC and TP and the cross product of the two variables. Interaction effect was established if the interaction terms revealed significant regression coefficients and if the increase in variance explained by the model ($\Delta R2$) after entering the interaction term in the regression equation is significant. Effects were then interpreted graphically via simple slope analysis, that is to say, by examining regression lines representing relationships between the predictor (time perspective) and the outcome variable (substance use) for representative groups created by dichotomizing the moderator variable (DC: +1 and -1 standard deviation above and below the mean; Cohen, Cohen, West & Aiken, 2003).

RESULTS

Descriptive Statistics and Measures Reliabilities

Sample characteristics are recapitulated in table 1. Participants reported lowest level of experimental use compared to those reported in national surveys performed on similar population (N=43 7999; 17 years old, 50,3 men; 49,7 women - 42% ever consumed) but higher rates for other levels of use (42% experimental, 24,7% occasional, 7,3 % regular, 3,2% intensive; Legleye, Spilka, LeNezet & Laffiteau, 2006).

Table 1. Sample Characteristics

Variable	Total	Men	Women
N	690	322	358
Age (m, SD)	16,7 (1,42)	16,7 (1,53)	16,6 (1,30)
Offer (N, %)			
No	169 (24,5)	59 (18,8)	110 (31,3)
Yes	497 (72)	254 (81,15)	241 (68,6)
Ever consumed (N, %)			
No	437 (63,3)	196 (61,4)	241 (68,1)
Yes	238 (34,5)	123 (38,5)	113 (31,9)
Consumption level (N, %)			
Experimental	64 (24)	27 (20,1)	37 (28,4)
Occasional	97 (36,4)	43 (32,1)	52 (40)
Repeated	54 (20,3)	28 (20,9)	26 (20)
Regular	24 (9)	19 (14,2)	5 (3,8)
Intensive	27 (10,1)	17 (12,7)	10 (7,7)
Time 2			
N	664	307	355
Response rate	96,3%	95,3%	99,1%
Offer (N, %)			
No	521 (78,5)	219 (71,3)	301 (84,8)
Yes	143 (21,5)	88 (28,7)	54 (15,2)
Consumption (N, %)			
No	556 (83,7)	239 (77,8)	315 (88,7)
Yes	108 (16,3)	68 (22,2)	40 (11,3)

Reliabilities for TPB measures appeared acceptable in the sample (subjective norms: N=4, α=.77 ; Control beliefs : N=4, α=.70 ; Attitude : N=4, α=.86 ; Intention : N=3, α=.94). ZTPI subscales reliabilities appeared low in the sample, but acceptable (PN: α=.66; PH: α=.63; F:

α=.60; PP: α=.60), except for PF (α=.41), this subscale was subsequently excluded from the analyses. General desire for control scale reliability appeared satisfactory (N=19; α=.65).

Intercorrelations between Measures

Intercorrelations between measures were computed and made appear significant links between TP and TCP components. Relations are in line with previous research, showing a relation between PH TP and positive attitude, norms and control related to cannabis use. DC appeared modestly but significantly positively correlated to PHTP, FTP and PPTD. No relation appeared between DC and TPB measures.

Table 2. Intercorrelations between measures

	PH	F	PP	PF	DC	NORM	CONTR	INTEN	ATT
ZTPI-PN	,167***	-,055	-,001	,191***	,032	,024	,085*	,041	,035
ZTPI-PH		-,081*	,206***	,159***	,181***	,187***	,289***	,187***	,222***
ZTPI-F			,116**	-,232***	,176***	-,131***	-,222***	-,237***	-,223***
ZTPI-PP				-,146***	,10**	-,023	-,049	-,100**	-,105**
DC						-,037	,078	,008	-,037
TCP-norm							,459***	,471***	,504***
TCP-control								,579***	,600***
TCP-intention									,667***

Distal and Proximal Predictors of Cannabis Use

In a first step of analyses, we explored how TP and DC constructs can predict the proximal predictors of intention (attitude, subjective norms and perceived behavioral control). In our model, given the constructs under study, it is hypothesized that TP and DC cannot be more or equally proximal determinants of intention or behaviors than attitudes, control and norms, but can instead participate at an upper level of prediction. Therefore, distal constructs are hypothesized as predicting intention through their impact on proximal TPB measures (i.e. a mediating effect). Hence, we first examined the relation of distal constructs to proximal TBP measures, by using a simultaneous multiple linear regression controlled for age and sex, with distal constructs as predictors and TPB measures as criterion. Results recapitulated in table 2 revealed that several TP subscales are significantly related to proximal predictors of cannabis use intention. Hence, in line with previous studies, PHTP appeared as positively related to attitudes, subjective norm and perceived control favoring cannabis use, whereas

FTP is negatively related to these constructs. Results also revealed a significant negative relation of PPTP to proximal predictors of cannabis use intention.

Table 3. Predictors of TPB components

	Attitude		Subjective Norm		Perceived Control	
	β	t	β	t	β	t
Gender	-,03	-1,00	-,00	-,12	-,06	-1,83t
Age	,14	3,85***	,07	1,89*	,13	3,60***
PNTP	-,01	-,24	-,01	-,29	,03	,89
PHTP	,23	6,11***	,19	4,98***	,27	7,19***
FTP	-,17	-4,74***	-,10	-2,67**	-,19	-5,39***
PPTP	-,11	-3,07**	-,04	-1,08	-,07	-1,98*
DCS	-,04	-1,16	-,05	-1,33	,05	1,47
R^2	.12***		.05***		.15***	

In a second step, hierarchical multiple linear regression were performed, by entering progressively all variables, from the most distal to the most proximal. In this model, TP and DC are assumed to share the same distal level, whereas substance perception is assumed to be a meso-level construct, and TPB measures are considered as the most proximal predictors. Regression equations were used to predict cannabis use intentions (linear multiple regression) and behaviors (binomial logistic multiple regression). Results (see Table 4) showed that FTP and PHTP are significant predictors of cannabis use intentions and subsequent behavior, whereas DC appeared to have no impact on intention or on behaviors. Step 2 and step 3 of the analyses revealed that the TP relation to cannabis use is mediated by proximal TPB measures of attitudes, perceived control and subjective norm. Sobel tests for indirect effects were significant in all cases (for PHTP : $z_{norm}=3.36^{***}$, $z_{attitude}=5.46^{***}$; $z_{control}=5.14^{***}$ and for FTP : $z_{norm}=2.29^{*}$; $z_{attitude}=4.35^{***}$; $z_{control}=4.28^{***}$).

Hence, if PHTP is positively related to cannabis use intention or behavior, it is trough its impact on attitudes, subjective norms and perceived control related to this behavior. For FTP, it must be noted that it remains a significant predictor of intention after having entered the TPB variables. Therefore, FTP has a direct impact on intention, which in turn mediate its relation to behavior. These results confirmed the predictive role played by time perspective in adolescent cannabis use as a distal dispositional construct leading to greater positive views on cannabis use, and to higher subsequent intentions and behaviors.

The Buffering Effect of Desire for Control

As in previous studies (Fieulaine & Martinez, 2010), Desire for Control appeared as having no direct effect on behaviour, and the present study extend this result by showing no effect on TPB measure. It remains to examine if we can observe in this sample the same buffering effect of DC as evidenced previously. In this aim, we entered in regression equations the interaction term TP X DC, created by multiplying scores after having centered the variables in order to reduce multicollinearity. To assess for an interaction effect, we examined the significance of the regression coefficient associated with the interaction term, and the significance of the increase in explained variance brought by the introduction of the interaction term.

Table 4. Synthesis of hierarchical multiple regressions

	Cannabis use intention		Cannabis use behavior	
Step 1	ß	t	OR	95% CI
Gender	-,08	-2,31[*]	,50	.32-.77[***]
Age	,10	2,67[**]	1.17	1.01-1.35[*]
PNTP	,00	,13	.91	.74-1.12
PHTP	,18	4,83[***]	1.83	1.40-2.38[***]
FTP	-,21	-5,58[***]	.63	.48-.82[***]
PPTP	-,10	-2,70[**]	.81	.63-1.03
DC	,01	,35	1.19	.81-1.78
R^2	.11[***]		.13[***]	
Step 2				
Gender	-,04	-1,71	,43	,24-,74[**]
Age	-,00	-,06	,95	,78-1,15
PNTP	,00	,14	.89	.68-1.17
PHTP	-,00	-,01	1.15	.85-1.56
FTP	-,07	-2,46[**]	.89	.64-1.24
PPTP	-,03	-1,23	.95	.69-1.31
DC	,03	1,13	1.06	.66-1.72
TPB-Norm	,14	4,57[***]	1.20	.97-1.48
TPB-Control	,25	7,15[***]	1,78	1.41-2.25[***]
TPB-Attitude	,40	11,56[***]	1.94	1.58-2.37[***]
R^2 (ΔR^2)	.51[***] (.40[***])		.53[***] (.40[***])	
Step 3 (Time 2)				
Gender			,46	,25-,84[**]
Age	- -	- -	,98	.80-1.21
PNTP	- -	- -	,84	.63-1.12
PHTP	- -	- -	1.21	.88-1.66
FTP	- -	- -	1.05	.73-1.50
PPTP	- -	- -	.96	.67-1.36
DC	- -	- -	.94	.56-1.59
TPB-Norm	- -	- -	1,02	.80-1.31
TPB-Control	- -	- -	1.36	1.06-1.75[**]
TPB-Attitude	- -	- -	1.53	1,21-1.93[***]
TPB-Intention	- -	- -	1,86	1.51-2.30[***]
R^2 (ΔR^2)	- -	- -	.58[***] (.05[**])	

Note: Gender was coded as 1:Men, 2:Women; Behavior was coded as 1: having consumed cannabis last week, 0: having not consumed cannabis last week.

Results showed a significant effect of PH X DC interaction on control beliefs (ß=.09, t=2.62, p<.01; ΔR^2=.02, p<.05) and on intention (ß=.10, t=2.80, p<.01; ΔR^2=.02, p<.05); and a tendencial effect of F X DC interaction on intention (ß=.06, t=1.89, p=.05; ΔR²=.02, p<.05). No significant effect appeared on subsequent behaviors. Complementary analyses showed that TPXDC interaction effects on intention remain significant even after having controlled for TPB measures. Hence, TP X DC interaction is a direct predictor of intention, even if the increase in explained variance is relatively low. Graphical interpretation of the interaction effects through simple slopes (see Figure 1) made appear that the positive relation PH maintain with intention was enhanced when individuals score higher on the DC dimension (.69 vs. .27 for low DC), and that the negative relation of FTP to intention was enhanced when individuals score higher on DC (-.66 vs. -.31 for low DC).

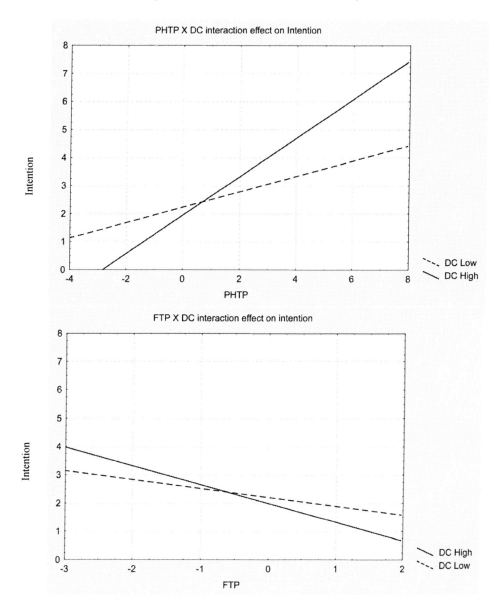

Figure 1. Interaction between TP and DC on cannabis use intentions.

Results are therefore in line with previous ones establishing the buffering effect of desire for control on the relationship between TP and substance use, giving further evidence of this effect in an adolescent sample and in regard with cannabis use.

CONCLUSION AND DIRECTIONS FOR FUTURE RESEARCH

In this chapter, we aimed at presenting new insights into the intervention of time and control in adolescents substance use. The results of this study are in line with previous ones and provide further support to the predictive role played by time perspective in substance use. Moreover, our study is the first, as far as we know, to establish the role of TP using a prospective design, with a large sample and for a specific behavior clearly defined in terms of its target, action, context, and time elements. Using such a design, the predictive role of PHTP and FTP find in our study strong evidence, and therefore challenge the main limitation often opposed to statements on the attention TP deserve in predicting and changing health behaviors. This is particularly true for present findings given they provide a clear view on the pathways through which TP impacts health behaviors. Using the theory of planned behavior model, TP appeared as a distal predictor of behavioral intention, mediated by proximal attitudes, behavioral control and subjective norms. In turn, behavioral intention was observed as the most predictive construct of subsequent behavior. These findings highlight the need to incorporate TP in existing model, not mainly in order to enhance their predictive power (TP contribution in this regard is relatively low), but to deeper our understanding of the antecedent of proximal behavioral edification. When considering interventions, identifying distal predictors of health behaviors allow for interventions designed for a variety of behaviours, and provide support for interventions aiming at changing broad dispositions to enhance health promotion practices.

Within the framework of self-regulation, results highlighted the ambiguous role desire for control may play in cannabis use. In line with our moderating hypothesis, desire for control appeared as having a buffering effect on the relation between TP and substance use. Hence, the well-established predictive role of future and present-hedonistic TP in substance use appears to be conditioned by the level of desire for control. Thus, if TP is a risk (for PH) and a protective (for F) factor in substance use, it is under the dependence of another psychological construct. In our study, the construct considered is not more proximal than TP. In relation to personal experiences, values and living conditions, TP and DC interact and thus establish what may be considered as social-psychological vulnerability profiles for cannabis use. High PHTP and high DC on the one hand, and low FTP and high DC on the other, appear as the most vulnerable profiles for substance use. It is important to note here that TP and DC are not highly intercorrelated, and furthermore do not represent overlapping factors. Thus, observed vulnerable profiles are not improbable, and one can't assume that TP is automatically linked to the less acknowledged construct of desire for control. Present findings highlight the importance of TP and DC constructs as distal predictors of cannabis use, and the role their interaction may play in establishing vulnerability profiles for substance use. High desire for control thus support the protective role of future orientation, but simultaneously reinforce the risk factor present hedonistic orientation represents. Self-control, as broadly defined, may bring to confusion between time and control, and lead to counterproductive interventions. Hence, there is a strong need to further our understanding of the role psychological time and control play in self-regulation processes and particularly in substance use. Time and control often appeared as the core concepts in self-regulation (Carver & Scheier, 2002; Hall & Fong, 2007) but few studies investigated these issues using the actual developments in research on these constructs. Conversely, there is a need to integrate self-regulation models in research on time or control, and to propose integrative approach, of time particularly, based not only on temporal dimensions, but also on recent models that incorporate time components. Temporal self-regulation (Hall & Fong, 2007), implementation intentions (Gollwitzer, 1999), construal levels (Trope & Liberman, 2010) have in common to place time and control at the heart of self-regulation processes.

One final and pressing issue may provide research avenues for future studies. If we emphasize how far distal constructs such as time perspective or desire for control deserve attention in self-regulation theory, this is in part because we seek to favor the establishment of a more "social" view on self-regulation, by incorporating social contexts, or their social-psychological proxys, in extended models of self-regulation or other models with time concerns. Two main issues, in our view under considered in self-regulation research, can easily illustrate the limitations of self-regulation theory if it remains disconnected to social surroundings. Both rely on the postulate that self-regulation capacity is socially grounded and shaped, and on the precautionary principle according to which we should reduce the risk of confusion between descriptive and normative findings, by reversing the traditional causal emphasis by placing the cause in the environment, at least as a working hypothesis. First, leaving conditions and socio-economic status lead to develop contrasting psychological dispositions. Whereas secured environment and resources allow the development of future orientation and planning competencies, social insecurity and deprivation lead to develop temporal coping strategies, by focusing on present or past, avoiding planning and psychologically leaving the future (Fieulaine, Apostolidis & Olivetto, 2006). Therefore, to understand more fully how self-regulation processes function in various contexts, there is a strong need to develop research on the intervention of environmental and socioeconomic factors. Second, from a social-psychological point of view, the normative component of self-regulation capacity deserves much more attention than actually. Well known for a long time is the social desirability of control and self-determination (Jellison & Green, 1981), but such a norm was also recently evidenced for future orientation and planning attitudes (Martinez & Fieulaine, 2011; Guignard, Apostolidis & Demarque, 2011). Hence, a strong limitation of actual research on self-regulation is that we don't know if it is not the social environment that is the principal cause of the impact of self-regulation capacities. If one assumes that self-regulation competencies are socially approved and that impulsivity and low self-control are not, then self-regulatory capacities are functional because of a norm favoring such kind of behaviors, attitudes, or self-presentation strategies. This is this kind of social causality we observed regarding future time perspective and academic achievement. In a self-presentation approach, we demonstrated that future orientation is not only rewarded by positive evaluations, but also lead to provide more help and academic support to a student presented as normative, namely as being future oriented (Martinez & Fieulaine, 2011). In the case of self-regulation processes, such an exploration of its normative components is lacking.

To open avenues for future research and interventions, we would like to end by a broader view on present findings and on the state of research on self-regulation. There are many reasons why self-regulation is still a fruitful and promising frame of work to understand and change health-damaging behaviors. But we are also convinced that the social roots of self-regulation deserve more attention, for several reasons. First, as for time perspective and desire for control, many of the dispositional constructs under study in social psychology are merely situational, but in the sense of Bourdieu's *habitus* (Bourdieu, 1998). Living conditions and social norms find their psychological counterpart through the objectification of social structure at the level of individual subjectivity. Hence, the *habitus* is, by definition, isomorphic with the structural conditions in which it emerged. The observed interaction between time perspective and desire for control, by defining vulnerability profiles, are not only informative for intra-personal processes, but also for the social contexts people live in. This is crucial for our understanding and for practical interventions. Challenging health-damaging behaviors need to explore how social inequalities lead to health inequalities. Self-regulation, and other related models, can be invaluable in this aim, by discovering social-psychological pathways through which socioeconomic status impacts health outcomes (Lachman & Weaver, 1998; Bailis & al. 2001; Fieulaine, Apostolidis & Olivetto, 2006; Adams & White, 2009; Guthrie & al., 2009). Another challenge is to build effective health communications. Present findings bring to support the inclusion of a double framing process in interventions or communications designed to prevent substance use. If temporal framing is well-known as a crucial determinant in health prevention (Orbell & Kyriakaki, 2008; Hall & Fong, 2007), it is necessary to consider also the possibility of simultaneous control framing, in order to make the former effective. Usually separated in health communications and interventions, time perspective and control could be more efficiently used as interactive factors in vulnerability-reduction or competence enhancement programs.

REFERENCES

Abdullatif, H.I., & Hamadah, L.N. (2005). The factorial structure of desirability of control scale among Kuwaiti subjects. *Social Behavior & Personality*, *33(3)*, 307-312.

Adams J. (2009). The role of time preference and perspective in socio-economic inequalities in health related behaviours. In S. Babones (ed.). *Social Inequality and Public Health* (pp. 9-25). Bristol, Policy Press.

Adams, J., & White, M. (2009). Time Perspective in Socioeconomic Inequalities in Smoking and Body Mass Index. *Health Psychology*, *28(1)*, 83-90.

Agarwal, A., Tripathi, K. K., & Srivastava, M. (1983). Social roots and psychological implications of time perspective. *International Journal of Psychology*, *18*, 367–380.

Agnew, C.R., & Loving, T.J. (1998). Future time orientation and condom use attitudes, intentions, and behavior. *Journal of Social Behavior & Personality*, *13*, 755-764.

Ajzen, I. (2002). *Constructing a TpB questionnaire: Conceptual and methodological considerations*. Retrieved April 27, 2011 from http://www-unix.oit.umass.edu/~aizen/pdf/tpb.measurement.pdf.

Apostolidis, T., Fieulaine, N., & Soulé, F. (2006). Future time perspective as predictor of cannabis use: Exploring the role of substance perception among French adolescents. *Addictive Behaviors, 31(12)*, 2339-2343.

Apostolidis, T., Fieulaine, N., Simonin, L., & Rolland, G. (2006). Cannabis use, time perspective and risk perception: Evidence of a moderating effect. *Psychology and Health*, *21*, 571-592

Armitage, C. J., & Conner, M. (2001). Efficacy of the theory of planned behaviour: A meta-analytic review. *British Journal of Social Psychology, 40*, 471-499.

Sheeran, P., Conner, M., & Norman, P. (2001). Can the theory of planned behavior explain patterns of health behavior change? *Health Psychology, 20,* 12–19.

Armitage, C. J., Conner, M., Loach, J., & Willetts, D. (1999). Different perceptions of control: Applying an extended theory of planned behavior to legal and illegal drug use. *Basic and Applied Social Psychology, 21*, 301-316.

Bailis, Segall, A., Mahon, M. J., Chipperfield, J. G., & Dunn (2001). Perceived control in relation to Socio-economic and behavioral resources for health. *Social Sciences and Medicine, 52*, 1661-1676.

Barber, L.K., Munz, D.C., Bagsby, P.G., & Grawitch, M.J. (2009). When does time perspective matter? Self-control as a moderator between time perspective and academic achievement. *Personality and Individual Differences, 46*, 250–253.

Baron, R.M., & Kenny, D.A. (1986). The moderator-mediator variable distinction in social psychological research: Conceptual, strategic, and statistical considerations. *Journal of Personality and Social Psychology, 51*, 1173-1182.

Baumeister, R. F., Vohs, K. D., & Tice, D. M. (2007). The strength model of self-control. *Current Directions in Psychological Science, 16*, 396-403.

Baumeister, R.F., Gailliot, M., DeWall, C.N., & Oaten, M. (2006). Self-Regulation and Personality: How Interventions Increase Regulatory Success, and How Depletion Moderates the Effects of Traits on Behavior. *Journal of Personality, 74*, 1773-1801.

Beck F., Legleye S., & Spilka S. (2006). Les drogues à 17ans, évolutions, contextes d'usage et prises de risqué. *Tendances, 49*, 4.

Beck, F., & Legleye, S. (2003). *Drogues et adolescence : usages de drogues et contextes d'usage entre 17 et 19 ans, évolutions récentes ESCAPAD 2002*. Paris, OFDT.

Björgvinsson, T., & Wilde, G.J.S. (1996). Risky health and safety habits related to perceived value of the future. *Safety Science, 22*, 27-33.

Bourdieu, P. (1998). *Practical Reason: On the Theory of Action*. Stanford, Stanford University Press.

Boyd, J. N., & Zimbardo, P. G. (2005). Time perspective, health, and risk taking. In A. Strathman, & J. Joireman, (Eds.), *Understanding Behavior in the Context of Time* (pp. 85-107). Mahwah, Erlbaum.

Brody, G. H., & Ge, X. (2001). Linking parenting processes and self-regulation to psychological functioning and alcohol use during early adolescence. *Journal of Family Psychology, 15*, 82-94.

Burger, J. M. (1992). *Desire for control: Personality, social and clinical perspectives*. New York, Plenum.

Burger, J. M., and H. M. Cooper (1979). The desirability of control. *Motivation and Emotion, 3*, 381-393.

Chapman, G.B. (2001). Time preferences for the very long term. *Acta Psychologica, 108(2)*, 95-116.

Chapman, G.B., & Coups, E.J. (1999). Time preferences and preventive health behavior. *Medical decision making, 19(3)*, 307-314.

Chapman, G.B., Brewer, N.T., Coups, E.J., Brownlee, S., Leventhal, H., & Leventhal, E.A. (2001). Value for the future and preventive health behavior. *Journal of experimental psychology Applied. 7(3)*, 235-250.

Cohen, J., & Cohen, P. (1983). *Applied multiple regression/correlation analysis for the behavioural sciences*. Hillsdale, Erlbaum.

Cohen, J., Cohen, P., West, S. G., & Aiken, L. S. (2002). *Applied multiple regression/correlation analysis for the behavioral sciences* (3rd ed.). Mahwah, NJ, Lawrence Erlbaum.

Conner, M., & Armitage, C. J. (1998). Extending the theory of planned behavior: A review and avenues for further research. *Journal of Applied Social Psychology, 28*, 1429-1464.

Cottle T. J. (1968). The location of experience : a manifest time orientation. *Acta Psychologica, 28*, 129-149.

Crockett, R.A., Weinman, J., Hankins, M., & Marteau, T. (2009). Time orientation and health-related behaviour: measurement in general population samples. *Psychology & Health, 24(3)*, 333-350.

De Ridder, D., & De Wit, J. (2006). Self-regulation of health behavior: Concepts. Theories and central issues. In D. De Ridder & J. De Wit (Eds.), *Self-regulation in health behavior* (pp. 1-23). Chichester, Wiley.

Fieulaine, N. & Martinez, F. (2010). Time under control: Time perspective and Desire for Control in Substance Use. *Addictive Behaviors, 35(8)*, 799-802.

Fieulaine, N., Apostolidis, T., & Olivetto, F. (2006). Précarité et troubles psychologiques : l'effet médiateur de la perspective temporelle. *Les Cahiers Internationaux de Psychologie Sociale, 72*, 51-64.

Fieulaine, N., Apostolidis, T. & Zimbardo, P.G. (submitted). Development and validation of a short form of the Zimbardo Time Perspective Inventory.

Finke, M. S. (2005). Time orientation and economics. In A. Strathman, & J. Joireman (Eds.), *Understanding Behavior in the Context of time* (pp. 109-123). Mahwah, Lawrence Erlbaum.

Fuchs, V.R. (1982). Time preference and health: An exploratory study. In: V.R. Fuchs (Ed.), *Economic aspects of health* (pp. 93-120). Chicago, University of Chicago Press.

Gebhardt, W.A., & Brosschot, J.F. (2002). Desirability of control: psychometric properties and relations with locus of control, personality, coping, mental and somatic complaints. *European Journal of Personality, 16*, 423-438.

Godin, G., & Kok, G. (1996). The theory of planned behavior: A review of its applications in health-related behaviors. *American Journal of Health Promotion, 11*, 87-98.

Gonzales, A., & Zimbardo, P.G. (1985, March). Time in perspective. *Psychology today*, 21-26.

Griva F, Anagnostopoulos F, Madoglou S. (2009). Mammography screening and the theory of planned behavior: suggestions toward an extended model of prediction. *Women Health, 49(8)*, 662-81.

Guignard, S., Apostolidis, T., & Demarque, C. (accepted). A socio-normative approach of the Future Time Perspective construct. *Communication presented at the 12th European Congress of Psychology, Istanbul, Turkey.*

Guthrie, L.C., Butler, S.C., & Ward, M.M. (2009). Time perspective and socioeconomic status: a link to socioeconomic disparities in health? *Social Science & Medicine, 68(12)*, 2145-2151.

Hagger, M. S. (2010). Self-regulation: An important construct in health psychology research and practice. *Health Psychology Review, 4*, 57-65.

Hall, P.A., & Fong, G.T. (2007). Temporal self-regulation theory: A model for individual health behavior. *Health Psychology Review, 1*, 6–52.

Henson, J.M., Carey, K.B., Carey, M.P., & Maisto, S.A. (2006). Associations Among Health Behaviors and Time Perspective in Young Adults: Model Testing with Boot-Strapping Replication. *Journal of Behavioral Medicine, 29(2)*, 127-137.

Holmbeck, G.N. (1997). Toward terminological, conceptual, and statistical clarity in the study of mediators and moderators: Examples from the child-clinical and psychology literatures. *Journal of Counseling and Clinical Psychology*, *65*, 399-410.

Joireman, J., Balliet, D., Sprott, D., Spangenberg, E., & Schultz, J. (2008). Consideration of future consequences, ego-depletion, and self-control: Support for distinguishing between CFC-immediate and CFC-future sub-scales. *Personality and Individual Differences, 48*, 15-21.

Keough, K.A., Zimbardo, P.G., & Boyd, J.N. (1999). Who's smoking, drinking and using drugs? Time perspective as a predictor of substance use. *Journal of Basic and Applied Social Psychology*, *21*, 149-164.

Kovač, V. B., & Rise, J. (2007). The relation between past behaviour, intention, planning and quitting smoking: the moderating effect of future orientation. *Journal of Applied Biobehavioral Research, 12(2)*, 82-100.

Lachman, M. E., & Weaver, S. L. (1998). The sense of control as a mod- erator of social class differences in health and well-being. *Journal of Personality and Social Psychology, 74*, 763–773.

Lewin, K. (1942). Time Perspective and Morale. In G. Watson (Ed.), *Civilian Morale* (pp. 48-70). Boston, Houghton Mifflin.

Martinez, F. & Fieulaine, N. (2011). *Time Perspective and Desire for Control as normative constructs: the social desirability of temporality and mastery.* Unpublished manuscript, University of Lyon.

McCutcheon, L.E. (2000). The desirability of control scale: still reliable and valid twenty years later. *Current Research in Social Psychology, 5(15)*, 225-235.

Muraven, M., & Baumeister, R. F. (2000). Self-regulation and depletion of limited resources: Does self-control resemble a muscle? *Psychological Bulletin, 126*, 247-259.;

Orbell, S. (2003) Personality systems interactions theory and the theory of planned behaviour: Evidence that self-regulatory volitional components enhance enactment of studying behaviour. *British Journal of Social Psychology, 42*, 95-112

Orbell, S. & Kyriakaki, M. (2008) Temporal framing and persuasion to adopt preventive health behavior: Moderating effects of individual differences in consideration of future consequences on sunscreen use. *Health Psychology*, *27*, 770-779,

Rasmussen, H. N., Wrosch, C., Scheier, M. F., & Carver, C. S. (2006). Self-regulation processes and health: The importance of optimism and goal adjustment. *Journal of Personality, 74*, 1721-1747.

Rhodes, R.E., Courneya, K.S. & Jones, L.W. (2005). The theory of planned behavior and lower-order personality traits: Interaction effects in the exercise domain. *Personality and Individual Differences, 38*, 251-265.;

Skinner, E. A. (1996). A guide to constructs of control. *Journal of Personality and Social Psychology*, 71, 549-570.

Sobel, M. E. (1982). Asymptotic intervals for indirect effects in structural equations models. In S. Leinhart (Ed.), *Sociological methodology 1982* (pp.290-312). San Francisco: Jossey-Bass.

Strathman, A., Gleicher, F., Boninger, D.S., Edwards, C. S. (1994). The consideration of future consequences: Weighing immediate and distant outcomes of behavior. *Journal of Personality and Social Psychology, 66(4),* 742-752.

Sundaramurthy, S., Bush, T. M., Neuwelt, C. M. & Ward, M. M. (2003). Time perspective predicts the progression of permanent organ damage in patients with systemic lupus erythematosus. *Lupus, 12(6),* 443-448.

Webb, T. L. & Sheeran, P. (2006). Does changing behavioural intentions engender behavior change? A meta-analysis of the experimental evidence. *Psychological Bulletin, 132,* 249-268.

Wills, T.A., Ainette, M.G., Stoolmiller, M., Gibbons, F.X., & Shinar, O. (2008).Good self-control as a buffering agent for adolescent substance use: an investigation in early adolescence with time-varying covariates. *Psychology of Addictive Behaviors, 22(4),* 459-471.

Wills, T.A., Sandy, J.M., & Yaeger, A.M. (2001). Time perspective and early-onset substance use: A model based on stress-coping theory. *Psychology of Addictive Behaviors, 15,* 118-125.

Wills, T. A., Sandy, J. M., & Yaeger, A. M. (2002). Moderators of the relation between substance use level and problems: test of a self-regulation model in middle adolescence. *Journal of Abnormal Psychology, 111(1),* 3–21.

Wills, T.A., & Stoolmiller, M. (2002). The role of self-control in early escalation of substance use. *Journal of Consulting and Clinical Psychology, 70,* 986–997. ;

Wills, T. A, Pokhrel, P., Morehouse, E. & Fenster, B. (in press). Behavioral and emotional regulation and adolescent substance use problems: A test of moderation effects in a dual-process model. *Psychology of Addictive Behaviors.*

Wills, T. A., Walker, C., Mendoza, D., & Ainette, M. G. (2006). Behavioral and emotional self-control: Relations to substance use. *Psychology of Addictive Behaviors, 20,* 265−278.

Zaleski,, Z. (1994). *Psychology of future orientation.* Lublin, Scientific Society.

Zimbardo, P.G., & Boyd, J.N. (1999). Putting time in perspective: A valid, reliable individual-differences metric. *Journal of Personality and Social Psychology, 77,* 1271-1288.

Zimbardo, P.G., & Boyd, J.N. (2008). *The Time Paradox.* New York, Free Press.

Reviewed by Thémis Apostolidis, PhD, Professor of Social and Health Psychology at the University of Provence.

In: Psychology of Self-Regulation
Editor: Vassilis Barkoukis

ISBN: 978-1-61470-380-8
© 2012 Nova Science Publishers, Inc.

Chapter 5

THE PROMOTION OF SELF-REGULATION THROUGH PARENTING INTERVENTIONS

Matthew R. Sanders[*] and Trevor G. Mazzucchelli

Parenting and Family Support Centre
The University of Queensland, Brisbane, Queensland, Australia

ABSTRACT

The capacity for a parent to self-regulate their own performance is argued to be a fundamental process underpinning the maintenance of positive, nurturing, non-abusive parenting practices that promote good developmental and health outcomes in children. Deficits in self-regulatory capacity which have their origins in early childhood are common in many psychological disorders and strengthening self-regulation skills is widely recognised as an important goal in many psychological therapies and is a fundamental goal in preventive interventions. Attainment of enhanced self-regulation skills enables individuals to gain a greater sense of personal control and mastery over their life. This paper illustrates how the application of self-regulatory principles can be applied to parenting and family based interventions for children and young people. The Triple P—Positive Parenting Program, which uses a self-regulatory model of intervention, is used as an example to illustrate the robustness and versatility of the self-regulation approach to all phases on the parent consultation process.

THE PROMOTION OF SELF-REGULATION THROUGH PARENTING INTERVENTIONS

A parent's capacity to change their own behaviour in response to cues and information about the current needs of their children is fundamental to successful adaptation to the role of

---

[*] Correspondence concerning this article should be addressed to Matthew R. Sanders, Parenting and Family Support Centre, University of Queensland, Brisbane, Queensland 4072, Australia. E-mail: matts@psy.uq.edu.au

being a parent. Although a parent's approach to raising their children is strongly rooted in the social, economic and cultural context surrounding parenthood, ultimately individual parents have the capacity to decide how they wish to raise their children. Parents can determine the specific behaviours, skills and values they wish to promote, and the methods of parenting they adopt including how they will encourage desirable behaviours and discourage problem behaviours (including limit setting and methods of disciplining their children).

The rationale for focusing on self-regulation is compelling. First, the capacity for self-regulation is associated with various positive life outcomes such as academic achievement, income, savings behaviour, physical and mental health, better interpersonal relationships and happiness (e.g., Aspinwall, 1998; Duckworth & Seligman, 2005; Fredrickson & Joiner, 2002; Mischel, Shoda, & Peake, 1988; Moffitt et al., 2011; Shoda, Mischel, & Peake, 1990; Tangney, Baumeister, & Boone, 2004; Tsukavama, Toomey, Faith, & Duckworth, 2010). Second, deficits in self-regulation are found in a large number of personal and social problems and psychological disorders including aggression, anxiety, criminal behaviour, depression, and impulse control problems such as binge eating and alcohol abuse (e.g., Avakame, 1998; Baumeister, Heatherton, & Tice, 1994; Moffitt et al., 2011; Tangney et al., 2004; Tremblay, Boulerice, Arseneault, & Niscale, 1995). Third, self-regulation seems to be an important mechanism in the success of many psychological interventions for mental health problems including acceptance and commitment therapy (Hayes, Stroshal, & Wilson, 1999), behavioural activation (Martell et al., 2001, 2010), dialectical behaviour therapy (Linehan, 1993), problem solving therapy (Nezu, 1986) and self-control therapy (Rehm, 1977), and in some positive psychology interventions (Kashdan & Rottenberg, 2010; Mazzucchelli, Kane, & Rees, 2010). Finally, deficits in self-regulation in early childhood predict adult health, economic and social behaviour (Moffitt et al., 2011).

The capacity to change one's parenting behaviour in a planned, self-initiated and deliberate way involves parents recognising that a change in their behaviour may be necessary. Sometimes the changes required of parents can be relatively minor, such as attending more frequently to a specific child behaviour they wish to encourage, while other changes can be more difficult to execute such as refraining from reacting to problem behaviour. Self-initiated change involves a complex but ill-defined interplay of cognitive, behavioural and affective processes; these changes include the capacity to plan and anticipate, to regulate one's own emotions, to solve problems, and where necessary to collaborate with significant others involved in the care or education of children (e.g., partners, child carers, teachers, grandparents). It also involves a set of planned actions, the execution of the plan, a review of whether the plan worked and, if necessary, further tailoring of the plan until the goal is attained. Despite the hypothesised importance of self-regulation to parenting (see Moffitt et al., 2011) little attention has been devoted to the issue of reliably measuring parents' capacity to self-regulate or to promote self-initiated behaviour change. This chapter seeks to fill that gap by defining the concept of parental self-regulation, by discussing the theoretical basis of the construct, and by discussing the clinical application and empirical basis of parental self-regulation. Finally we discuss the implications of self-regulation for practice, policy and future research on parenting intervention.

SELF-REGULATION: A UNIFYING FRAMEWORK FOR STRENGTHENING PARENTING

We have argued previously that the development of an individual's capacity for self-regulation should be a central goal of parenting interventions (Sanders, 2008). Self-regulation is a process whereby individuals acquire the skills they need to change their own behaviour and become independent problem solvers and controllers of their own destiny. Capacity for self-regulation can be enhanced in a broader social environment that supports parenting and family relationships (Karoly, 1993). The approach to self-regulation discussed here is derived from social-cognitive theory. According to Bandura, the development of self-regulation is related to personal, environmental and behavioural factors; these factors operate separately but are interdependent (Bandura, 1986; Bandura, 1999). Self-regulation has an important role in the delay of gratification, emotional expression, moral development, compliance, adjustment, social competence, empathy and academic performance (Eisenberg, 2004). Social cognitive learning is the route to developing good self-regulatory skills (Bandura, 1977).

This self-regulation framework draws heavily on Bandura's cognitive social learning theory (e.g., Bandura, 1991). This model describes both the processes by which individuals can change their behaviour and the social interactional contexts that promote the capacity to change. Self-regulation is usefully defined by Karoly (1993) as:

> ...those processes, internal and or transactional, that enable an individual to guide his/her goal directed activities over time and across changing circumstances (contexts). Regulation implies modulation of thought, affect, behaviour or attention via deliberate or automated use of specific mechanisms and supportive metaskills. The processes of self-regulation are initiated when routine activities impeded or when goal directedness is otherwise made salient (e.g. the appearance of a challenge, the failure of habitual action patterns, etc). (p.25).

In the case of parents learning to change their parenting practices, the self-regulation process is operationalised as a multi-component process involving five key elements.

Self-management Tools

Parents learn to utilise different tools and skills to change their parenting practices. These skills include self-determination of parenting goals (what changes parents seek to make), self-monitoring of specific parent and child behaviours over the course of an intervention (how often specific target behaviours occur), self-selection of change strategies (a specific parenting plan to execute), self-evaluation of whether a parent achieved some performance criterion (what they set out to achieve) and self-reward (parent congratulates themselves for goal attainment). In this approach each parent is responsible for choosing from a range of options introduced in a parenting program which aspects of their own and their child's behaviour they wish to change.

Parental Self-efficacy

Many parenting interventions seek to increase parents' confidence in their capacity to solve personally relevant problems. Parents of children with significant behavioural and emotional problems often enter parenting programs with low self-efficacy in their capacity to handle specific child behaviours (e.g., aggression, tantrums, fearfulness). Parents of children with behaviour problems tend to have lower task specific self-efficacy in managing their daily parenting responsibilities (Sanders & Woolley, 2005). Over the course of a parenting program parents' self-efficacy typically improves and they develop global and task specific positive expectations that they have the knowledge and skill to change their child's and their own behaviour.

Personal Agency

Parents develop explanations as to why change did or did not occur during a parenting intervention. A self-regulation approach encourages parents to "own" the change process. This involves encouraging parents to attribute changes or improvements in their family situation to their own or their child's efforts rather than to chance, age, maturational factors, the practitioner's skills or efforts or other uncontrollable events (e.g., a spouse's poor parenting or genes). It is tempting for practitioners to feel reassured and pleased when a parent says that their child is so much better since coming to see the therapist. The practitioner should prompt the parent to identify what they are doing differently that has enabled the child's behaviour to change.

Self-sufficiency

The ultimate goal of a parenting intervention is that the parent becomes an independent problem solver who has the personal resources, knowledge and skills to maintain any gains achieved and to tackle future problems with the same child or other children in the family. Self-sufficient parents are not heavily reliant on others to successfully execute their daily parenting responsibilities and have the necessary resilience and personal resources to parent effectively with minimal or no additional support from services or social networks. This pursuit of self-sufficiency does not mean that parenting is undertaken in a disconnected way from essential support networks (e.g., childcare, good health care) or is viewed as an insular, private activity even though most parenting is undertaken in the privacy of people's homes. On the contrary, parents are encouraged to build healthy support networks including extended family support and other people from within their community. However parents are encouraged to view most of the key parenting decisions they take with their children as their own responsibility and as an exercise of personal judgement and choice.

Problem Solving

Successful parenting requires parents to become troubleshooters and active problem solvers. Intervention equips parents to define problems more clearly, formulate options, develop a parenting plan, execute the plan, and evaluate the outcomes achieved and to revise the plan as required. However, an intervention process needs to assist parents to generalise the knowledge, principles and skills they have learned so they can apply them to future problems, at different points in a child's later development, and to other relevant siblings in a family.

These self-regulation principles are very robust and apply equally to all program participants including parents and children, service providers, disseminators, program developers and researchers. The self-regulation skills outlined above can be taught to children by parents in developmentally appropriate ways. For instance, attending and responding to child-initiated interactions and prompting, modeling and reinforcing children's problem solving efforts promotes emotional self-regulation, independence, and problem solving in children. Self-regulation principles can also be applied in the training of service providers to deliver different levels of the intervention, in troubleshooting implementation difficulties, or overcoming staffing problems within an organisation (Sanders & Turner, 2005).

PARENTAL SELF-REGULATION IN ACTION: TOWARDS AN OPERATIONAL DEFINITION

In order to further operationalise the concept of self-regulation as it applies to parenting it is useful to consider the characteristics of a parent who has strong self-regulatory capability. Such a parent would have a clear sense of the sorts of behaviours, skills and values she wishes to manifest in herself as a parent and adult, instil in her child, and foster in her home and broader community. She would have realistic expectations of herself, of others in a caring role for her child, and knowledge as to what she could reasonably expect of her child at different points of his or her development. Monitoring her performance against these standards would be automatic, rather than conscious or deliberate.

Upon detecting a discrepancy between a personal standard and current performance (be it performance of herself, her child, or a significant other), goal-relevant habitual behaviour would be brought under her volitional control. Deliberately attending to these behaviours would provide information from which she develops hypotheses as to why the discrepancy has come about and clarity with regard to her objectives. The parent would have a rich repertoire of knowledge and skills from which to draw on when formulating options and developing a plan or new way of responding. These would not only include parenting and interpersonal skills (such as clear instructions, descriptive praise, planned ignoring), but also personal management skills (such as verbal self-cueing, attentional control, and ideas on how to arrange her environment to prompt and reinforce her own behaviour). The parent would proceed to execute the plan and evaluate the outcome, revising the plan as required until a desirable outcome has been achieved. At this point the parent would allow the new behaviour(s) to come under the control of new environmental stimuli—that is, her behaviour would again become automatic.

The self-regulating parent would have positive expectations that she could successfully enact her plan and bring about future positive outcomes. She would be self-reflective, open to and capable of identifying personal strengths and weaknesses, successes and failures, without being unhelpfully critical. Her self-evaluations and attributions would be constructive and serve to increase her competence and confidence for addressing future challenges.

Affect is naturally linked to goal-directed behaviour. Diverse feeling states arise as a result of success, failure, frustration, slowing, or delay in the pursuit of goals (Carver, 2004). If necessary, the self-regulating parent would be capable of managing these affective states concurrently with other goal pursuits. However, and importantly, rather than ploughing through life with a stony grimness she would mostly enjoy the process. Having genuinely high self-regulatory capacity she would have the ability to deploy her self-regulation skills when required and suspend them when they're not required. On occasion she would let go of her end-state-cognitions in order to enjoy the moment, experience contentment and flow (Csikszentmihalyi, 1990).

SELF-REGULATION AS A SKILL

Although there may be some inherited elements, there is strong evidence that self-regulatory capacity is a learned skill and can be strengthened with practice and training (e.g., Gollwitzer, 1999; Muraven, Baumeister, & Tice, 1999; Richards & Gross, 2000; Tomaka, Blascovich, Kibler, & Ernst, 1997). There is also evidence that parental behaviours are associated with the development of self-regulatory capacity in children (e.g., Avakame, 1998; Cochran, Wood, Sellers, Wilkerson, & Chamlin, 1998; Finkenauer, Engels, & Baumeister, 2005; Gibbs, Giever, & Martin, 1998; Jang & Smith, 1997; McCord, 1979; Sanders, 1998; Taylor & Biglan, 1998).

THE DEVELOPMENT OF SELF-REGULATION SKILLS

The capacity for self-regulation including parental self-regulation emerges in a developmental context at a very young age. The foundations of children's success at school, in their relationships, and in life in general are laid down in the early years of a child's life. Emergence of self-regulation capacity in early childhood is a strong predictor of long term development outcomes for children. For example, Moffitt et al. (2011) found that a composite measure of children's self-control (that included independent observation of children's behaviour) assessed at age three predicted a wide variety of indices of adult wellbeing at age thirty after controlling for social class and the child's IQ. These outcomes included their physical health, their adult income, substance abuse and criminal behaviour. Furthermore, children who had improved their self-control by age 11 had significantly better longer-term developmental outcomes then children who had not, suggesting the possibility that improving self-control outcomes for children through early intervention could be a common pathway to prevention of a variety of adverse developmental outcomes in young people and adults.

Building self-regulation capacity and skills in children is important and lays the foundation for the capacity for self-regulation as an adult. If parents can help children develop self-regulatory skills, they will equip them with powerful and important life tools to alter their behaviour and responses and overcome undesirable genetic, peer and other social influences throughout life.

Positive parenting skills influence children's self regulation. Table 1 provides examples of specific parenting practices that can be used to promote self-regulation in children and adolescents.

Table 1. Parenting Practices and the Development of Self-Regulation in Children

Self regulation skill being promoted	Specific parenting strategy	Parent-child interaction situation	Application	Likely outcome
Independent problem solving of homework	Incidental teaching	When a 7-year-old child asks for help, the parent pays attention and prompts the child to solve a problem for themselves by giving a clue without giving the answer.	Child: *"Mum, how do you spell necessary?"* Mother: *"How do you think you spell it? Have a try yourself....* *You've got the beginning right, what about the ending? Is it ery or ary? That's right ary. Well done!"*	Child solves the problem with minimal parental assistance.
Independent brushing of teeth	Ask-say-do	Parent initiates an interaction to teach a child to brush their teeth and uses the least intrusive prompt needed to help the child execute the task.	Mother: *"What's the first thing you do when you brush your teeth?"* Child: *"I don't know."* Mother: *"Well you get your toothbrush and squeeze some toothpaste on the brush. Can you do that?"* Child: *"No. I can't do it."* Mother: *"Having trouble are you? I squeeze the paste up here"* (using manual guidance prompt, with parent hand over child's hand). *"That's right. Well done."*	Child more likely to try again in the future
Emotion regulation	Positive attending to child's attempts to regulate emotion	Parent provides positive attention following a child showing restraint in a situation of provocation from sibling.	*"James, I really like the way you ignored Aaron just then when he was teasing you."*	Child learns to develop a plan to deal with other children who are annoying or irritating.

Table 1. (Continued)

Self regulation skill being promoted	Specific parenting strategy	Parent-child interaction situation	Application	Likely outcome
Self monitoring of own behaviour	Prompting the child to review or reflect on own performance or achievement	Parent asks child to review and report on how they have been going with the practise of a skill or a behaviour.	Parent: *"How many stickers have you got on your chart now?"* or *"Tell me what you have done to get all those stickers"*	Child learns to track and report on their own behaviour.
Self-evaluation of accomplishments	Asking child to describe their accomplishment while listening carefully to child's statements	Child approaches parent to show them a painting they have just completed.	Parent: *"Well now, that does look like an interesting painting. Tell me about it... What about this part up here?"*	Child learns to describe their own accomplishments and self-evaluate what they have accomplished. Becomes less reliant on praise or attention.
Creating a positive expectancy for change	Parent asks child to talk about their child's expectation	After a discussion with a 9-year-old on how to deal with teasing at school, the parent conveys their confidence in the child's capacity to deal with the situation.	Parent: *"Do you think you can use your plan tomorrow?"* Child: *"I think so."* Parent: *"I agree with you, I think you really can do it. Sounds like it's sure worth a try."*	Child anticipates they can follow the plan and that it will work.

APPLYING SELF-REGULATION PRINCIPLES TO WORKING WITH PARENTS

There a range of ways parents can enhance children's self-regulation skills, but a parent's capacity to regulate his or her behaviour is essential to consistently model and apply these principles. It is therefore important that parenting interventions enhance parents' own self-regulatory capacity. Some of the ways that parenting programs can achieve this are described below.

Modelling

Parenting practitioners have an opportunity to demonstrate the skills that they wish to instil in parents. These include being organised and prepared for sessions, negotiating goals for the intervention as a whole and for each session, and monitoring and reviewing progress in a systematic fashion during sessions. When obstacles or problems arise practitioners can attempt to understand the difficulty in a nonjudgmental way, generate ideas to overcome the issue, formulate a plan and enact it before reviewing the outcome. All this can be done while conveying optimism that change is possible and providing encouragement for both the parent's and the practitioner's own efforts.

Instruction in Social Learning Principles

Parenting interventions based on social learning principles provide parents with explicit information regarding why children behave the way they do (e.g., Sanders, 1999; Webster-Stratton, 1998). These principles are then reinforced by instruction in how these principles may be applied in a parenting context through a range of adaptive parenting strategies. If parents have an understanding of these principles and strategies they may then recognise that these principles and strategies do not just apply to parents and children, but to all human behaviour including one's own.

Guidance through the Change Process

As parents participate in a parenting intervention they are supported through a definite sequence in behaviour change. They are provided guidance in: (a) specifying the behaviours to be targeted for change and selecting a goal, (b) making observations about these target behaviours, (c) selecting parenting strategies and formulating a parenting plan, (d) reviewing progress and making adjustments to the plan as required, and finally (e) taking steps to ensure that desired changes are maintained. Over the course of a parenting intervention, there is often the opportunity for a number of target behaviours to be worked on in this manner. Thus the principle of sufficient exemplars is employed whereby the goal is for parents to have worked through a sufficient number of examples to facilitate the generalisation of this process (see Stokes & Baer, 1977).

Graduated Prompting Format to Strengthen Self-regulation Skills

Parenting competence and self-regulatory capacity can be enhanced simultaneously through a feedback process that adopts a "least-to-most" structured prompting format (Sanders, Mazzucchelli, & Ralph, in press). In this model a parent's parenting and self-regulatory knowledge and skills are constantly assessed and the least amount of prompting and information is provided that is necessary for the parent to successfully manage their own performance. For instance, after practising a particular parenting skill, if a parent does not spontaneously evaluate his or her performance and identify goals for change, the practitioner would provide the least amount of prompting to assist them to constructively do so. Over successive sessions this prompting would be faded so that the parent independently engages in these self-evaluation, planning and goal setting skills.

Promoting Self-regulation and Workforce Development

Another potential application of self-regulation principles relates to the clinical supervision of practitioners (Sanders, McGee, Loureio, & Murphy-Brennan, 2011). The successful translation into practice of evidence-based interventions requires practitioners to be able to deliver interventions competently. Competent delivery of programs requires a workplace culture that values evidence-based practices, organisational support from line management and access to supervision. Parenting interventions are delivered by a wide range of practitioners many of who do not have a workplace culture of regular supervision. Even in disciplines that have such a culture, as in clinical psychology and social work, supervision is not always available and the traditional model of having an experienced and expert clinical supervisor available is rarely attained.

An alternative is the use of a peer support self-regulation approach to supervision. Sanders and Murphy-Brennan (2010) described a peer support system of supervision that utilises self-regulation principles. In this approach, structured peer supervision sessions are conducted in small groups (5-6 practitioners) which are led by a rotational peer facilitator. Each practitioner is assigned on a rotational basis to be the leader and to structure the sessions. Each member of the group has to bring along a videotape or audiotape of an interview with a parent and be prepared to review the tape with the assistance of peers.

In undertaking the review the practitioner whose tape is being reviewed previews the tape and then begins a formal process of self-evaluation and reflection. For example, "*What were my goals?.... What did I do well?.... What should I do differently?.... What are my practise goals for next time?....*" At each stage of the process the peer facilitator prompts the practitioner to review their own performance then invites comments and suggestions from other group members to assist the practitioner identify future practice goals. This process parallels closely the process parents go through in individual coaching sessions with a therapist.

Applying Self-regulation to Organisations

Self-regulation principles also have relevance to organisations providing parenting support. It is not uncommon for an organisation to lack coherence in its aims and practice, and to be managed in a "top-down" fashion with decisions regarding services being imposed on service delivery staff in the absence of consultation, input or ownership by those staff. This can increase resistance to policy decisions (Webster-Stratton & Taylor, 1998). A lack of consultation between staff and management can also result in logistical barriers to service provision to go unresolved. Further, often there are no mechanisms in place to feedback outcomes being achieved with families. This can lead to a continuation of services that are not demonstrably effective and management to rely on organisational "spin" to satisfy consumer, political and media demands for accountability.

In contrast, organisations adopting self-regulation principles have a clear mission and supporting procedural guidelines and performance targets which are collaboratively determined with staff. Mechanisms are in place to collect output and outcome data and measures of program fidelity. Reviews of performance targets are undertaken on a routine and regular basis to inform training and support efforts and to inform decision making at a policy level. Staff accomplishments in delivering services are recognised and celebrated and, if necessary, management assist staff to identify and overcome barriers to the implementation of services. These organisations support staff by ensuring access to adequate training, supervision and resources, providing strategies and materials for service promotion (e.g., brochures, posters and press releases). Organisational management take action to support the financial, organisational and human resources required to support the work of practitioners. These organisations are also likely to be proactive in seeking to influence the future development of programs in which they have invested. Organisations might provide feedback to program developers and researchers regarding implementation successes and difficulties, and how programs could be developed to better meet the needs of specific client groups. Collaboration with research groups to examine field-generated questions are typically encouraged (Fixsen, Blase, Naoom, & Wallace, 2009; Fixsen, Naoom, Blase, Friedman, & Wallace 2005; Sanders & Turner, 2005).

Programs or new innovations may not be adopted if there is a lack on congruence between its theory or practical implementation and the orientation and practices of an organisation (Backer, Liberman, & Kuehnel, 1986; Sanders, Prinz, & Shapiro, 2009). Consequently, the dissemination of empirically supported parenting programs must not only involve adequately training practitioners in the content and processes of an intervention, it must also engage participating organisations to ensure that the accurate delivery of the intervention is supported.

PROMOTING SELF-REGULATION VIA PARENTING INTERVENTIONS: ADVANTAGES AND OPPORTUNITIES

There is evidence that self-regulatory capacity as measured in early childhood predicts a wide variety of indices of adult wellbeing and social behaviour (Mischel et al., 1988; Moffitt et al., 2011; Shoda et al., 1990; Tremblay et al., 1995). This, combined with the absence of any evidence that one can have too much self-regulatory capacity (Grant & Schwartz, 2011), has implications for policy-makers who seek to enhance the physical, mental and financial health of the population and reduce the crime rate. Large-scale or universal interventions aimed at enhancing self-regulation may improve the welfare of the entire population and reduce a range of problems that burden modern society.

While a range of psychological and behaviour change interventions increase participants' self-regulatory skills, there may be advantages to building self-regulatory capacity through a parenting intervention. Parenting interventions can be made universally available, making participation normative and non-stigmatising and increasing the likelihood that large portions of the population will be reached (Sanders et al., 2008; Prinz, Sanders, Shapiro, Whitaker, & Lutzker, 2009). Developmentally, these interventions can target children during critical periods of their development such as early childhood and adolescence when they are most likely to have a beneficial impact (Knudsen, Heckman, Cameron, & Shonkoff, 2006; Smart et al., 2005). Further, the costs of establishing the infrastructure to implement a public health parenting intervention are modest and substantially less than the amount of government expenditure it would save (Foster, Prinz, Sanders, & Shapiro, 2008; Mihalopoulos, Sanders, Turner, Murphy-Brennan, & Carter, 2007).

The benefits of parenting interventions may also extend beyond children who have more adaptive skills and less problem behaviour. By enhancing parents' self-regulatory capacity parents may also reap a range of additional benefits. For example, parents who participate in parenting programs typically report fewer personal adjustment problems and higher relationship satisfaction (e.g., Dadds, Schwartz, & Sanders, 1987; Sanders & McFarland, 2000; Zubrick et al., 2005). We have also observed apparent cascading effects such that some parents generalise their self-regulatory skills to other life domains. For instance one parent, as she neared completion of a parenting program, demonstrated enhanced interpersonal skills with adults by making an appointment with her child's teacher at school and raising concerns regarding bullying in a clear and non-escalatory fashion. Another parent, after achieving improvements in his child's behaviour, brainstormed and followed through on solutions to a number of obstacles that had previously prevented him from obtaining employment.

The potential of parenting interventions to have a range of collateral benefits for parents and families suggests a whole new research agenda. How far reaching are the benefits of parenting interventions? What strategies might be further incorporated within a parenting intervention to enhance these benefits? How can we best assess self-regulatory capacity and evidence of collateral benefits in a parenting context?

EFFICACY OF A SELF-REGULATION APPROACH TO PARENTING

The early demonstration of the role of the self-regulation approach to parenting was reported in the early eighties by Sanders and Glynn (1981). They trained five parents of preschoolers with disruptive behaviour problems to modify their own behaviour through the use of self-regulation skills (goal setting, self-monitoring, monitoring of implementation of a parenting plan to enable self-evaluation). When parents were taught self-management skills they were more likely to generalise their skills to untrained childcare situations than when they simply received instruction and feedback. This early study was a foundation study for the development of the Triple P—Positive Parenting Program which is a tiered multilevel system of parenting intervention using a self-regulation approach within a public health model of intervention. A large number of studies have attested to the efficacy of this approach to working with parents and several independent meta-analyses have been published demonstrating positive child and parent outcomes (see Nowak & Heinrichs, 2008).

More recently the self-regulation approach has been successfully applied to media and technology assisted approaches to parenting. For example, Sanders, Joachim, and Turner (2011) recently evaluated the effects of an eight-session web-version of Triple P that employed a self-regulation approach and demonstrated a significantly greater sustained improvement in the web conditions compared to controls on measures of conduct problems, parenting self-efficacy, dysfunctional parenting and parental anger. The same process of promoting self-regulation can also be employed in running parenting groups, individually administered therapy, parenting interventions delivered over the phone and through self-help text based interventions.

FUTURE DIRECTIONS

Although the clinical methods for delivering parenting interventions using a self-regulation framework have been well articulated in practitioner manuals (e.g., Sanders, Turner, & Markie-Dadds, 1998), there continues to be a gap in how to best measure self-regulation processes. Although measures of task specific parental self-efficacy have been developed and validated and shown to be sensitive to the effects of intervention (e.g., Sanders & Woolley, 2005), other aspects of the self-regulation approach articulated here require better measures to be developed. Self-regulation measures are required to assess the occurrence of competencies used as part of a method of producing behaviour change and an explanation for that change. Do practitioner strategies that theoretically should promote parental self-regulation (e.g., prompting of parental goal setting) actually do so and does change in self-regulatory capacity mediate change in desired parenting and/or child outcomes? Research is needed to develop sound measures of the components of self-regulation processes (e.g., goal setting, self-evaluation, self-monitoring).

CONCLUSIONS

Self-regulation predicts future health, wealth, and social behaviour. Enhancing self-regulation at a population level is likely to benefit society by improving citizens' health and wealth and reducing a range of societal problems. Parenting programs based on cognitive-behavioural and social learning principles would seem to represent a viable way of achieving these goals. They have been demonstrated to be capable of promoting positive health and developmental outcomes in children, capable of being disseminated at a universal level, and with a desirable cost-benefit ratio.

Parents who have strong self-regulatory capacity and who use positive parenting practices are likely to benefit their children by promoting their children's self-regulation skills. We have argued that the integration of a self-regulation perspective into parenting interventions is a powerful method of training parents to change their parenting practices. The approach enables parents to become independent and less reliant on others to produce and maintain change. Further, it is argued that self-regulatory principles are robust and apply to all other participants of the parent consultation process including service providers, managers, program disseminators, program developers and researchers.

A self-regulation perspective to parenting has a range of implications for practice and leads to a number of predictions that are yet to be empirically tested. However, in order to test these predictions sound measures of the components of self-regulation processes need to be developed.

REFERENCES

Aspinwall, L. G. (1998). Rethinking the role of positive affect in self-regulation. *Motivation and Emotion, 22,* 1–32.

Avakame, E. F. (1998). Intergenerational transmission of violence, self-control, and conjugal violence: A comparative analysis of physical violence and psychological aggression. *Violence and Victims, 13,* 301-316.

Backer, T. E., Liberman, R. P., & Kuehnel, T. G. (1986). Dissemination and adoption of innovative psychosocial interventions. *Journal of Consulting and Clinical Psychology, 54,* 111-118.

Bandura, A. (1977). *Social learning theory.* Englewood Cliffs, NJ: Prentice-Hall.

Bandura, A. (1986). *Social foundations of thought and action: A social cognitive theory.* Englewood Cliffs, NJ: Prentice Hall.

Bandura, A. (1991). Social cognitive theory of moral thought and action. In W. M. Kurtines & J. L. Gewirtz (Eds.), *Handbook of moral behavior and development* (Vol. 1, pp. 45-103). Hillsdale, NJ: Lawrence Erlbaum.

Bandura, A. (1999). Social cognitive theory: An agentic perspective. *Asian Journal of Social Psychology, 2,* 21-41.

Baumeister, R. F., Heatherton T. F., & Tice, D. M. (1994). *Losing control: How and why people fail at self-regulation.* San Diego, CA: Academic Press.

Carver, C. S. (2004). Self-regulation of action and affect. In R. F. Baumeister & K. D. Vohs (Eds.) *Handbook of self-regulation: Research, theory, and applications* (pp. 13-39). New York, NY: Guilford Press.

Cochran, J. K., Wood, P. B., Sellers, C. S., Wilkerson, W., & Chamlin, M. B. (1998). Academic dishonesty and low self-control: An empirical test of a general theory of crime. *Deviant Behavior, 19,* 227-255.

Csikszentmihalyi, M. (1990). *Flow: The psychology of optimal experience.* New York, NY: Harper Perennial.

Dadds, M. R., Schwartz, S., & Sanders, M. R. (1987). Marital discord and treatment outcome in the treatment of childhood conduct disorders. *Journal of Consulting and Clinical Psychology, 55,* 396-403.

Duckworth, A. L., & Seligman, M. E. P. (2005). Self-discipline outdoes IQ in predicting academic performance of adolescents. *Psychological Science, 16,* 939-944.

Eisenberg, N. (2004). Prosocial and moral development in the family. In T. A. Thorkildsen & H. J. Walberg (Eds.) *Nurturing morality* (pp. 119-135). New York, NY: Kluwer Academic/Plenum Publishers.

Finkenauer, C., Engels, R. C. M. E., & Baumeister, R. F. (2005). Parenting behaviour and adolescent behavioural and emotional problems: The role of self-control. *International Journal of Behavioral Development, 29,* 58-69.

Fixsen, D. L., Blase, K. A., Naoom, S. F., & Wallace, F. (2009). Core implementation components. *Research on Social Work Practice, 19,* 531-540.

Fixsen, D. L., Naoom, S. F., Blase, K. A., Friedman, R. M., & Wallace, F. (2005). *Implementation research: A synthesis of the literature.* Tampa, FL: University of South Florida, Louis de la Parte Florida Mental Health Institute, The National Implementation Research Network.

Foster, E. M., Prinz, R. J., Sanders, M. R., & Shapiro, C. J. (2008). The costs of a public health infrastructure for delivering parenting and family support. *Children and Youth Services Review, 30*, 493-501.

Fredrickson, B. L., & Joiner, T. (2002). Positive emotions trigger upward spirals toward emotional well-being. *Psychological Science, 13,* 172–175.

Gibbs, J. J., Giever, D., & Martin, J. S. (1998). Parental management and self-control: An empirical test of Gottfredson and Hirschi's general theory. *Journal of Research in Crime and Delinquency, 35*, 40-70.

Gollwitzer, P. M. (1999). Implementation intentions: Strong effects of simple plans. *American Psychologist, 54,* 493-503.

Grant, A. M., & Schwartz, B. (2011). Too much of a good thing: The challenge and opportunity of the inverted U. *Perspectives on Psychological Science, 6,* 61-76.

Hayes, S. C., Strosahl, K. D., & Wilson, K. G. (1999). *Acceptance and commitment therapy: An experiential approach to behavior change.* New York, NY: Guilford.

Jang, S. J., & Smith, C. A. (1997). A test of reciprocal causal relationships among parental supervision, affective ties, and delinquency. *Journal of Research in Crime and Delinquency, 34*, 307-336.

Karoly, P. (1993). Mechanisms of self-regulation: A systems view. *Annual Review of Psychology, 44*, 23-52.

Kashdan, T. B., & Rottenberg, J. (2010). Psychological flexibility as a fundamental aspect of health. *Clinical Psychology Review, 30*, 467-480.

Knudsen, E. I., Heckman, J. J., Cameron, J. L., & Shonkoff, J. P. (2006). Economic, neurobiological, and behvioral perspectives on building America's future workforce. *Proceedings of the National Academy of Sciences of the United States of America, 103*, 10155-10162.

Linehan, M. M. (1993). *Cognitive-behavioral treatment of borderline personality disorder.* New York, NY: Guilford Press.

Martell, C.R., Addis, M. E., & Jacobson, N. S. (2001). Depression in Context: Strategies for Guided Action. New York: Norton

Martell, C. R., Dimidjian, S., & Herman-Dunn, R. (2010). Behavioral Activation for Depression: A Clincian's Guide. New York: Guilford

Mazzucchelli, T. G., Kane, R. T., & Rees, C. S. (2010). Behavioral activation interventions for well-being: A meta-analysis. *The Journal of Positive Psychology, 5*, 105-121.

McCord, J. (1979). Some child-rearing antecedents of criminal behavior in adult men. *Journal of Personality and Social Psychology, 37*, 1477-1486.

Mihalopoulos, C., Sanders, M. R., Turner, K. M. T., Murphy- Brennan, M., & Carter, R. (2007). Does the Triple P-Positive Parenting Program provide value for money? *Australian and New Zealand Journal of Psychiatry, 41*, 239–246.

Mischel, W., Shoda, Y., & Peake, P. K. (1988). The nature of adolescent competencies predicted by preschool delay of gratification. *Journal of Personality and Social Psychology, 54*, 687-696.

Moffitt, T. E., Arseneault, L., Belsky, D., Dickson, N., Hancox, R. J., Harrington, H.,... Caspi, A. (2011). A gradient of childhood self-control predicts health, wealth, and public safety. *Proceedings of the National Academy of Sciences of the United States of America, 108*, 2693-2698.

Muraven, M., Baumeister, R. F., & Tice, D. M. (1999). Longitudinal improvement of self-regulation through practice: Building self-control strength through repeated exercise. *The Journal of Social Psychology, 139*, 446-457.

Nezu, A. M. (1986). Efficacy of a social problem-solving therapy approach for unipolar depression. *Journal of Consulting and Clinical Psychology, 54*, 196-202.

Nowak, C., & Heinrichs, N. (2008). A comprehensive meta-analysis of Triple P—Positive Parenting Program using hierarchical linear modeling: Effectiveness and moderating variables. *Clinical Child and Family Psychology Review, 11,* 114-144.

Prinz, R. J., Sanders, M. R., Shapiro, C. J., Whitaker, D. J., & Lutzker, J. R. (2009). Population-based prevention of child maltreatment: The US Triple P system population trial. *Prevention Science, 10*, 1-12.

Rehm, L. P. (1977). A self-control model of depression. *Behavior Therapy, 8*, 787-804.

Richards, J. M., & Gross, J. J. (2000). Emotion regulation and memory: The cognitive costs of keeping one's cool. *Journal of Personality and Social Psychology, 79*, 410-424.

Sanders, M. R. (1998). The empirical status of psychological interventions with families of children and adolescents. In L. L'Abate (Ed.), *Family psychopathology: The relational roots of dysfunctional behavior* (pp. 427-465). New York, NY: Guilford Press.

Sanders, M. R. (1999). Triple P-Positive Parenting Program: Towards an empirically validated multilevel parenting and family support strategy for the prevention of behavior and emotional problems in children. *Clinical Child & Family Psychology Review, 2*, 71-90.

Sanders, M. R. (2008). Triple P—Positive Parenting Program as a public health approach to strengthening parenting. *Journal of Family Psychology, 22*, 506-517.

Sanders, M. R., & Glynn, E. L. (1981). Training parents in behavioral self-management: An analysis of generalization and maintenance effects. *Journal of Applied Behavior Analysis, 14*, 223–237.

Sanders, M. R., Joachim, S., & Turner, K. M. T. (2011). *A randomised controlled trial evaluation of the effects of Triple P Online for parents of children with conduct problems.* Manuscript in preparation.

Sanders, M. R., Mazzucchelli, T. G., & Ralph, A. (in press). Promoting parenting competence through a self-regulation approach to feedback. In R. M. Sutton, M. M. Hornsey, & K. M. Douglas (Eds.) *Feedback: The communication of praise, criticism, and advice.* New York, NY: Peter Lang.

Sanders, M. R., & McFarland, M. (2000). Treatment of depressed mothers with disruptive children: A controlled evaluation of cognitive behavioral family intervention. *Behavior Therapy, 31*, 89-112.

Sanders, M. R., McGee, E., Loureiro, T., & Murphy, M. (2011). *Supervision and the implementation of evidence-based parenting programs: Towards a self-regulation approach.* Manuscript in preparation.

Sanders, M. R., & Murphy-Brennan, M. (2010). Creating conditions for success beyond the professional training environment. *Clinical Psychology: Research and Practice, 17*, 31-35.

Sanders, M. R., Prinz, R. J., & Shapiro, C. J. (2009). Predicting utilization of evidence-based parenting interventions with organizational, service-provider and client variables. *Administration and Policy in Mental Health and Mental Health Services Research, 36*, 133-143.

Sanders, M.R., Ralph, A., Sofronoff, K., Gardiner, P., Thompson, R., Dwyer, S., & Bidwell, K. (2008). Every Family: A population approach to reducing behavioral and emotional problems in children making the transition to school. *Journal of Primary Prevention, 29*, 197-222.

Sanders, M. R., & Turner, K. M. T. (2005). Reflections on the challenges of effective dissemination of behavioural family intervention: Our experience with the Triple P—Positive Parenting Program. *Child and Adolescent Mental Health, 10*, 158-169.

Sanders, M. R., Turner, K. M. T., & Markie-Dadds, C. (1998). *Practitioner's manual for enhanced Triple P*. Brisbane, Australia: Families International Publishing.

Sanders, M. R., & Woolley, M. L. (2005). The relationship between maternal self-efficacy and parenting practices: Implications for parent training. *Child: Care, Health and Development, 31*, 65-73.

Shoda, Y., Mischel, W., & Peake, P. K. (1990). Predicting adolescent cognitive and self-regulatory competencies from preschool delay of gratification: Identifying diagnostic conditions. *Developmental Psychology, 26*, 978-986.

Smart, D., Richardson, N., Sanson, A., Dussuyer, I., Marshall, B., Toumbourou, J. W.,... Oberklaid, F. (2005). *Patterns and precursors to adolescent antisocial behaviour: Outcomes and connections*. Melbourne, Australia: Australian Institute of Family Studies.

Stokes, T. F., & Baer, D. M. (1977). An implicit technology of generalization. *Journal of Applied Behavior Analysis, 10*, 349-367.

Tangney, J. P., Baumeister, R. F., & Boone, A. L. (2004). High self-control predicts good adjustment, less pathology, better grades, and interpersonal success. *Journal of Personality, 72*, 271-322.

Taylor, T. K., & Biglan, A. (1998). Behavioral family interventions for improving child rearing: A review of the literature for clinicians and policy makers. *Clinical Child and Family Psychology Review, 1*, 41-60.

Tomaka, J., Blascovich, J., Kibler, J., & Ernst, J. M. (1997). Cognitive and physiological antecedents of threat and challenge appraisal. *Journal of Personality and Social Psychology, 73*, 63-72.

Tremblay, R. E., Boulerice, B., Arseneault, L., & Niscale, M. J. (1995). Does low self-control during childhood explain the association between delinquency and accidents in early adolescence? *Criminal Behaviour and Mental Health, 5*, 439-451.

Tsukayama, E., Toomey, S. L., Faith, M. S., & Duckworth, A. L. (2010). Self-control as a protective factor against overweight status in the transition from childhood to adolescence. *Archives of Pediatrics & Adolescent Medicine, 164*, 631-635.

Webster-Stratton, C. (1998). Preventing conduct problems in head start children: Strengthening parenting competencies. *Journal of Consulting and Clinical Psychology, 66*, 715-730.

Webster-Stratton, C., & Taylor, T. K. (1998). Adopting and implementing empirically supported interventions: A recipe for success. In A. Buchanan & B. L. Hudson (Eds.), *Parenting, schooling and children's behaviour: Interdisciplinary approaches* (pp. 127-160). Aldershot, England: Ashgate.

Zubrick, S. R., Ward, K., Silburn, S. R., Lawrence, D., Williams, A. A., Blair, E.,... Sanders, M. R. (2005). Prevention of child behavior problems through universal implementation of a group behavioral family intervention. *Prevention Science, 6*, 287-304.

In: Psychology of Self-Regulation
Editor: Vassilis Barkoukis

ISBN: 978-1-61470-380-8
© 2012 Nova Science Publishers, Inc.

Chapter 6

COGNITIVE PERSISTENCE: REFINING THE ROLE OF CONSCIOUSNESS WITHIN SELF-REGULATION

Derek Dorris

School of Applied Psychology, University College Cork, Ireland

ABSTRACT

Self-regulation is assumed to be achieved through both conscious and nonconscious processes. It has recently been argued (Dorris, 2009; Baumeister, Masicampo, & Vohs, 2011) that consciousness plays only an indirect role in self-regulation in that it selects a behaviour to be executed and, from that selection, a series of integrated downstream behavioural processes are set in motion so that the execution of the selected behaviour is carried out nonconsciously. It is argued here, that this refined notion of consciousness is most clearly demonstrated in self-regulatory persistence and that the act of persistence amounts to the same thing as the conscious process described by Dorris (2009) and Baumeister et al. (2011). It is argued, that such a conflation bolsters the notion that consciousness is simply a selector in that it allows us to see selection as a more effortful and, therefore, more organising process.

Traditionally consciousness has been strongly linked to the self-regulation of our thoughts, emotions, and behaviour. However, this link seems to have been grounded in intuition more than actual experimental observation. Though, consciousness is typically intuited to be involved in the recognition of the need to control and the formation of the intention to control, knock-on intuitions have also appeared to implicate it in the on-line implementation of intended behaviour. As the issue was never clearly addressed in the academic literature, it would seem that that intuition became presupposition. However, in recent years there has been a reaction against this assumption as several studies demonstrated a host of nonconscious processes that are each capable of implementing intended behaviour in the absence of consciousness. On the back of this research, it was argued by some that consciousness has no role to play in self-regulatory implementation whatsoever. The present work builds on a new approach to consciousness within self-regulation (see Dorris, 2009;

Baumesiter, Masicampo, & Vohs, 2011). This approach sees conscious self-regulation as being functionally involved in self-regulatory implementation not by assuming on-line control over that behaviour but by selecting that behaviour and allowing a series of downstream nonconscious plans to carry out its execution. Where this work builds on that idea is by linking this refined notion of conscious selection with cognitive persistence. Cognitive persistence refers to the process of commanding or willing oneself to engage in given task behaviour. It will be argued in this chapter that the conscious selection that Dorris (2009) describes and integration that Baumeister et al. (2011) describe is the same process involved in cognitive persistence. However, it will be further argued that the latter more fully captures the typical intuitions we hold about consciousness. Specifically, that consciousness is effortful and that consciousness acts as an organiser of our behaviour.

CONSCIOUS AND NONCONSCIOUS SELF-REGULATION

Self-regulation refers to the intentional control over our own behaviour so that it accords with our goals and desires. The literature describes self-regulation as capable of being driven both consciously and nonconsciously (Fitzsimons & Bargh, 2004). For example, when one is learning to drive a car it is generally assumed that one must initially attend to and co-ordinate the different sub-skills consciously. However, with repeated practicing of that skill, it is assumed that one can begin to execute the desired behaviour nonconsciously. Nonconscious self-regulation is thought to be capable of being initiated both consciously, through the intentional activation of the nonconscious behavioural routine (e.g., deciding to drive), and automatically, by environmental stimuli appropriate to that nonconscious routine (e.g., the sound of the engine turning over). Chen, Lee-Chai, and Bargh (2001) demonstrated the latter when they showed that "communally orientated" participants (those with a chronic tendency to use power fairly and responsibly) who were seated in a position of high power (a professor's chair in the professor's office) made more socially desirable responses than those who were seated in a position of low power (a guest's chair). These findings indicated that the professor's chair preconsciously cued the participants' chronic representation for communal behaviour so that they behaved in accordance with that frequently pursued goal.

In recent years, more subtle forms of nonconscious self-regulatory processes have been uncovered by investigations into intentions formation. For example, research into prospective memory (our memory to complete future intentions) found that the formation of intentions makes words related to those intentions more accessible to nonconscious activation during a lexical decision task (Marsh, Hicks, & Bink, 1998; Marsh, Hicks, and Bryan, 1999). Furthermore, research into implementation intentions showed that planning the implementation of an intention allows that intention to be implemented nonconsciously (Coehn & Gollwitzer, 2008). For example, Gollwitzer and Brandstätter (1997) showed that participants, who had formed implementation intentions which specified the right time to present a counter-argument to an argument made by a opponent, responded with counter-arguments faster than those participants who had not formed an implementation plan.

As increasingly more examples of nonconscious self-regulation were identified, some began to question if consciousness has any role to play in self-regulation at all. Bargh's (1990) *auto-motive model of goal-directed behaviour* which postulated that the majority of our behaviour is initiated and carried out in the absence of conscious awareness acted as the platform for this new approach. Although Bargh's (1990, see also Bargh, 1997) model left some scope for conscious processing, he suggested that this scope might continue to be narrowed as investigations into nonconscious control proceeded. His conclusions began to resonate with assertions coming from the related field of cognitive neuroscience: - that consciousness was too slow to be meaningfully involved in the on-line control of our own behaviour (Jeannerod, 1997 & 2006). Thus, the idea that consciousness was a non-functional by-product of nonconscious activity became popular once again as the argument that "behaviour does not originate with a conscious decision" (Dijksterhuis, Chartrand, & Aarts, 2007, p. 52) gained momentum within the literature.

INDIRECT CONSCIOUS CONTROL

Although nonconscious self-regulation does appear to be a particularly important feature of our system for cognitive control, an even newer approach has emerged that brings consciousness right back into the fold. Dorris (2009) and Baumeister et al. (2011) have both recently outlined a notion of self-regulation that frames consciousness as an indirect driver of intended behaviour. Specifically, Dorris (2009) argued that Clark's (2001, 2002, 2006) *experience-based selection model of motor control* (which holds that fine-tuned motor movements are only indirectly controlled by conscious experience) could be used a model for the wider field of self-regulation. Similarly, Baumeister et al. (2011) concluded that, based on an in-depth review of experimental literature, the role of consciousness is not to directly control human behaviour but to indirectly influence it. Importantly, both of these approaches maintain that consciousness affects behaviour not by maintaining on-line control over it but by selecting and integrating desired behaviour which sets in motion a series of nonconscious processes, the function of which, are to implement the intended behaviour.

For instance, Dorris (2009) reviews a number of self-regulatory theories from Metcalf and Mischel's (1999) *hot/cool systems model of self-regulation* to Miller and Wallis' (2009) theory of prefrontal function and concludes that, according to many such theories, the "direct activation of goal-representations puts in place a constellation of biases the aggregate effect of which is....promoting or priming appropriate responses" (p. 745). For example, Metcalf and Mischel's (1999) model (see also, Ayduk & Kross, 2009) describe a system of control wherein the manner in which one decides to perceive a stimulus can give rise to different types of automatic processes. An emotional or "hot" perception gives rise to impulsive reactions towards that stimulus while a more abstract or "cool" perception creates something similar to an implementation intention which allows for a more "controlled" reaction towards that stimulus. Similarly, Baumeister et al. (2011) described a number of diverse mechanisms through which conscious thought indirectly influences behaviour. They pointed to work on mental practice or visualisation that showed imagining oneself executing a behaviour subsequently led to more efficient physical manifestations of that behaviour (see Kosslyn and Moulton's, 2009 for a review). They also pointed out that when consciousness intrudes on the direct control over our own behaviour that behaviour tends to be impaired as in the case of choking.

In both papers, therefore, a more refined notion of consciousness is reinserted back into the self-regulatory process. In refining the idea of consciousness, both Dorris (2009) and Baumeister et al. (2011) reigned in the scope of its operation. According to these mutually compatible perspectives, consciousness is not framed as a broadly integrated organiser of behaviour responsible for the every aspect of the self-regulatory process. Instead, it is framed as an initiator, a process that gets the ball rolling so to speak. It is this narrower reformulation of the conscious process in self-regulation that the present work focuses on. Specifically, it is agued here that in attempting to distil consciousness down to its essence, Dorris (2009) and Baumeister et al. (2011) have identified a construct that appears very like cognitive persistence as viewed from the research into ego depletion.

SELECTION AS PERSISTENCE AND PERSISTENCE AS SELECTION

Self-regulatory depletion or "ego depletion" is a phenomenon observed when one's attempt to persist at a self-regulatory task is negatively affected by one's recent self-regulatory exertions. In one of many examples, Muraven, Tice, and Baumeister (1998) found that participants who constantly suppressed a target thought whilst engaging in a writing task persisted at a subsequent ostensibly solvable (but in reality unsolvable) anagram task for shorter periods of time than those who did not have to suppress a target thought. To explain such observations, Muraven and Baumeister (2000) and Baumeister (2003) postulated that our ability to self-regulation is dependent on a finite resource much in the same way that our physical muscles are dependent on a physical energy. Thus, he maintained that when we self-regulate our thoughts and behaviour we tap into and deplete a self-regulatory strength, which like our physical muscles, requires a period of replenishment before it can properly tackle any subsequent tasks.

Importantly, to the current focus of this chapter, Vohs and Baumeister (2004) concluded that from a review of the literature, only conscious self-regulation is dependent on the self-regulatory resource. Of course, this makes sense as ego depletion is very much an indicator of effortfulness and one of the most often cited attributes of consciousness is that it requires effort. Webb and Sheeran (2003) confirmed this when they demonstrated that participants who completed a Stroop task that they had planned their performance on (i.e., formed implementation intentions) subsequently persisted for longer on three unsolvable tracing puzzles than those who completed a Stroop task unaided. Webb and Sheeran (2003) concluded that the nonconscious operations that the implementation planning put in place allowed the participants to complete the Stroop task without depleting the self-regulatory resource.

Interestingly, in the same way that Dorris (2009) and Baumeister et al. (2011) reduce consciousness to an initiator of behaviour, the research on ego depletion can be understood to be similarly (if not identically) reductive. Within the paradigm of ego depletion, causing ego depletion is *the* criteria for consciousness and persisting or not persisting at a task is always assumed to be the cause or effect of depletion respectively. Though experiments have demonstrated that ego depletion can negatively affect task performance, it is explicitly assumed that the poorer performance is due to an inability to persist. For example, Baumeister, Bratslvsky, Muraven, and Tice (1998) predicted and demonstrated that participants who suppressed their emotions while watching a funny or sad movie subsequently completed fewer solvable anagrams than those who were not given any instructions to control their emotions while watching the same movies. To explain these results Baumeister et al. (1998) argued that during anagram performance, "One must keep breaking and altering the tentative combinations of letters one has formed and must make oneself keep trying despite multiple initial failures" (p. 1258). In other words, in the ego depletion literature, it is not the controlling of the process that is assumed to require conscious effort. It is the initiation of the process or the "pushing" of the process into effect.

Cognitive persistence can, therefore, be contrasted with other aspects of the self-regulatory process as the only process that requires effort and, therefore, by the standards of the wider literature on consciousness, it is the only process that is truly conscious. What is interesting from the standpoint of Dorris' (2009) and Baumeister et al.' (2011) frameworks is that persistence closely matches the notion of selection that features so strongly in those frameworks. After all, what is selection if not the commitment to the doing of a task and what is persistence if not the decision to do one thing over another? Can we, therefore, assume selection (as the above frameworks describe it) and persistence (as the ego depletion paradigm frames it) to be reflections of the same process? It is argued here that we can. It is also argued that by conflating the two we are left with a better understanding of how selection might represent the entire functional responsibilities of consciousness within self-regulation.

One of the most important implications that conflating selection with persistence has for the above frameworks of indirect control is that it makes selection effortful. Thus, not only does our new understanding of selection fit traditional definitions of consciousness more closely but its capacity to initiate a series of subsequent cognitive processes can be more easily intuited because the thrust of our mental energy can now be assumed to be behind it. Baumeister et al.'s (1998) explanation of how the self-regulatory resource is employed to aid performance in tasks such anagram completion seems to describe mental effort as being useful in generating psychological momentum that continues until the task is completed or until it stalls and needs to be generated again. By viewing selection in a similar light it becomes easier to conceptualise it as a functional processes within the self-regulatory domain. In this light, selection is not simply "deciding" to do one thing over another but instead it is an active and forceful process setting in motion a train of events capable of achieving a goal. In short it is an organiser. Importantly, this complements much of what Baumesiter et al. (2011) say when specifying the way in which the conscious decision to control ultimately achieves that goal. For example, "Consciousness serves integrative functions that can have downstream effects on behaviour. It seems to bridge general, abstract ideas to specific actions..." (p. 20).

Though, it is argued here that the proposed conflation can bolster our understanding of selection, it might also augment our understanding of persistence from the perspective of the literature on ego depletion. It is reasonable to say that, from a self-regulatory standpoint, persistence is viewed as a very straightforward nonconceptual operation. This has undoubtedly appealed to the many who have undertaken experimental testing in this field. Its clear-cut nature allows for reliable measurements and emphatic conclusions. However, in the same way that the proposed conflation allows us the see a more functional side to selection/integration, it also highlights a conceptual element to persistence that is perhaps ignored by typical accounts of ego depletion. Persistence is a cognitive driver, and so it is shaped and actualised through intention. By seeing persistence as a form selection/integration we can imbue it with the sort of conceptual elements that justify it being viewed as the manifestation of our conscious capacity. Thus, when one persists, we can view that process more fully as one's decision to continue pouring one's mental effort into a task because of its relative, immediate and/or long-term significance to one's goals and ambitions.

DISCUSSION

The different and shared roles that conscious and nonconscious processes play within self-regulation are both complex and still somewhat mysterious. Though, there has been an attempt to explain self-regulation by mainly referring to the latter in recent years, reviews of the relevant literature such as those carried out by Dorris (2009) and Baumeister et al. (2011) suggest that consciousness does play an indirect yet nonetheless critical role in self-regulation. Specifically, they argue that it integrates and sets in motion the series of nonconscious processes that ultimately allow the desired behaviour to be executed. It has been suggested in this chapter that the refined notion of consciousness proffered by those reviews can be related to the refined notion of consciousness found in the ego depletion literature. Specifically, it is suggested that selection as Dorris (2009) describes it and integration as Baumeister et al. (2011) describe it can be likened to persistence as demonstrated in that literature.

Thus, under the proposed conflation comes a more functional notion of selection. What were formerly separate processes are, here, understood to be two sides of the same coin which drives the broader process of self-regulation as both its initiator and its organiser. Under the proposed conflation, conscious intention manifests itself as nothing more than the beginning of persistence. Importantly, this accords with our intuitions regarding consciousness being an effortful process of will. It also complements traditional cognitive concepts of consciousness as an accommodator or "re-shaper" of mental representations. Rather than being an automatic process of assimilation, consciousness within self-regulation can be more readily intuited as an active driver and orchestrator of activity.

A more phenomenal side to persistence is also illuminated under this conflation as the priming and integrating powers of selection and conscious intention become critically linked to it. Thus, persistence is not merely an initiator but also an organiser and creator of downstream nonconscious self-regulatory processes. Although, phenomenal accounts of consciousness are not often provided when discussing persistence within the ego depletion literature, this does not mean that the former has no place within the latter. On the contrary, it might be argued that phenomenal or experiential awareness of one's situation is fundamental to persistence as the recognition of the need to strive for a goal gives persistence direction and meaning. By linking it with selection or intention formation (and the perceived discrepancies between current state and intended state), the proposed conflation can be understood to support such a wider notion of persistence.

When it comes to the wider implications for the proposed conflation it can be argued that bringing both selection and persistence together provides us with a new conceptual/methodological framework for investigating and interpreting consciousness within self-regulation. For example, using the more refined notion of selection, related phenomena such as indecisiveness could be framed as a possible function of ego depletion rather than solely a character trait. Thus, our ability or inability to persist would have important implications for socio-cognitive constructs such as sedentary behaviour and laziness as they become related to our ability and inability to intend. Furthermore, as persistence is impaired by ego depletion, then degrees of downstream nonconscious behavioural integration, could too be related to degrees of ego depletion at the time of selection so that extended and uninterrupted performance (if not facilitated by chronic/practiced automatic routines), could be accounted for by reference to unimpaired implementational priming.

Self-regulation will continue to be approached by those who wish to see it primarily as a nonconscious process and those who favour more intuitive conscious accounts. The notion of indirect conscious control described by both Dorris (2009) and Baumeister et al. (2011) provides a sort of middle ground between both approaches. The present chapter expands on that framework by refining both the critical features of selection/integration and cognitive persistence to better explain the mechanism that allows conscious intentions to be enacted nonconsciously. The result is a slightly broader conceptual/methodological framework that will hopefully facilitate continued investigations into indirect conscious control.

REFERENCES

Ajzen, I. (1991). The theory of planned behaviour. *Organizational Behavior and Human Decision Processes, 50*, 179–211.

Bargh, J. A. (1990). Auto-motives: Preconscious determinants of thought and behaviour. In E. T. Higgins & R. M. Sorrentino (Eds.). *Handbook of motivation and cognition* (Vol. 2, pp. 93–130). New York: Guilford.

Bargh, J. A. (1997). The automaticity of everyday life. In Advances in social cognition. In R. S. Wyer (Ed.). *The automaticity of everyday life* (Vol. X, pp. 1–61). New Jersey: Lawrence Erlbaum Associates, Inc.

Baumeister, R. F. (2003). Ego Depletion and Self-Regulation Failure: A Resource Model of Self-Control. *Alcoholism: Clinical and Experimental Research, 27(2)*, 1-4.s

Baumeister, R. F., Masicampo, E. J., & Vohs, K. D. (2011). Do conscious thoughts cause behavior? *Annual Review of Psychology, 62*, 331-361.

Baumeister, R. F., Bratslavsky, E., Muraven, M., & Tice, D. M. (1998). Ego depletion: Is the active self a limited resource? *Journal of Personality and Social Psychology, 74*, 1252–1265.

Clark, A. (2001). Visual experience and motor action: Are the bonds too tight? *The Philosophical Review, 110*, 495–519.

Clark, A. (2002). Is seeing all it seems? Action, reason and the grand illusion. *Journal of Consciousness Studies*, 9, 181–202.

Clark, A. (2006). Vision as dance? Three challenges for sensori-motor contingency theory. *PSYCHE, 12(*1). <http://www.psyche.cs.monash.edu.au>.

Cohen, A., & Gollwitzer, P. M. (2008). The cost of remembering to remember: Cognitive load and implementation intentions influence ongoing task performance. In M. Kliegel, M. A McDaniel, & G. O. Einstein (Eds.), *Prospective memory* (pp. 367–390). New York: Lawrence Erlbaum Associates.

Dijksterhuis A., Chartrand T. L., Aarts H. (2007). Effects of priming and perception on social behavior and goal pursuit. In *Social psychology and the unconscious: The automaticity of higher mental processes,* Ed. J. A. Bargh, pp. 51-132. Philadelphia: Psychology Press.

Chen S, Lee-Chai AY, Bargh JA (2001) Relationship orientation as a moderator of the effects of social power. *Journal of Personality Social Psychology, 85,* 173–187.

Dorris, D (2009). Self-regulation and the hypothesis of experience-based selection: Investigating indirect conscious control. *Consciousness and Cognition,18,* 740-753.

Fitzsimons, G. M., & Bargh, J. A. (2004). Automatic self-regulation. In R. F. Baumeister & K. D. Vohs (Eds.), *Handbook of self-regulation* (pp. 151–170). New York: Guilford Press.

Gollwitzer, P. M., & Brandstätter, V. (1997). Implementation intentions and effective goal pursuit. *Journal of Personality and Social Psychology, 73,* 186–199.

Jeannerod, M. (1997). *The Cognitive Neuroscience of Action.* Wiley-Blackwell.

Jeannerod, M. (2006) Consciousness of action as an embodied consciousness. In *Does consciousness cause behavior?* Eds. S. Pockett, W. Banks, S. Gallagher, pp. 25-38. Cambridge, MA: MIT Press.

Kosslyn S. M, Moulton S. T. (2009). Mental imagery and implicit memory. In *The Handbook of Imagination and Mental Simulation*, Ed. K. D. Markman, W. M. P. Klein, J. A. Suhr, pp. 35-51. New York: Psychology Press.

Marsh, R. L., Hicks, J. L., & Bryan, E. S. (1999). The activation of unrelated and cancelled intentions. *Memory and Cognition, 27,* 320–327.

Marsh, R. L., Hicks, J. L., & Cook, G. I. (2008). On beginning to understand the role of context in prospective memory. In M. Kliegel, M. A. McDaniel, & G. O. Einstein (Eds.), *Prospective memory* (pp. 77–100). New York: Lawrence Erlbaum Associates.

Metcalfe, J., & Mischel, W. (1999). A hot/cool system analysis of delay of gratification: Dynamics of willpower. *Psychological Review, 106,* 3–19.

Miller, E. K., & Wallis, J. D. (2009). Executive function and higher-order cognition: Definition and neural substrates. *Encyclopedia of Neuroscience, 4,* 99–104.

Muraven, M.R., & Baumeister, R.F. (2000). Self-regulation and depletion of limited resources: Does self-control resemble a muscle? *Psychological Bulletin, 126,* 247-259.

Muraven, M., Tice, D.M., & Baumeister, R.F. (1998). Self-control as limited resource: Regulatory depletion patterns. *Journal of Personality and Social Psychology, 74,* 774-789.

Vohs, K. D., & Baumeister, R. F. (2004). Understanding self-regulation: An introduction. In R. F. Baumeister & K. D. Vohs (Eds.), *Handbook of self-regulation* (pp. 1–12). New York: Guilford Press.

Webb, T. L., & Sheeran, P. (2003). Can implementation intentions help to overcome ego-depletion? *Journal of Experimental and Social Psychology, 39,* 279–286.

In: Psychology of Self-Regulation
Editor: Vassilis Barkoukis

Chapter 7

ANTECEDENTS AND CONSEQUENCES OF SELF-REGULATED LEARNING IN PHYSICAL EDUCATION

Vassilis Barkoukis, Kondilenia Katsani, and Despoina Ourda*

Aristotle University of Thessaloniki,
Department of Physical Education and Sport Sciences

ABSTRACT

Self-regulation is an important factor affecting the learning process and achievement in education. Although there is ample empirical evidence on the effects of self-regulation on learning in the general education literature, related research in the context of physical education is limited. The present study used a cross-sectional survey-based design to investigate the motivational antecedents and affective consequences of self-regulated learning in physical education lessons. Participants were 345 high school students attending the 8th and 9th grades of typical co-educational secondary schools in Greece. The survey included measures of achievement goals, motivational climate, basic psychological needs, motivational regulation, self-regulation, as well as enjoyment and boredom. Linear regression analysis was used, and showed that approach achievement goals, perceptions of learning motivational climate and satisfaction of basic psychological needs were positive predictors of self-regulated learning in physical education. Also, self-regulated learning positively predicted enjoyment, but had a negative predictive effect on boredom. The findings of the present study highlight the role of motivational variables in self-regulated learning strategies and on student's affective responses within the context of physical education lessons.

Keywords: achievement goals, motivational climate, basic psychological needs, motivational regulations, enjoyment, boredom

* Correspondence should be addressed to Vassilis Barkoukis, Aristotle University of Thessaloniki, Greece, email: bark@phed.auth.gr, telephone: +30 2310 992225.

ANTECEDENTS AND CONSEQUENCES OF SELF-REGULATED LEARNING IN PHYSICAL EDUCATION

Several approaches and theoretical frameworks have been developed to study self-regulation of human behaviour. There is a consensus in these approaches that self-regulation reflects the ability of the self to override and alter its responses and includes proactively initiated thoughts, feelings, and behaviors (Zimmerman, 2000). Regulation corresponds to change in order to make behaviour consistent to a standard such as an ideal or goal. It is a process by which individuals attempt to constrain unwanted urges in order to gain control of the inchoate response (Baumeister & Vohs, 2007).

In the context of general education, self-regulated learning has become an important aspect of the learning environment, and involves students' active participation in the learning process. This is realized through the effective management of behavioral, emotional, cognitive, attentional, and environmental resources in order to accomplish the desirable learning outcomes (Pintrich, 2000; Zimmerman, 2000). Most, if not all, intervention designs aiming to improve the learning process incorporate self-regulated learning strategies. Practices that guide students to engage in academic tasks, set academic goals, foster self-monitoring and self-evaluation and adjust goals are common in education interventions (Barkoukis, Tsorbatzoudis & Grouios, 2008; Boekaerts & Corno, 2005).

Motivation and affect are considered to be important aspects of self-regulated learning. As Efklides (2011) and Volet, Vauras and Salonen (2009) pointed out, motivation and affect interact with meta-cognitive skills, and these interactions have important implications for self-regulated learning. However, despite the ample research evidence on the association between motivation, affect and self-regulated learning in general education, there is only limited evidence in the context of physical education (Ommundsen, 2003; Theodosiou, Mantis & Papaioannou, 2008; Theodosiou & Papaioannou, 2006). Thus, the aim of the present study was to investigate the motivational antecedents and the consequences of self-regulated learning in the context of school physical education. Towards this end, current developments on the more prominent theories of motivation in the area of physical education (i.e., achievement goal and self-determination theories) are briefly described as follows.

ACHIEVEMENT GOAL THEORY

According to the pioneering work of Nicholls (1989) on achievement goal theory, individuals in a specific context strive to achieve their personal goals. In this process, two main achievement goal orientations have been identified, namely task and ego goal orientation. People with task orientation engage in an activity in order to improve mastery of the task at hand. On the other hand, ego oriented individuals engage in an activity aiming the demonstration of high competence and outperforming their opponents (Nicholls, 1989). Elliot and colleagues (e.g. Elliot, 1997; Elliot & Church, 1997; Elliot & Thrash, 2001) incorporated the approach and avoidance distinction provided by the achievement motive approach (Atkinson, 1964) into this so called dichotomous, achievement goal approach and developed the hierarchical model of approach and avoidance achievement motivation. This model includes mastery goals, which are similar to task orientation and reflect focus on personal improvement and task mastery. The model further posits the distinction of ego orientation into two different achievement goals, namely performance-approach and performance-avoidance goals. Performance-approach goals represent the engagement in an activity as a means to display higher competence against others, whereas performance-avoidance goals reflect the tendency to avoid displaying low competence compared to other participants. Research in sport and physical education using this trichotomous approach of achievement goals indicated that mastery goals relate to more positive patterns of responses (i.e., state anxiety, perceptions of competence and effort) relative to performance-approach goals, which, in turn have a more positive pattern compared to performance-avoidance goals (Cury, Da Fonseca, Rufo, Peres, & Sarrazin, 2003). This approach was further extended with the inclusion of an avoidance direction in mastery goals. The newly added mastery-avoidance goal reflected the tendency to avoid lack of improvement and task failure. Further research suggested that mastery-avoidance goals displayed worse cognitive, affective and behavioral responses in education compared to mastery-approach goals, but more positive ones compared with performance-avoidance goals (Cury, Elliot, Da Fonseca & Moller, 2006; Elliot & McGregor, 2001).

The concepts described in the achievement goal theory have been used to operationalize the situation-induced environment that directs the goals of an action, the so-called motivational climate) (Ames, 1992a, 1992b). Motivational climate is considered to affect a person's interpretation of the criteria of success and failure in achievement environments and, based on Nicholls (1989) distinction, can be either task- or ego-involving (Duda, 2001; Duda & Hall, 2001). Task-involving climate is assumed to have positive cognitive, affective and behavioural outcomes, whereas an ego-involving climate results into negative outcomes, such as lower enjoyment and effort, and higher anxiety (Barkoukis et al., 2008; Duda & Whitehead, 1998; Jaakkola & Digelidis, 2007).

Newton and Duda (1993, 1999) proposed the existence of subdimensions of task- and ego-involving climate, and noted that these dimensions can provide more thorough understanding of motivational climate. Specifically, they argued that a task-involving climate includes the dimensions of cooperative learning, important group role for the students, and an emphasis on effort and improvement. The ego-involving climate, on the other hand, encompasses punishment for mistakes, unequal recognition of group role, and intra-team member rivalry.

SELF DETERMINATION THEORY

Self-determination is a macro-theory of motivation that seeks to explain the 'why' questions of human behaviour. The theory incorporates several sub-theories such as the of basic psychological needs theory. According to Deci and Ryan (2000) psychological needs represent "innate psychological nutriments that are essential for ongoing psychological growth, integrity, and well-being" (p. 229) and guide human behaviour. The theory identified three basic psychological needs: needs for autonomy, competence, and relatedness. The need for autonomy corresponds to the desire of individuals to choose their actions and feel that their behaviour is self-endorsed. The need for competence reflects individuals' propensity to feel efficient and effective, and to experience opportunities to experience mastery of their environment. The need for relatedness refers to the desire to feel connected with others, treated with sensitivity, cared for, and supported by significant others (Ryan & La Guardia, 2000; Deci & Ryan, 2000; Ryan and Deci, 2000).

The satisfaction of these needs leads to adaptive motivational-related outcomes, such as high interest and enjoyment from activity participation. In self-determination theory three fundamental facets of motivation have been identified: intrinsic motivation (individuals participate in a behavior for the pleasure and satisfaction derived from doing so displaying high interest and enjoyment from the activity), extrinsic motivation (individuals participate in a behavior in order to obtain external rewards or avoid negative situations and emotions), and amotivation (the absence of a contingency between one's actions and outcomes; Deci & Ryan, 2002). According to Vallerand et al. (1992) these facets represent higher order dimensions of motivation that include more specific intrinsic and extrinsic motives. Intrinsic motivation includes the motive to gain more knowledge (e.g., satisfaction derived from exploration and learning), experience accomplishment (e.g., reaching new standards or creating something new) and stimulation (e.g. engaging in sensation seeking activities). Similarly, extrinsic motivation encompasses the motives of external regulation (e.g., involvement in an activity to gain rewards or avoid punishment), introjection (e.g., involvement in behaviors to alleviate the internal stress produced by feelings of guilt or anxiety) and identification (e.g., engagement in behaviors that have been valued as important by the person).

PRESENT STUDY

The present study examined the effects of several motivational-related variables on indices of self-regulated learning. In line with Efklides (2011) and Volet et al. (2009), motivational-related variables were considered to be antecedents of self-regulated learning, because exercising control requires cognitive effort, which, in turn, draws on motivation resources. Past research in physical education has examined the effect of achievement goals and motivational climate on self-regulated learning. Ommundsen (2003) showed that junior high school students adopting task orientation goals displayed higher levels of self-regulated learning (i.e., metacognitive/elaboration strategies, regulation of effort and help seeking), as compared to students adopting an ego orientation. Similar findings were provided by more recent studies with high school students in Greece (i.e., Theodosiou, et al., 2008; Theodosiou & Papaioannou, 2006). The aforementioned studies employed Nicholls' dichotomous approach of achievement goals. Ommundsen (2006) used Elliot's trichotomous approach, and showed that performance avoidance goals had a negative association with self-regulated learning, without, however, excluding the possibility for a positive effect of performance approach goals. Nevertheless, so far there is no evidence on the effect of mastery avoidance goals on self-regulated learning.

Similarly, research examining the effect of motivational climate on self-regulation used the two core perceptions of mastery and performance motivational climate (Gano-Overway, 2008; Theodosiou, et al., 2008; Theodosiou & Papaioannou, 2006). In all these studies, perceived mastery motivational climate displayed a large and positive effect on self-regulated learning, whereas the effect of perceived performance climate was neutral (Gano-Overway, 2008), or small and marginal one (Theodosiou & Papaioannou, 2006). Yet, Newton, Duda and Yin (2000) argued that the use of more dimensions of mastery and performance motivational climate could offer a more elaborated view of motivational climate's effect.

Overall, past research on achievement goal theory has not taken into account the current theoretical advancements. The aim of the present study was to extend previous research by employing the 2 X 2 achievement goal approach, and an extended approach of motivational climate. Based on previous research and the tenets of achievement goal theory, it was assumed that approach goals (mastery and performance) will positively predict, whereas avoidance goal (mastery and performance) would negatively predict self-regulated learning (hypothesis 1). Regarding motivational climate, it was hypothesized that task orientation dimensions and intra-team member rivalry would positively predict self-regulated learning, but unequal recognition and punishment for mistakes would have a negative effect (hypothesis 2).

Furthermore, despite the important role of motivation in self-regulated learning (Efklides, 2011; Volet et al., 2009), there is no evidence on the effect of basic psychological need satisfaction and motivational regulations. To the best of the authors' knowledge, only Theodosiou (2004) investigated this association in a physical education setting, but he measured interest rather than motivational regulations. Based on the tenets of self-determination theory it was expected that satisfaction of the basic psychological needs, intrinsic motivation and identified regulation would have a positive effect on self-regulated learning, while external regulation and amotivation a negative one (hypothesis 3).

Contrary to Efklides (2011) and Volet et al. (2009), affective responses from participation in physical education lessons, such as enjoyment and boredom, were used as consequences of self-regulated learning. Efklides (2011) argued that several facets of self-regulated learning have affective elements, and, as such, they interact with motivation to influence self-regulated learning. However, in the present study enjoyment and boredom were operationalized as affective responses to a particular activity that reflected generalized feelings described as "enjoy", "happy", "bored", and "distracted". These constructs are more differentiated than global affect, but more general than a specific emotion, such as excitement or anxiety (Scanlan & Simons, 1992). It was hypothesized that the use of self-regulatory strategies will be positively associated with enjoyment and negatively with boredom (hypothesis 4).

METHOD

Participants

The sample of the study consisted of 345 junior high school students ($M = 14.16$, $SD = .98$). The students were attending typical co-educational schools in an urban city of Northern Greece. All students were Caucasians and native Greek nationals.

Measures

Achievement goals. The 2 X 2 Achievement Goals in Physical Education Questionnaire (AGPEQ; Wang, Biddle & Elliot, 2007) was used to measure students' achievement goals. This measure is an adaptation of the original Achievement Goals Questionnaire (Elliot & McGregor, 2001) to be directly applicable to physical education. The AGPEQ measures four achievement goals in terms of both valence and definition of competence (a total of 12 items; 3 per subscale); Mastery approach (example item: 'It is important to me to learn as much as possible from physical education class'), Mastery avoidance (example item: 'I worry that I may not learn all that I possibly could in physical education class'), Performance approach (example item: 'It is important for me to do better than other students in physical education class') and Performance avoidance (example item: 'My goal in physical education class is to avoid performing poorly'). Participants responded on a 7-point Likert scale ranging from *not at all true of me* (1) to *very true of me* (5). Wang et al. (2007) have demonstrated evidence on the factorial validity and reliability of the scale.

Motivational climate. An adapted to physical education version of the Perceived Motivational Climate in Sport Questionnaire-2 (PMCSQ-2; Newton, et al., 2000) was used to assess the dimensions of mastery and performance climates. Each higher order dimension consists of 3 subscales. The mastery climate dimension includes cooperative learning (e.g., the teacher encourages students to help each other), effort/improvement (e.g., the teacher wants us to try new skills), and important role (e.g., each student contributes in some important way). The performance climate dimension encompasses intra-team member rivalry (e.g., students are encouraged to outplay the other students), unequal recognition (e.g., the teacher gives most of his or her attention to the best students), and punishment for mistakes (e.g., the teacher gets mad when a player makes a mistake). The students responded to the stem 'In this PE class...' on a -point Likert-type scale ranging from *strongly disagree* (1) to *strongly agree* (7). PMCSQ-2 has been found to have adequate internal reliability and factorial validity with athletes (Newton et al., 2000). In addition, Georgainas and Daroglou (2008) provided evidence on the psychometric properties of the scale regarding its use with Greek adolescents.

Basic psychological needs. A shortened and adapted for a physical education version of Ntoumanis' (2005) scale was used to measure satisfaction of basic psychological needs. The scale includes 9 items measuring autonomy (e.g., 'I feel that my choices are based on my true interests and values'), competence (e.g., 'I feel that I can successfully complete difficult tasks and projects'), and relatedness (e.g., 'I feel a sense of contact with people who care for me, and whom I care for'). Responses were anchored on a 7-point Likert-type scale ranging from *not true at all* (1) to *very true* (7). The scales showed satisfactory levels of internal consistency for competence ($\alpha = .70$) and relatedness ($\alpha = .74$) but low for autonomy ($\alpha = .40$). The autonomy scale was retained for the shake of complete investigation of the effect of basic psychological needs, but results should be interpreted with caution.

Motivational regulations. Students' motivational regulations were measured via Situational Motivation Scale (SIMS; Guay, Vallerand & Blanchard, 2000). The SIMS is consisted of 16 items assessing four dimensions of situational motivation (i.e., intrinsic motivation, identified regulation, external regulation, and amotivation). Participants responded to the stem 'Why did you participate in the PE lesson?' on a 7-point Likert scale, ranging from 1 (*does not correspond at all*) to 7 (*corresponds exactly*). Example item for intrinsic motivation is 'because the lesson was fun', for identified regulation 'by personal choice', for external regulation 'because I fell that I had to participate', and for amotivation 'I don't know; I don't see what PE lessons brings me'. Guay et al. (2000) provided evidence on the validity and reliability of the scale. Previous use of SIMS with Greek students supported its factor structure and internal consistency ($as > .70$; Katsani, 2010).

Self-regulated learning strategies. The use of self-regulatory strategies by the students was measured with the Motivated Strategies for Learning Questionnaire (MSLQ) scale (Pintrich, Smith, Garcia, & McKeachie, 1993). The original questionnaire includes 15 scales representing different learning strategies. In the present study we employed the three self-regulation scales: a) metacognitive self-regulation with 9 items (e.g., 'if the activities or exercises are difficult to understand, I change the way I approach them'), c) regulation of effort with 3 items (e.g., 'when the activities or exercises are difficult, I give up or take only the easy ones') and d) help seeking with 4 items (e.g., 'when I can't understand something in PE, I ask the PE teacher for help'). The items were modified appropriately to reflect situations in PE lessons. Responses were anchored on a 5-point Likert scale, ranging from 1 (*don't agree at all*) to 5 (*agree completely*). The internal consistency was satisfactory for metacognitive regulation ($\alpha = .76$) and marginally adequate for regulation of effort ($\alpha = .61$) and help seeking ($\alpha = .61$) (see Pallant, 2007).

Affective responses. A modified to the PE context version of the scale developed by Duda, Fox, Biddle, and Armstrong (1992) to measure children's affective responses in sport was used to measure boredom and enjoyment. Boredom was assessed with 3 (e.g., 'When playing in this PE class I am usually bored') and enjoyment with 4 items (e.g., 'I usually have fun in this PE class'). Participants responded on a 7-point scale with endpoints of (*totally disagree* (1) and *totally agree* (7). In a longitudinal study with Greek high school students Ntoumanis, Barkoukis and Thøgersen-Ntoumani (2009) indicated adequate internal consistency coefficients for both boredom (as ranged from .69 to .73) and enjoyment (as ranged from .76 to .81).

Procedure

Approval from school's principals was obtained to conduct the study in their schools. Students were informed that they have been chosen to participate in a large scale study measuring their perceptions about physical education. Informed consents were administered to the students with the instruction to return them signed by their parents, if they didn't want their child to participate in the study. No informed consent was returned signed. Both oral and written instructions were provided to students to enhance the comprehension of the items, and they were encouraged to ask clarifying questions. Students were also informed that their responses would be strictly confidential and will be used only for research purposes.

RESULTS

Descriptive statistics of the study's variables are presented in Table 1. The analysis of correlation is presented in Table 2.

Table 1. Descriptive statistics of the study's variables

	Mean	SD	Skewness	Kurtosis	Cronbach α
Intrinsic Motivation	5.16	1.58	-.854	.083	.83
Identified regulation	4.87	1.41	-.664	.215	.69
External regulation	3.64	1.72	.142	-.844	.82
Amotivation	3.40	1.60	.178	-.796	.77
Metacognitive regulation	4.43	1.07	.020	.019	.76
Regulation of effort	4.49	1.59	-.265	-.715	.61
Help seeking	4.43	1.36	-.403	-.321	.61
Enjoyment	5.00	1.56	-.826	-.067	.82
Boredom	3.00	1.66	.673	-.349	.68
Competence	5.20	1.18	-.539	-.347	.70
Autonomy	3.83	1.39	.021	-.460	.40
Relatedness	5.07	1.48	-.748	-.165	.74
Cooperative learning	4.83	1.51	-.513	-.482	.79
Effort/Improvement	5.19	1.19	-.852	.543	.81
Important role	5.22	1.39	-.847	.298	.78
Intra-team member rivalry	4.03	1.39	.008	-.402	.42
Unequal recognition	3.00	1.55	.524	-.721	.84
Punishment for mistakes	3.09	1.47	.415	-.704	.71
Mastery approach	5.51	1.50	-1.113	.627	.74
Mastery avoidance	4.63	1.55	-.417	-.646	.67
Performance approach	4.00	1.89	-.022	-1.098	.74
Performance avoidance	4.33	1.60	-.217	-.631	.65

Table 2. Analysis of correlation.

	2	3	4	5	6	7	8	9	10	11	12	13	14	15	16	17	18	19	20	21	22
1. Intrinsic Motivation	.76	-.45	-.41	.47	.12	.37	.58	-.40	.29	.23	.51	.59	.62	.60	.13	-.31	-.35	.68	.18	.04	.16
2. Identified regulation		-.28	-.26	.45	-.02	.36	.49	-.26	.33	.35	.45	.50	.49	.51	.14	-.14	-.18	.59	.16	.17	.19
3. External regulation			.67	-.04	-.43	-.04	-.29	.36	-.20	-.05	-.27	-.30	-.27	-.34	.22	.47	.43	-.30	.05	.08	.13
4. Amotivation				-.01	-.46	-.00	-.24	.44	-.15	.09	-.16	-.22	-.25	-.24	.20	.56	.45	-.29	.14	.18	.12
5. Metacognitive regulation					-.28	.67	.46	-.12	.24	.30	.38	.47	.49	.46	.25	.10	.01	.50	.32	.25	.30
6. Regulation of effort						-.22	.03	-.35	.14	-.16	-.01	.02	.05	.14	-.35	-.55	-.47	.12	-.21	-.34	-.24
7. Help seeking							.43	-.08	.18	.27	.36	.45	.35	.31	.22	.10	.01	.28	.31	.18	.17
8. Enjoyment								-.46	.44	.40	.61	.53	.52	.56	.17	-.16	-.28	.53	.23	.14	.15
9. Boredom									-.33	-.10	-.30	-.30	-.34	-.36	.03	.42	.49	-.39	-.03	.13	.02
10. Competence										.32	.31	.27	.33	.37	.04	-.07	-.12	.35	-.01	.14	.09
11. Autonomy											.40	.32	.21	.34	.22	.09	.02	.25	.16	.22	.07
12. Relatedness												.57	.46	.57	.11	-.17	-.24	.47	.09	-.01	.04
13. Cooperative learning													.60	.64	.11	-.23	-.27	.49	.18	.02	.13
14. Effort														.67	.16	-.24	-.32	.60	.25	-.01	.21
15. Important role															.07	-.28	-.32	.61	.20	.01	.16
16. Intra-team member rivalry																.38	.34	.09	.18	.29	.21
17. Unequal recognition																	.67	-.24	.08	.33	.09

Table 2. (Continued)

	2	3	4	5	6	7	8	9	10	11	12	13	14	15	16	17	18	19	20	21	22
18. Punishment for mistakes																		-.30	.02	.31	.02
19. Mastery approach																			.35	.13	.32
20. Mastery avoidance																				.32	.38
21. Performance approach																					.43
22. Performance avoidance																					

Note: coefficients above .14 are significant at the 0.01 level; coefficients between .10 and .14 are significant at the 0.05 level; coefficients below .10 are not statistically significant

Antecedents of Self-Regulation

A set of linear regression analyses were used to investigate the possible effect of motivational-related variables on the dimensions of self-regulation examined in the present study. The motivational related variables were set as the independent variables and self-regulated learning strategies as the dependent ones. With respect to metacognitive regulation, the results of the analysis indicated that mastery approach, performance approach and mastery avoidance goals were significant predictors ($F(3,337) = 48.58$, $p < .001$). In addition, metacognitive regulation was predicted by effort/improvement, unequal recognition, cooperative learning and important role ($F(2,343) = 38.78$, $p < .001$ in terms of motivational climate), relatedness and autonomy ($F(2,344) = 35.31$, $p < .001$; in terms of basic psychological needs), and intrinsic motivation, amotivation and identified regulation ($F(3,344) = 44.68$, $p < .001$; in terms of motivational regulations) (see Table 3).

Table 3. Antecedents of metacognitive regulation.

Predictor	F	df	p	R^2	R^2 change	b	p
Achievement goals	48.58	3, 337	< .001	.30			
Mastery approach					.26	.25	< .001
Performance approach					.03	.15	< .01
Mastery avoidance					.01	.10	< .05
Motivational climate	52.30	4, 343	< .001	.38			
Effort/Improvement					.24	.29	< .001
Unequal recognition					.05	.29	< .001
Cooperative learning					.06	.25	< .001
Important role					.01	.19	< .01
Psychological needs	35.31	2, 344	< .001	.17			
Relatedness					.14	.31	< .001
Autonomy					.03	.17	< .001
Motivational regulations	44.68	3, 344	< .001	.28			
Intrinsic motivation					.26	.42	< .001
Amotivation					.04	-.21	< .001
Identified regulation					.01	.18	< .01

Regarding regulation of effort, the results of the analysis indicated that performance approach, mastery approach, mastery avoidance and performance avoidance goals were significant predictors ($F(4,337) = 20.28$, $p < .001$). Furthermore, regulation of effort was predicted by unequal recognition, intra-team member rivalry, punishment for mistakes and cooperative learning ($F(4,344) = 47.41$, $p < .001$ in terms of motivational climate), autonomy and competence ($F(2,344) = 13.66$, $p < .001$; in terms of basic psychological needs), and amotivation, external regulation and identified regulation ($F(3,344) = 42.67$, $p < .001$; in terms of motivational regulations) (see Table 4).

Table 4. Antecedents of regulation of effort.

Predictor	F	Df	p	R^2	R^2 change	b	p
Achievement goals	20.28	4,337	< .001	.19			
Performance approach					.11	-.25	< .001
Mastery approach					.03	.27	< .001
Mastery avoidance					.03	-.16	< .01
Performance avoidance					.02	-.16	< .01
Motivational climate	47.41	4,344	< .001	.35			
Unequal recognition					.30	-.40	< .001
Intra-team rivalry					.02	-.11	< .05
Punishment for mistakes					.01	-.19	< .01
Cooperative learning					.01	-.11	< .05
Psychological needs	13.66	2,344	< .001	.07			
Autonomy					.03	-.24	< .001
Competence					.04	.22	< .001
Motivational regulations	42.67	3.344	< .001	.27			
Amotivation					.21	-.34	< .001
External regulation					.03	-.25	< .001
Identified regulation					.03	.18	< .001

Table 5. Antecedents of help seeking.

Predictor	F	Df	p	R^2	R^2 change	b	P
Achievement goals	25.76	2,336	< .001	.13			
Mastery avoidance					.10	.24	< .001
Mastery approach					.03	.19	< .001
Motivational climate	42.59	3,342	< .001	.27			
Cooperative learning					.20	.41	< .001
Unequal recognition					.05	.24	< .001
Effort/Improvement					.02	.17	< .01
Psychological needs	30.79	2,343	< .001	.15			
Relatedness					.13	.30	< .001
Autonomy					.02	.15	< .01
Motivational regulations	24.47	3.343	< .001	.17			
Intrinsic motivation					.13	.30	< .001
Amotivation					.03	-.17	< .01
Identified regulation					.03	.18	< .05

With respect to help seeking, the results of the analysis indicated that mastery avoidance and mastery approach goals were significant predictors ($F(2,336) = 25.76$, $p < .001$).

Furthermore, help seeking was predicted by cooperative learning, unequal recognition, and effort/improvement ($F(4,344) = 47.41$, $p < .001$ in terms of motivational climate), relatedness and autonomy ($F(2,343) = 30.79$, $p < .001$; in terms of basic psychological needs), and intrinsic motivation, amotivation, and identified regulation ($F(3,343) = 24.47$, $p < .001$; in terms of motivational regulations) (see Table 5).

Consequences of Self-Regulation

A set of linear regression analyses were used to investigate the possible effect of the dimensions of self-regulation examined in the present study on students' affective responses from participation in physical education lessons. The self-regulated learning strategies acted as the independent variables and enjoyment and effort as the dependent ones. Regarding enjoyment the results of the analysis indicated a significant effect of all the self-regulation dimensions ($F(3,343) = 42.03$, $p < .001$). The results of the analysis indicated that only effort and metacognitive regulation were significant predictors of boredom ($F(2,343) = 38.78$, $p < .001$) (see Table 6).

Table 6. Consequences of self-regulation.

Consequence	Predictor	F	df	p	R^2	R^2 change	b	p
Enjoyment		42.03	3, 343	< .001	.27			
	Metacognitive regulation					.21	.35	< .001
	Regulation of effort					.03	.18	< .001
	Help seeking					.03	.23	< .001
Boredom		38.78	2, 343	< .001	.18			
	Regulation of effort					.12	-.43	< .001
	Metacognitive regulation					.06	-.24	< .001

DISCUSSION

Motivation and affect are considered to be important aspects of self-regulated learning (Efklides, 2011). However, there is only limited evidence on the association between motivation, affect and self-regulated learning in physical education settings. The present study aimed to investigate the motivational-related antecedents of self-regulated learning in physical education lessons, and the effect of self-regulated learning on students' affective responses to lesson participation. The results of the regression analyses indicated that motivational-related variables significantly predicted the adoption of self-regulated learning strategies. In turn, these strategies influenced affective responses from lesson participation.

With respect to achievement goals, the results of the analyses partially supported the study's first hypothesis and showed that mastery approach goals positively predicted self-regulated learning strategies, while performance avoidance goals did not exert significant predictive effects. Performance approach and mastery avoidance goals displayed a mixed pattern with positive effect on one but negative on another strategy. For instance, they displayed a positive effect on metacognitive regulation but negative on regulation of effort.

These findings are consistent with the theoretical postulates of the 2 X 2 achievement goal approach (Elliot, 1997; Elliot & McGregor, 2001) and related research (Wang, et al., 2007; Ommundsen, 2003; Theodosiou & Papaioannou, 2006), thus suggesting that mastery approach goals are the most adaptive type of goals, while performance avoidance the most maladaptive one. Regarding performance approach and mastery avoidance goals the present findings are in congruence with previous research showing a mixed pattern of responses, a positive effect on some responses and a negative effect on other ones. In fact, the mixed effect of these goals on self-regulated learning strategies might explain the mixed effect of these goals on several outcomes from lesson participation. As Pintrich (2000) argued self-regulation may mediate the effect of motivation on the outcomes of activity involvement. Hence, if a specific outcome is associated with regulation of effort (for instance, effort exerted in a difficult exercise), then performance approach and mastery avoidance goals would be expected to have a negative effect. But if this specific outcome is associated with help seeking (for instance, asking help from the teacher), then mastery avoidance goals would be expected to have a positive effect. Therefore, it seems that achievement goals can be potential antecedents of self-regulated learning, yet the self-regulated learning strategies act as regulators of their effect on activity outcomes.

With respect to motivational climate, the results of the present study supported our hypothesis that different climate dimensions will have distinct effect on self-regulated learning strategies. More specifically, mastery oriented dimensions positively predicted self-regulated learning strategies, while performance oriented dimensions had negative effects. This is consistent with both theoretical predictions (Ames, 1992a, 1992b) and research evidence (Theodosiou et al., 2008; Theodosiou & Papaioannou, 2006) showing that the adaptive role of mastery oriented motivational climate. Contrary to our hypothesis, unequal recognition showed the most adaptive profile of performance oriented dimensions. This finding might imply that students who feel wrongly judged by their teacher try harder to prove their abilities and role during the lesson. Interestingly, cooperative learning was negatively associated with regulation of effort. This finding is difficult to interpret. A possible explanation might lie on social loafing (Duda & Ntoumanis, 2003). Students might rely on their classmates during collaborative exercises and avoid exerting maximum effort. There is only limited evidence on social loafing in physical education lessons (Swain, 1996). Cooperative learning has been promoted as a very effective instructional format in education (Hänze & Berger, 2007; Hijzen, Boekaerts & Vedder, 2007). Future research should investigate social loafing in physical education when cooperative learning practices are used. Overall, these findings imply that mastery oriented climate was the most adaptive, and physical educators should foster student's perceptions of such a climate.

The effect of satisfaction of basic psychological needs on self-regulated learning was also examined. In line with the study's second hypothesis, Three basic psychological needs significantly predicted self-regulated learning dimensions. Only relatedness and autonomy predicted both metacognitive regulation and help seeking. With respect to relatedness, this finding shows that students who feel socially accepted by their classmates tend to be more likely to use self-regulated learning strategies to improve performance (i.e., metacognitive regulation), or ask for their classmates' help to overcome difficulties. Similarly, satisfaction of autonomy also predicted the use of self-regulated learning strategies, but negatively predicted regulation of effort. There is no clear explanation for this finding. Perhaps exercise or certain situations during physical education courses are not attractive to students who have satisfied the need for autonomy. Nevertheless, more evidence to warrant this effect. Anyway, results pertaining to autonomy should be interpreted with caution due to low internal consistency of the scale.

On the other hand, competence predicted only regulation of effort. This finding shows that students, who feel competent, tend to exert more effort during the physical education lesson. This is consistent with past research (Deci & Ryan, 2000; Ryan & Deci, 2000) and indicates satisfaction of competence need is essential for students participating in activities in order to improve. Hence, physical educators should provide opportunities for all students to feel competent during the lesson in order to maximize effort and subsequent performance (Barkoukis et al., 2008). Overall, these findings imply that basic psychological needs can have a unique effect on self-regulated learning. More research is needed, however, to further investigate the effect of basic psychological need satisfaction on several dimensions of self-regulated learning in physical education lessons.

With respect to motivational regulations the results of the analyses supported our assumptions and were in line with theoretical predictions (Deci & Ryan, 2002). Intrinsic motivation and identified regulation were positive predictors of self-regulated learning strategies, whereas external regulation and amotivation exerted significant but negative effects. Self-determined motivation is the most adaptive type of motivation. Students participating in physical education lessons out of intrinsic motivation are more susceptible in using self-regulated learning strategies such as regulation of effort, help seeking, and metacognitive strategies. On the other hand, students with extrinsic motivation avoid using such practices. These findings have important practical implications for the learning process in physical education, as they imply that educators should foster intrinsic motivation and self-determined forms of motivation. Taking into consideration the findings of the present study regarding motivational climate these findings indicate that educators should develop a mastery oriented motivational climate that leads to the formation of intrinsic motivation. Interventions programs, such as TARGET (Ames, 1992a, 1992b, Barkoukis et al., 2008), may offer useful guidelines in order to promote several aspects of a mastery oriented motivational climate.

Another important aim of the study was to investigate the effect of self-regulated learning practices on the affective responses of the students from physical education lessons' participation. The results showed that students using self-regulated learning practices experienced higher enjoyment and less boredom, compared to those who did not utilize self-regulation. These findings demonstrate that self-regulated learning fosters an adaptive learning environment. The use of self-regulated learning strategies during the physical education lesson made students derive more pleasure and satisfaction from the lesson. Consequently this was associated with lower levels of boredom. Clearly, physical educators should teach, promote and facilitate the use of such strategies in order to enhance the experience of positive affective states during the lesson. Practices such as goal setting, cooperative learning, and self-evaluation can foster the use of self-regulated learning strategies and lead to positive affective responses.

The present study offers a preliminary investigation on the antecedents and consequences of self-regulated learning in physical education lessons. Future research should expand these findings by examining more complex associations between self-regulation-related variables. For instance, the Metacognitive and Affective model of Self-Regulated Learning (MASRL) developed by Efklides (2011), proposes that the interaction between motivation and affect influences the formation of self-regulated learning. According to Efklides, these interactions exist in two levels, the Person and the Person × Task levels. The investigation of these interactions in the context of physical education could offer a better understanding of the mechanism underlying the formation of self-regulation. Furthermore, there is substantial evidence (Vallerand, 2007) that motivational regulations influence students' affective responses. Perhaps self-regulated learning strategies can mediate this relationship, and accordingly, explain the mechanism through which motivation influences affect. In addition, the results of the present study indicated that self-regulated learning strategies influence the affective outcomes resulting from participation in physical education lessons. An important outcome of the physical education lesson is leisure-time physical activity (Hagger & Chatzisarantis, 2007). Hence, it would be interesting to investigate whether self-regulated learning in physical education lessons influences directly, or indirectly, leisure-time physical activity. In sum, the findings of the present study indicated that motivation-related variables significantly predicted self-regulated learning strategies in physical education. Approach achievement goals, mastery oriented motivational climate, basic psychological needs and self-determined motivation exerted a significant positive effect, whereas avoidance goals, performance oriented motivational climate and extrinsic motivation had either a neutral or negative effect. Furthermore, the use of self-regulated learning strategies was positively associated with enjoyment, and negatively with boredom from participation in physical education lessons. Physical education teachers are encouraged to foster mastery oriented motivational climate using interventions such as TARGET.

REFERENCES

Ames, C. (1992a). Classrooms: Goals, structures and student motivation. *Journal of Educational Psychology, 84*, 261-271.

Ames, C. (1992b). The relationship of achievement goals to student motivation in classroom settings. In G. Roberts (Ed.) *Motivation in sport and exercise* (pp. 161-176). Champaign, IL: Human Kinetics.

Atkinson, J. W. (1964). *An introduction to motivation.* Princeton, NJ: Van Nostrand.

Barkoukis, V., Tsorbatzoudis, H., & Grouios, G. (2008). Manipulation of motivation climate in physical education: Effects of a seven-month intervention. *European Physical Education Review, 14*, 373-394.

Baumeister, R.F., & Vohs, K.D. (2007). Self-regulation, ego depletion, and motivation. *Social and Personality Psychology Compass, 1*, 1–14.

Boekaerts, M., & Corno, L. (2005). Self-regulation in the classroom: A perspective on assessment and intervention. *Applied Psychology: An international review, 54*, 199-231.

Cury, F., Da Fonséca, D., Rufo, M., Peres, C., & Sarrazin, P. (2003). The trichotomous model and investment in learning to prepare for a sport test: A mediational analysis. *British Journal of Educational Psychology, 73*, 529–543.

Cury, F., Elliot, A.J., Da Fonseca, D., & Moller, A. (2006). The social-cognitive model of achievement motivation and the 2 X 2 achievement goal framework. *Journal of Personality and Social Psychology, 90,* 666–679.

Deci, E.L., & Ryan, R.M. (2000). The 'what' and 'why' of goal pursuits: Human needs and the self-determination of behavior. *Psychological Inquiry, 11*, 227-268.

Deci, E.L., & Ryan, R.M. (2002). *Handbook of self-determination research.* Rochester, NY: University of Rochester Press.

Duda, J.L. (2001). Achievement goal research in sport: Pushing the boundaries and clarifying some misunderstandings. In G. C. Roberts (Ed.), *Advances in motivation in sport and exercise* (pp. 129-182). Champaign, IL: Human Kinetics.

Duda, J.L., Fox, K., Biddle, S., & Armstrong, N. (1992). Children's achievement goals and beliefs about success in sport. *British Journal of Educational Psychology, 62*, 313-323.

Duda, J.L., & Hall, H. (2001). Achievement goal theory in sport: Recent extensions and future directions. In R. N., Singer, H. A., Hausenblas, & C.M. Janelle, (Eds.), *Handbook of sport psychology* (2nd ed.) (pp. 417-443). New York: Wiley.

Duda, J.L., & Ntoumanis, N. (2003). Correlates of achievement goal orientations in physical education. *International Journal of Educational Research, 39,* 415-436.

Duda, J.L., & Whitehead, J. (1998). Measurement of goal perspectives in the physical domain. In J. L. Duda (Ed.), *Advances in sport and exercise psychology measurement* (pp. 21–48). Morgantown, WV: Fitness Information Technology.

Efklides, A. (2011). Interactions of metacognition with motivation and affect in self-regulated learning: The MASRL model. *Educational Psychologist, 46*, 6-25.

Elliot, A.J. (1997). Integrating "classic" and "contemporary" approaches to achievement motivation: A hierarchical model of approach and avoidance achievement motivation. In P. Pintrich & M. Maehr (Eds.), *Advances in motivation and achievement* (vol. 10, pp. 143–179). Greenwich, CT: JAI Press.

Elliot, A.J. & Church, M.A. (1997). A hierarchical model of approach and avoidance achievement motivation. *Journal of Personality and Social Psychology, 72*, 218–232.

Elliot, A.J., & McGregor, H.A. (2001). A 2 X 2 achievement goal framework. *Journal of Personality and Social Psychology, 80*, 501-519.

Elliot, A.J., & Thrash, T.M. (2001). Achievement goals and the hierarchical model of achievement motivation. *Educational Psychology Review, 13*, 139–156.

Gano-Overway, L.A. (2008). The effect of goal involvement on self-regulatory processes. *International Journal of Sport and Exercise Psychology, 6*, 132-156.

Georgainas, G., & Daroglou, G. (2008). The relationship between achievement goal and perceptions of motivational climate in Greek handball athletes. *Hellenic Journal of Physical Education & Sport Science*, 28, 43-54. [in Greek]

Guay, F., Vallerand, R.J., & Blanchard, C. (2000). On the assessment of situational intrinsic and extrinsic motivation: The Situational Motivation Scale. *Motivation and Emotion, 24*, 175-213.

Hagger, M.S., & Chatzisarantis, N.L.D. (2007b). The trans-contextual model of motivation. In M. S. Hagger & N. L. D. Chatzisarantis (Eds.), *Intrinsic motivation and self-determination in exercise and sport* (pp. 54-70*)*. Champaign, IL: Human Kinetics.

Hänze, M., & Berger, R. (2007). Cooperative learning, motivational effects, and student characteristics: An experimental study comparing cooperative learning and direct instruction in 12th grade physics classes. *Learning & Instruction, 17*, 29-41.

Hijzen, D., Boekaerts, M. & Vedder, P. (2007). Exploring the links between students' engagement in cooperative learning, their goal preferences and perceptions of contextual factors in the classroom. *Learning and Instruction, 17,* 673–687.

Jaakkola, T., & Digelidis, N. (2007). Establishing a positive motivational climate in physical education. In L. Liukkonen, Y. V. Auweele, B. Vereijken, D. Alfermann, Y., & Theodorakis (Eds.), *Psychology for physical educators* (pp. 3-20). Champaign, IL: Human Kinetics.

Katsani, K. (2010). *Effect of different teaching approaches on students' learning strategies in secondary education.* Unpublished Master Thesis. Aristotle University of Thessaloniki. Greece. [in Greek]

Newton, M., & Duda, J.L. (1993). Elite adolescent athletes' achievement goals and beliefs concerning success in tennis. *Journal of Sport and Exercise Psychology, 15,* 437-448.

Newton, M., & Duda, J.L. (1999). The interaction of motivational climate, dispositional goal orientations, and perceived ability in predicting indices of motivation. *International Journal of Sport Psychology, 30,* 63-82.

Newton, M. Duda, J.L. & Yin Z. (2000). Examination of the psychometric properties of the Perceived Motivational Climate in Sport Questionnaire - 2 in a sample of female athletes. *Journal of Sports Sciences, 18,* 275 – 290.

Nicholls, J. (1989). *The competitive ethos and democratic education.* London: Harvard University Press.

Ntoumanis, N. (2005). A prospective study of participation in optional school physical education based on self-determination theory. *Journal of Educational Psychology, 97,* 444-453.

Ntoumanis, N., Barkoukis, V., & Thogersen-Ntoumani, C. (2009). Developmental trajectories of motivation in physical education: Course, demographic differences, and antecedents. *Journal of Educational Psychology, 101,* 717-728.

Ommundsen, Y. (2003). Implicit theories of ability and self-regulation strategies in physical education classes. *Educational Psychology, 23,* 141-157.

Ommundsen, Y. (2006). Pupils' self-regulation in physical education: the role of motivational climates and differential achievement goals. *European Physical Education. Review, 2,* 289-315.

Pallant, J. (2007). *SPSS survival manual: A spet by step guide to data analysis using SPSS for Windows* (3rd edition). Berkshire. Open University Press.

Pintrich, P.R. (2000). The role of goal orientation in self-regulation learning. In M. Boekarts, M. P. R. Pintrich, & M. Zeidner (Eds), *Handbook of Self-regulation (pp.451-502).* San Diego, CA: Academic Press.

Pintrich, P.R., Smith, D.A., Garcia, T., & McKeachie, W.J. (1993). Reliability and predictive validity of the Motivated Strategies for Learning Questionnaire (MSLQ). *Educational and Psychological Measurement, 53,* 801-813.

Ryan, R.M., & Deci, E.L. (2000). Self-determination theory and the facilitation of intrinsic motivation, social development, and well-being. *American Psychologist, 55,* 68-78.

Ryan, R.M., & La Guardia, J.G. (2000). What is being optimized over development?: A self-determination theory perspective on basic psychological needs across the life span. In S. Qualls & N. Abeles (Eds.), *Psychology and the aging revolution* (pp. 145-172). Washington, DC: APA Books.

Scanlan, T.K., & Simons, J.P. (1992). The construct of sport enjoyment. In: G. Roberts (Ed.), *Motivation in sport and exercise* (pp. 199–215). Campaign, IL: Human Kinetics.

Swain, A. (1996). Social loafing and identifiability: The mediating role of achievement goal orientations. *Research Quarterly for Exercise and Sport, 67*, 337–344.

Theodosiou, A. (2004). *Metacognitive strategies and motivational climate in physical education.* Unpublished doctoral dissertation. Democritus University of Thrace, Komotini, Greece.

Theodosiou, A., Mantis, K., & Papaioannou, A. (2008). Student self-reports of metacognitive activity in physical education classes. Age-group differences and the effect of goal orientations and perceived motivational climate. *Educational Research and Review, 3*, 353-364.

Theodosiou, A., & Papaioannou, A. (2006). Motivational climate, achievement goals and metacognitive activity in physical education and exercise involvement in out-of-school settings. *Psychology of Sport and Exercise, 7*, 361-379.

Vallerand, R.J. (2007). Intrinsic and extrinsic motivation in sport and physical activity. A review and a look at the future. In G.C. Tenenbaum, & R.C. Eklund (Eds.), *Handbook of sport psychology* (3rd ed., pp. 59-83). New York: John Wiley.

Vallerand, R.J., Pelletier, L., Blais, M., Briere, N., Senecal, C., & Vallieres, E. (1992). The Academic Motivation Scale: A measure of intrinsic, extrinsic and amotivation in education. *Educational and Psychological Measurement, 52*, 1003-1017.

Volet, S., Vauras, M., & Salonen, P. (2009). Psychological and social nature of self- and co-regulation in learning contexts: An integrative perspective. *Educational Psychologist, 44*, 1-12.

Wang, C.K.J., Biddle, S., & Elliot, A.J. (2007). The 2 X 2 achievement goal framework in a physical education context. *Psychology of Sport and Exercise*, 8, 147-168.

Zimmerman, B.J. (2000). Attainment of self-regulation: A social cognitive perspective. In M. Boekaerts, P.R. Pintrich, & M. Zeidner (Eds.), *Handbook of self-regulation* (pp. 13-39). San Diego, CA: Academic Press.

In: Psychology of Self-Regulation
Editor: Vassilis Barkoukis

ISBN: 978-1-61470-380-8
© 2012 Nova Science Publishers, Inc.

Chapter 8

SELF-CONTROL, SELF-REGULATION, AND JUVENILE DELINQUENCY

Martha Frías-Armenta[1,], Jorge Borrani[2], Pablo Valdez[2], Hugo Tirado[2] and Xochitl Ortiz Jiménez[2]*

[1]Universidad de Sonora, Mexico
[2]Universidad Autónoma de Nuevo León, México

ABSTRACT

Several theories have been proposed to explain delinquency; some include environmental factors and others consider personal variables. Personal, cognitive, and emotional deficits have been associated to delinquent or antisocial behavior. It has been argued that low self control is an internal system that manages antisocial behavior; self control is also understood as a tendency to pursue instant gratification. Besides, self-regulation has been related to violent behavior. Self regulation is conceptualized as the capacity to modulate emotions, attention and behavior; this concept has also been linked to emotional control. Effortful control is another term used for emotional regulation, which is associated to modulation of emotional reactivity and behaviors. Control or regulation of emotions and cognitions are the factors related to delinquent behavior. The aim of this chapter is to test a model including self-control and self-regulation as predictors of antisocial behavior. The sample was integrated by 164 participants, 58 were juvenile delinquents internalized in an institution and 106 were selected from the general community in a northern Mexican city. All of them reported some kind of antisocial behavior. Scales investigating impulsivity, risk, self-regulation and antisocial behavior were administered to the participants. The data were analyzed using structural equation modeling. Two factors were constructed: *self –control*, with impulsivity, sensation seeking, and risk indicators, and *self –regulation*, with indicators of emotional volatility, emotional intensity and activity regulation. Both factors exhibited a negative effect on antisocial behavior. We conclude that self-control is an important factor in the prediction

---

[*] Correspondence regarding this chapter should be sent to: Martha Frías Armenta, Departamento de Derecho, Universidad de Sonora, Blvd. Luis y Encinas y Rosales S/N, Hermosillo, Sonora, 8300, Mexico. E-mail: marthafrias@sociales.uson.mx

of antisocial behavior; however there are additional variables that should be included in explanatory models of juvenile delinquency in prospective studies.

INTRODUCTION

Around the world, 199,000 homicides of young people were produced in 2000 (The Annual Report on Violence and Health 2002; Krug, Dahlberg, Mercy, Zwi, & Lozano, 2002). From January to May, 2008, 4048 adolescents were incarcerated in treatment centers of Mexico (Secretaría de Seguridad Pública, Consejo de Menores, 2008). Katzmann (2002) details that in the United States 309 juveniles out of 100,000 are arrested due to violent crime, including homicide, aggravated assault, and robbery. The Unified Reporting Program (UCR) of that country report 1,560,289 arrests of juvenile offenders (Burfeind & Bartusch, 2006). The FBI indicates that the arrest of juveniles for murder increased 2.8 percent in 2007 compared to 2006 and the total arrest frequency for juveniles resulted in 9,347,086 cases (Crime in the United States, 2007). In Rome, according to the police, 2 percent of juveniles committed a crime (Roucek, 1970). Israel sources indicate that the rate of violent injuries in young people is 196 per 100,000 (Krug, Dahlberg, Mercy, Zwi, & Lozano, 2002). England estimated an annual increase of delinquency of 5 and 6% (Maguire, Morgan & Reiner, 2002).

Cognitive and emotional deficits have been associated to children and adolescent violent or antisocial behavior. One of most cited theories is Gottfredson & Hirschi's (1990) low self control theory. A number of studies have tried to demonstrate the relationship between low self-control and delinquency, with some of them failing and other succeeding. Gottfredson & Hirschi (1990) argue that low self control is the crucial factor predicting delinquency. However, the existence of additional explanatory variables has been demonstrated. Emotional self-regulation is, for instance, associated to antisocial behavior. Emotions can change the way the individual interact with the environment and emotions can also change motivations. Moreover, emotional regulation correlates with adaptive functioning; that is, emotional control helps in responding adequately to social requirements, and helps to interact with society. Alternatively, emotional disregulation could incite violence (Valiente, Lemery-Chalfant, & Reiser, 2007). Low self control and self regulation are causes of violence in young people (Gottfredson & Hirschi, 1990).

A number of studies relate self control to delinquency; however, the relationship between emotional self-regulation has not been studied, and there is no study combining both self control theory and self-regulation in a due explanatory model. Therefore, the objective of this chapter is to test a model that includes both predictors of antisocial behavior.

SELF- CONTROL THEORY

Gottfredson, & Hirschi (1990) proposed the Low Self Control Theory. This argues that self control is an internal system that manages antisocial behavior. Low self control is also understood as a tendency to pursue instant gratification (MacDonald, Piquero, Valois, & Zullig, 2005). Thus, it is assumed that this trait tends to be stable across time (Marcus, 2004). Individuals lacking self-control are impulsive, risk taking, of volatile temper, and tend to get involved in criminal acts because they cannot anticipate/think the long term consequences of their behavior (Gottfredson, & Hirschi.2009). The Classical Theory of Crime (CTC) establishes that humans have a natural tendency to seek pleasure and search for their immediate satisfaction, crime being an uncontrolled propensity for gratification while self control restrains this tendency, (Muraven, Pogarsky, & Shmueli, 2006). Consequently, CTC assumes that human beings have a natural tendency to be aggressive and that criminals follow this natural propensity (Idem). According to this theory, two key factors explain criminal conduct: low self-control and opportunity (Cauffman, Steinberg, & Piquero, 2005). Hirschi and Gottfredson (1994) define self-control as "the tendency to avoid acts whose long term costs exceed the momentary advantages." Individual differences in self-control determine participation in criminal activities, low self-controlled individuals are impulsive, insensitive and risk-taking and more prompt to be involved in criminal acts (Gottfredson & Hirschi, 1990). Therefore, individuals do not seek the opportunity for crime; they act when the possibility arises, and low self-control persons are more likely to offend. Thus, individuals with low self control tend to respond immediately to the environment; they are active, physical, adventuresome, and insensitive to suffering and to the needs of others, pursue immediate pleasure, and are tolerant to physical pain. In addition, classical control theories argue that criminals are not restrained by social norms and posit that they are asocial (Gottfredson, & Hirschi, 2009). The weakness of criminals social bonds are related to criminal behavior and similarly legal norms do not exert influence on criminals. Thus, these theories establish that criminals are insensitive to social and legal norms. In this sense, empirical research has also demonstrated that self-control is a relevant factor in predicting criminal and deviant behavior (Pratt, & Cullen, 2000). However, in these studies self-control has been defined in several forms, which could cause inconsistent results. In some of them self control is highly related to criminal behavior and in others this relation is nonexistent.

Gottfredson & Hirschi (2009) suggest that the main predictor of self-control is an ineffective child-rearing practices. Parents have to inculcate self-control to their children, and they have to follow some procedures to reach that goal, such as supervision, recognition, and regulation of deviant behavior. Inappropriate parenting fails in creating self control in children (Burfeind, & Bartusch, 2005). Empirical studies have shown that parents' conduct and supervision, as well as their rearing practices are important factors in preventing delinquency from occurring and in eliminating its sources (Ngai & Cheung, 2005; Frías-Armenta, Ramirez, Soto, Castell, & Corral-Verdugo, 2000). Parental warmth and concern are indispensable conditions for effective child rearing (Gottfredson & Hirschi, 2009). Mother's competences and father's interactions with family are also related to juvenile delinquency inhibition (McCord, 2009). The straight of the parent-child relationship also prevent juvenile delinquency from being developed (Burfeind, & Bartusch, 2005). Valiente, Lemery-Chalfant, and Reiser (2007) assessed the effect of parental effortful control (the ability to control dispositional reactivity) on externalized behavior and found a negative relationship between these two constructs.

Family environment and childrearing practices play an important role in child behavior problems. Consequently, harsh parenting has been associated to antisocial behavior and delinquency. Family separation and family violence facilitate juvenile delinquency (Ngai & Cheung, 2005). A longitudinal study conducted by Rebellon and Van-Gundy (2005) found that child abuse was a predictor of violent and property crimes. Besides, antisocial behavior is one of the short term consequences of child abuse (Frías, Ramírez, Soto, Castell, & Corral, 2000). Other studies indicate that a history of child abuse increases the risk for antisocial behavior in adolescence and adulthood (Cicchetti & Manly, 2001; Lansford, Dodge, Pettit, Bates, Crozier, & Kaplow, 2002). Another longitudinal study by Gushurst (2003) reported that 74% of adolescents who had been abused presented at least one of the following problems: high levels of aggression, anxiety, depression, problems with the police, runaway, gang involvement, unwanted pregnancy, compared with 43% of the adolescents who had not been abused. In addition, the likelihood of being arrested on charges of violent acts was 1.9 times higher for child abuse victims than for the controls. Experimenting abuse during childhood has been related to carrying arms during adolescence (Leeb, Barker, & Strine, 2007). Victims of child abuse present a higher risk of developing psychopathology, depression (Putnam, 2003) and aggressive behaviors (Baldry, 2007). Aversive and inept parenting and inconsistent discipline are also related to juvenile delinquency (Meeus, Branje, & Overbeek, 2004).

Social control is indirectly related to individual self-control through parental supervision (Gottfredson & Hirschi, 2009). During childhood, such supervision prevents further involvement in antisocial behavior or criminal acts from occurring (Hoffman, 2002). The recognition of deviant behavior is an essential component of supervision; parents should be able to distinguish the lack of self control of their children in order to monitor their behavior (Gottfredson & Hirschi, 2009). Burfeind & Bartusch (2005) argue that criminal parents possess a deviant lifestyle; they drink excessively, steal things, etc.; thus they will not be able to recognize the antisocial acts of their children. Parental imprisonment is related to juvenile delinquency; parent-child separation is a risk factor for antisocial behavior, apparently it affects the quality of care, also producing stigma, and the reduction of family income (Murray & Farrington, 2005). Supervision and discipline is almost inexistent in families with separated or imprisoned parents. Moreover, parents that stay at home might use harsh corrective methods or inconsistent punishment (Burfeind & Bartusch, 2006). Control theories stress the need of sanctions to misbehavior for the prevention of criminal behavior (Idem). Formal or direct control is established by the imposition of formal rules, supervision, and sanction. However, punishment it not always desirable; disapproval from valuable people could be a more potent sanction. Control theories are concerned with the informal social control exerted by the family, friends and other members of the community (Idem). Parental supervision is also considered as an informal social control for children.

Hirschi (2009) proposes the Control Theory of Delinquency trying to elucidate the factors that reduce delinquency. According to such theory, individuals that develop social bonds to people (parents) or conventional institutions (schools) are less likely to engage in delinquency. The establishment of these bonds prevents delinquency from occurring because crime put people in danger to lose both their social position and bonds gained. Four bounds are expected to prevent delinquency: attachment, commitment, involvement and belief. Attachment consists of the affection of the individual towards other(s) as a member of society; it is the internalization of social norms. Social norms are shared by the group the individual belongs to, and they establish an external influence: the perception of what others are doing or what they should do (Schultz, 2002). Grasmick and Bursik (1990) operationalize the concept of social norm as the loss of respect from socially valuable people (friends or acquaintances) since violating a social norm is to act contrary to the desires, standards, and customs of other members of society. The internalization of the social norm has been operationalized as personal norm. A personal norm has been identified as a sentiment of moral obligation (Schwartz, 2002). In these terms, social norms indicate the external pressure (the perception of what others are doing or what they have to do), and personal norms are the internalized self-expectations (what I should do). Therefore, attachment is the dimension related to the individuals' bond to conventional social norms and its internalization as a personal norm to prevent criminal behavior from occurring.

Commitment is defined by Hirschi (2009) as the fear of consequences. People invest money, education, and social bonds to acquire a reputation; the fear to destroy their reputation prevents them from being involved in criminal acts. Individuals assess the costs and benefits of criminal behavior, based on their status. When the cost exceeds the benefits, crime is not committed. Rational choice theory also establishes a similar hypothesis, indicating that crime likelihood will expand when an individual encounters a suitable situation whose expected benefits surpass costs and risks (Wortley & Mazarolle, 2008). The process of living in a society pursuing a conventional status is identified as commitment to conformity and it will prevent crime. Involvement in conventional activities is a deterrent of delinquency because people do not have time to engage in criminal activity (Hirschi, 2009). For juveniles, the time they spent in conventional activities for satisfying their recreational interest makes the difference in terms of juvenile delinquency. Informal or unconventional activities in leisure time for adolescent may create a set of values that inhibit delinquency (idem). Sharing a universal value system in society constitutes the beliefs dimension of the control theory of crime. It is assumed that every person is socialized in a group wherein they define what is good or wrong (Idem). Self-categorization theory (Sigala, Burgoyne, & Webley, 1999), in turn, proposes that social identity is the way people are socialized. This theory establishes that there are three levels of abstraction that can be used to categorize identity: personal identity (the being as individual), social identity (the being as member of a group), and intra-species identity (oneself as part of the human race). Each level is as valid as the subsequent (or precedent); the being is also defined as "individual" and "social member of the group." In essence, people are more prone to be influenced by whom they consider members of their relevant self-categorization (Hornsey, 2008). These influences mean that the points of view and behavioral tendencies of the members of the group are going to be internalized as their social convictions (Abrams & Hogg, 1990). Control theory indicates that variations in the internalization of norms exist: the less a person believes in obeying society's rules, the more likely that s/he will violate them (Hirschi, 2009). Self-categorization theory argues that internalization is affected by the group's identification. According to this theory, criminal behavior will depend on the identification of the group, the attachment with the group, the level of internalization of social norms and the fear of losing the social status inside the group. Social Control theories (SCT) indicate that behavior is motivated by external consequences, which are perceived as punishments and rewards (Tyler, 2006). Classical theories established that criminality is a natural tendency of humans. This propensity is indicated by two variables: low self control and opportunity; however, for social control theories, behavior can be controlled by external consequences. Theorists such as Hirschi (2009) recognize the role of environmental factors in the emergence and maintenance of self-control. Therefore, parental practices and supervision could help to develop this individual's capacity.

IMPULSIVITY

Gottfredson and Hirschi (2009) proposed some elements to identify self-control and impulsivity is one of the key components of their theory. Dickman (1990) defines impulsivity as the tendency to deliberate less than most people before engaging in action; it is also a characteristic of people that act without thinking of the risk of their behavior (Miller, Joseph, Tudway, 2004). Impulsivity has been also defined as the incapacity to forecast consequences, to wait, and to inhibit inappropriate behaviors (Reynolds, Ortengren, Richards, & de Wit, 2006). In addition, it is conceived as lack of self-control and a tendency to immediate gratification (Carrasco, Barker, Tremblay, & Vitaro, 2006). Impulsivity is associated with responding before a question is concluded, with difficulty in waiting turn, and with interrupting others (Enticott & Ogloff, 2006).

The structure of impulsivity has been discussed in regard to the unidimensionality or multi-dimensionality of the construct. Some researchers characterize three different components: the first is structured by the tendency to manifest spontaneous thoughts and behaviors, the second as the propensity to be disorganized and unprepared in everyday activities, and the third as carefree attitudes and behaviors (Miller, Joseph, & Tudway, 2004). Whiteside and Lynam (2001) studied impulsivity and found four facets: urgency, premeditation, perseverance, and sensation seeking and they defined urgency as the tendency to feel strong impulses, premeditation as the tendency to think about the consequences of acts before engaging in them, perseverance is the ability to remain focused in a task, and sensation seeking is the tendency to look for exciting activities. Reynolds, Penfold, and Patak (2008) evaluated the dimensions of impulsivity in a group of adolescents and identified three behavioral elements: Impulsive decision-making, impulsive inattention and impulsive disinhibition. Therefore, impulsivity has been rather conceptualized as a multifaceted construct including verbal, cognitive and behavioral dimensions (Avila, Cuenca, Felix, Parcet, & Miranda, 2004).

Cognitive and behavioral impulsivity has been related to delinquency (Avila, Cuenca, Felix, Parcet, & Miranda, 2004) and has been seen as a key aspect of violence, aggression, and substance abuse (Vigil-Colet & Codorniu-Raga, 2004). Impulsivity is positively related to substance abuse and drug consumption (Slater, 2003). Smokers, cocaine users, alcoholics, and opiate addicts score higher on impulsive measures and behavioral inhibitions tasks (Reynolds, Richards, Horn, & Karraker, 2004). Billieux, Van der Linden, and Ceschi, (2007) used the Impulsive Behavior Scale and Questionnaire Smoke Urges in 40 undergraduate students and found that the urgency dimension of impulsivity was significantly related to smoking craving. Impulsivity and sensation seeking also predict unsafe driving (Dahlen, Martin, Ragan, & Kuhlman, 2005). Children and adolescents consuming drugs show higher rates of impulsivity (Moeller & Dougherty, 2002).

Impulsive aggression has been described as an affective emotional response. Stanford, Houston, Villemarette-Pittman, and Greve, (2003), in a study conducted with 80 psychiatric aggressive patients, found that they exhibited higher scores in personality pathology, impulsivity, anger, psychoticism, neuroticism and hostility. Carrasco, Barker, Tremblay, and Vitaro (2006) examined personality traits in 868 adolescent boys finding impulsivity and extraversion traits being related to antisocial behavior. A longitudinal study conducted with 400 boys, measuring impulsivity and antisocial behavior, showed an association between antisocial behavior and behavioral impulsivity (White, Moffitt, Caspi, Bartusch, Needles, & Stouthamer-Loeber, 1994). Fossati, Barratt, Carretta, Leonardi, Grazioli, and Maffei (2004) conducted a study with 747 undergraduate students and found that the impulsivity facets were linked to different aggressive dimensions. Offenders showed significant differences in diverse measures of impulsivity in a research investigating 129 adolescents, 86 institutionalized and 43 regular school students (Carroll, Hemingway, Bower, Ashman, Houghton, & Durkin, 2006). Impulsivity also increases health risk behaviors such as alcohol use and smoking (Grano, Virtanen, Vahtera, Elovainio, & Kivimaki, 2004). Another study showed that both behavioral and cognitive impulsivity were associated to delinquency (Herba, Tranah, Rubia, & Yule, 2006). Impulsive children also exhibit sensation seeking behaviors (Gatzke-Kopp, Raine, Loeber, Stouthamer-Loeber, & Steinhauer, 2002).

SELF-REGULATION

Self-regulation is conceptualized diversely in the literature. Rafaelli and Crockett (2003) define it as the capacity to regulate emotions, attention and behavior, while Dawes, Tarter and Kirisci (1997) use the term *behavioral self-regulation* defining it as the level of control of individuals' reactivity or activity before environmental stimuli, which can be manifested as inattention, impulsivity, and hyperactivity. This concept has also been related to emotional control (Zeanah, 2005). Effortful control is another term used for emotional regulation, which is associated to the modulation of emotional reactivity and behaviors (Valiente, Lemery-Chalfant, & Reiser, 2007). Individuals with high EC tend to voluntarily control their attention and behavior.

Eisenberg and Fabes (1998) argue that self-regulated individuals are social competent and pro-social, even if they experience negative emotions. Rafaelli & Crockett (2003) studied sexual risky behaviors in adolescents and found that self-regulation was associated with sexual risk taking. The lack of children effortful control correlated with children problem-behaviors (Valiente, Lemery-Chalfant, & Reiser, 2007). Attentional control is considered another aspect of EC, which is also associated to delay in gratification (Sethi, Mischel, Aber, Shoda, & Rodriguez, 2000). Behavioral self regulation is also related to substance abuse (Dawes, Tarter, & Kirisci, 1997).

Emotion regulation is one recent paradigm for studying emotions, and it is defined as the way a person uses emotional experiences for adaptive functioning (Thompson, 1994). This contruct has been linked to emotional control and coping strategies for modifying emotion reaction (Galambus & Costigan, 2003). Emotional regulation is understood as the way individuals deal with their feelings and how they reach positive emotions and modulate distress (idem). This theory also establishes that flexibility and responsiveness are necessary skills for the control of emotions, and another skill included is the awareness of emotional states, the capacity to understand others' emotions, and empathy (Thompson, 1994). Adolescents are more able than children to regulate their emotions, and they can assume the point of view of others (Galambus & Costigan, 2003). Emotional regulation includes strategies to modify, intensify, dismiss, or transform emotional reactions to adapt to social requirements. Therefore, it is contextual dependent, since different environments represents diverse emotional challenges. Emotional regulation will depend on the goals of the individual and the environmental requirements (Thompson, 1994). Campos, Mumme, Kermoian, and Campos (1994) consider emotional regulation as an interpersonal phenomenon rather than an intrapsychic one. It is argued that beliefs about the availability of support and the likelihood of others' response will facilitate emotional regulation throughout constructing strong relations with others (Thompson, 1994). The ability to experience emotions and the control of intensity and duration is also conceived as emotional regulation (Zeanah, 2005). Alternatively, emotional disregulation is defined as the impairment of the control of emotional practices and expression (Zeanah, 2005).

Emotions could function as a contextual factor for parenting (Forgatch & Stoolmiller, 1994). The parent-child relationship is essential for emotional development (Oatley & Jenkins, 2006). Warm parenting creates an affective atmosphere that helps children to develop skills to manage emotions, and emotion regulation is essential for the adaptation to social environments.

EMOTIONS

The definition of emotion has proven difficult to establish. A number of researchers conceive it as a psychological state that prepares the organism to react adaptively to different relevant physical conditions for survival (Ortiz, Ramirez, & Valdez, 2009). Kelley (2005) indicates that emotion involves "motivational states, shaped by natural selection that allows modulation of physiological and behavioral responses ensuring survival, reproduction and fitness" which corresponds to valence affective states (Ortony & Turner, 1990). Frijda (1986) defines emotions as the "change in readiness for action". However, it is also considered as a communication process from one member of the species to another (Barlow, 2004). Communication patterns have the same signal value within species. Campos *et al.* (1994) consider emotion as the process that establishes, maintains, changes, and terminates the individual relation with the environment or other matters. Emotions are also conceived as states that are elicited by rewards and punishments (Rolls, 2005).

Emotions are viewed as the essential motivation for human behavior (Izard, 1998). Emotions may change the way people act (Posner, 2001); abilities, preferences, and beliefs are sometimes modified during emotional states. Moreover, there are emotional dispositions that moderate these emotional states (Posner, 2001). In addition, it is possible both to "cultivate" emotional dispositions and to control emotions (Cacioppo & Gardner, 1999). Emotions are also seen as intense and adaptive changes in response to an environmental stimulus (Adolphs, 2005). Adolphs (idem) argues that emotions are "representational states" because they characterize the connotation for the organism's homeostasis of a set of sensory inputs and behavioral outputs.

Charles Darwin hypothesized that a small number of emotional states were innate and present from birth in humans (Zeanah, 2005), showing consistencies across and within species (Barlow, 2004). There are six to nine universal human expressions. However, these universal expressions could be subject to modification through socialization (Izard & Read,

1982). Some behavioral mechanisms establish a quick and appropriate (i.e., adaptive) response accompanying an emotion. For instance, escape from an imminent physical danger is the best possible reaction. However, controlling emotional reactions serves better the individuals' adaptation in facing social stimuli, regardless of their perceived dangerous nature. Darwin also pointed out that humans express emotions in the same way from childhood to adulthood (Idem). Evidence has been found of three emotional states in two year-old babies (Izard & Read, 1982). Emotion facial expression seems to be consistent across cultures (Idem). Thus, innate emotional states have been called *primary emotions*, while the emotions that individuals acquire through their lifespan are identified as *secondary emotions* (Damasio, 1995). Ultimately, any stimulus possesses an affective meaning (Simon, 1997). Since emotions regulate social behavior in groups they are also considered as a social adaptation (Adolphs, 2005). Humans have to survive within a social group and self-regulation of emotions is a tool for adaptation of this social group. Emotions as adaptive processes are diverse in different cultures; one stimulus may elicit distinct emotions in people from different cultures because its differential meaning. Emotions are seen as signals ruling social communication (Adolphs, 2005). Emotions are also related to long term plans since individuals evaluate and select the available rewards and their costs, avoiding punishments (Rolls, 2005).

Additionally, the discussion continues about the independence of cognition from emotion, in which some researchers consider emotions as a separate mechanism (Zajonc, 1984) and others believe that emotions and cognition are functions of the same system (Lazarus, 1984). Lazarus (1991) argues that cognition precedes emotions because individuals evaluate emotions before a behavioral response. Since differential neuroanatomical structures have been identified for emotion and cognition, appraisal and affect are often uncorrelated: affective reactions can be manifested without appraisal. Therefore, some emotional states can be invoked without the mediation of a cognitive process (Zajonc, 1984).

Considering these results offered by the literature, the aim of this study is to analyze the relationship between self-control, self-regulation and antisocial behavior. Having this in mind, we specified and tested a model including self-control and self-regulation as predictors of antisocial behavior in juvenile delinquents.

METHOD

Participants

The sample included 164 participants; 58 were juvenile delinquents internalized in a juvenile court) and 106 were selected from the general community of a middle-sized Mexican city (population = 700,000 inhabitants). All of them reported some kind of antisocial behavior. The mean age for the total sample was 14 years old, 13.82 (SD=1.35) for the control group and 14.33 (SD=1.34) for minors at the juvenile court. Twenty four percent of the participants in the juvenile delinquent group were females and 76% were males.

Instruments

Self Regulation

Self-regulation was assessed using Raffaelli and Crockett's (2003) scale, which consists of 14 items based on the theory that self regulation is a multi-dimensional construct. The items measured emotional volatility and intensity, and activity regulation, using a 5 point scale, ranking from 0 to 4, where 0=Totally disagree and 4=Totally agree. Raffaelli and Crockett (2003) conducted a confirmatory factor analysis, which indicated construct validity of the instrument. These items are intended to assess emotional volatility, attention and activity regulation. In the pilot study an alpha of .86 was obtained.

Risk Taking

The Grasmick et al.'s (1993) instrument was used. The instrument includes 4 items in a 7-point scale (0="never", 1="once", 2="two times"... to 6="more than 20 times") detailing risky actions. Vazsonyi, Pickering, Junger, and Hessing, (2001) reported an alpha of .62 for the instrument.

Impulsivity

This construct can be defined as the tendency to respond quickly to a specific stimulus without thinking or evaluating the possible consequences of such responding. Grasmick et al's (1993) scale was used to assess it. This instrument includes 19 items with 7 point-scale response options from 0 to 6, 0 meaning "never", 1 "once", 2 "two times"... to 6 "more than 20 times" the individual reported actions such as acting impulsively, acting without thinking, planning trips, etc. Varsonyi, Pickering, Junger, and Hessing (2001) reported an alpha of .62 for this scale. We piloted it with high school students obtaining an alpha of .86.

Antisocial Behavior

Twenty six items of the antisocial behavior scale by Grasmick *et al.* (1993) were utilized. They were first piloted with high school students, obtaining a Cronbach's alpha of .70. By responding to this scale, participants have to select an option out of 7 points, ranking from 0 to 6, where 0 indicates "never" and 6 "more than 20 times" they engaged in a particular antisocial action during the last six months. "Steal something," "damage public property," "smoke," and "avoid paying for something consumed" are examples of this scale's items.

Procedure

The authorization from the president of the Minor Tutelary Counsel (Juvenile Court) was obtained in order to have access to the Court's building for the administration of the instruments to the institutionalized minors. This authorization was granted by school principals for the control group. Clinical psychologists, trained in psychological interview, administered the instruments in approximately 15 to 20 minutes. The voluntary consent to participate was obtained from both groups, minors and their parents, and they were advised that they could stop the interview at any moment. The arrested juveniles were interviewed first; once we obtained the demographic data of this group we located the participants for the control group and they were interviewed at the school they were attending.

Data Analysis

First, we conducted univariate analysis (means, standard deviations, minimum and maximum values) from the demographic data and the scales used as well as Cronbach's alphas to indicate internal consistency for those scales. Indexes of each sub-scale were computed (an index is the average response of the sub-scale items). Three indexes of the self-regulation scale (emotional volatility, emotional intensity, and activity regulation) were computed as well as five indexes of antisocial behavior (general deviance, thief, assault, school problems, and property crimes) and four indexes for impulsivity and risk seeking (motor impulsivity, no plan impulsivity, sensation seeking and risk taking). In addition, a structural equation model (SEM) was specified to estimate the relationships between self-control, self-regulation and antisocial behavior. The specified hypothetical model considered the direct and indirect effects of self-regulation and self-control on antisocial behavior. In order to test the pertinence of this hypothesized model, goodness of fit indicators were considered. These indicators show whether the specified relations in the model are supported by the data, and included the statistical indicator χ^2, expecting a non-significant p value (p >.05) associated to this indicator. Practical indicators were also considered, including the Non-Normed Fit Index (*NNFI*) and the Comparative Fit Index (*CFI*)) which are expected to produce a value higher than .90 (Bentler, 2006). To assess the reasonable error of approximation in terms of goodness of fit, the index root mean squared error (RMSEA) was obtained, requiring a <.08 value (Browne & Cudeck, 1993).

RESULTS

The univariate statistics of the scale of risk's items (means and standard deviations) are shown in Table1.

Table 2 exhibits the univariate statistics of the impulsivity scale. The highest mean was for "having an active life (mean 3.07).

In turn, Table 3 displays univariate statistics for the self-regulation scale. "Very active" (mean=2.15, range 0 to 4), "swift change of humor" (mean =2.14, range 0 to 4), and "worries too much" were the items with the highest means.

Table 1. Univariate statistics from responses to the risk scale

Items	N	Mean	sd	Min	Max
Experimenting risk-taking	162	2.06	1.535	0	4
Taking risks for fun	162	1.78	1.527	0	4
Do things that cause problems	162	1.44	1.532	0	4
Having fun is more important	162	1.14	1.367	0	4

Table 2. Univariate statistics from responses to the impulsivity scale

Items	N	Mean	sd	Min	Max
Start a work without planning	158	1.73	1.35	0	4
Think what to do before starting it	158	2.95	1.24	0	4
Acting impulsively	158	2.01	1.35	0	4
Spending no time for planning	158	2.11	1.30	0	4
Having new and excitement experiences	158	2.30	1.44	0	4
Planning before starting a new job	158	2.89	1.17	0	4
Traveling without planning routs and times	158	2.62	1.45	0	4
Getting into new situations	158	1.85	1.46	0	4
Doing things just for emotion	158	1.80	1.49	0	4
Changing interest frequently	158	1.99	1.24	0	4
Doing scaring things	158	2.07	1.48	0	4
Trying anything even if it is dangerous	158	1.90	1.53	0	4
Having a very active life	158	3.07	1.25	0	4
Doing craziness just for fun	158	2.02	1.54	0	4
Exploring a strange place	158	1.50	1.55	0	4
Prefer unpredictable friends	158	1.97	1.44	0	4
Excitation without thinking consequences	158	1.63	1.36	0	4
A crazy person	158	1.66	1.51	0	4
Likes parties without inhibitions	158	1.56	1.59	0	4

Table 3. Univariate statistics from responses to the self-regulation scale

Items	N	Mean	sd	Min	Max
Suddenly changes humor	162	2.14	1.369	0	4
Fearful and anxious	162	1.79	1.480	0	4
Feels happy	162	1.40	1.497	0	4
Cries frequently	162	.99	1.35	0	4
Nervous or stressed	162	1.67	1.44	0	4
Irritable	162	1.61	1.45	0	4
Strong Temperament	162	1.45	1.53	0	4
Problems to concentrate	162	1.46	1.37	0	4
Confounding feelings	162	1.86	1.39	0	4
Acts without thinking	162	1.49	1.48	0	4
Difficulty to stop thinking	162	1.88	1.48	0	4
Very active	162	2.15	1.50	0	4
Worries too much	162	2.05	1.51	0	4

Table 4 presents the univariate statistics of the antisocial scale. The highest levels of antisocial behavior were for fights (mean=2.26, range 0 to 4) and goes out without permission (mean=1-87, range 0 to 4). Finally, Table 5 exhibits the means, standard deviation, and alphas of all the scales. All alphas were higher than .70, which is considered an appropriate internal consistence.

Figure 1 shows the results of the structural model; all the proposed factors seem to evidence convergent construct validity of the used measures, manifested by the salient and significant values of the factor loadings. Self- control affected positively antisocial behavior (structural coefficient = .25) self-regulation had a direct effect on antisocial behavior (structural coefficient = .29) as well as on self-control (structural coefficient = .55). The practical goodness of fit indicators met the required criterion values, evidencing the adequacy of the tested model. Although the X^2 was significant ($\chi^2(43) = 80.68$; $p < .000$), the practical indexes demonstrated that the model fit the data (Bentler, 2006).

Table 4. Univariate statistics from responses to the risk-taking scale

Items	N	Mean	sd	Min	Max
Gets inside forbidden place	136	1.10	1.740	0	4
Goes out without permission	136	1.87	2.139	0	4
Does not return money	136	.88	1.417	0	4
Dirties the streets	136	1.57	2.053	0	4
Cheats a cashier	136	.43	1.203	0	4
Bothers unfamiliar persons	136	1.12	1.795	0	4
Cheats	136	1.01	1.671	0	4
Takes tires' air off	136	.66	1.545	0	4
Lies about age	136	.68	1.464	0	4
Makes inappropriate calls	136	.60	1.307	0	4
Avoids to pay	136	.70	1.405	0	4
Starts alarms	136	.75	1.429	0	4
Damages public places	136	.60	1.390	0	4
Abuses animals	136	.95	1.502	0	4
Graffiti	136	1.15	2.092	0	4
Destroys things of another person	136	1.07	1.696	0	4
Makes heavy jokes	136	1.49	1.901	0	4
Answers wrong to an authority	136	1.32	1.805	0	4
Smokes in a prohibited place	136	.77	1.789	0	4
Refuses to do homework	136	1.32	1.763	0	4
Fights	136	2.26	2.329	0	4
Threats people to get Money	136	.62	1.674	0	4
Gets into a close store	136	.47	1.377	0	4
Uses fake money	136	.55	1.343	0	4
Steals things to a family member	136	.56	1.349	0	4
Steals something of little value	136	.78	1.538	0	4

Table 5. Means and reliabilities of all used scales

Scale	N	Mean	SD	Alpha
Risk	136	6.42	4.46	.74
Impulsivity	136	39.63	14.29	.86
Self-regulation	136	21.95	11.50	.86
Antisocial behavior	136	25.28	29.24	.95

CONCLUSION

The General Theory of Crime considers self-control as a unique determinant of criminal behavior (Gottfredson & Hirschi, 1990). However, research results indicate a limited explanatory power of the former variable on the variance of the latter; this would indicate the existence of additional variables predicting antisocial behavior. Marcus (2004) argues that behavior is the product of intricate determinants from different sources. Criminal behavior is initiated and maintained by multiple determinants and self-control is just one of these factors. Marcus also indicates that investigations trying to demonstrate that self-control is a unique variable predicting criminal behavior have failed, although other studies have supported and documented the uni-determined nature of criminal actions (Gottfredson & Hirschi, 1990; Pratt & Cullen, 2000).

Low self-control is clearly an important predictor of delinquent behavior (Pratt & Cullen, 2000; Vitacco & Rogers , 2001). Nevertheless, these studies explain less than 20% of the variance in such behavior (Vazsonyi, Pickering, Junger, & Hessing, 2001). In view of the abovementioned results, we were committed to study the explanatory role of variables other than self control, yet also including this important determinant in our model of antisocial behavior.

Since theory establishes that individuals lacking self control are impulsive and risk taking (Gottfredson & Hirschi, 1990), in the study reported in this chapter these variables constituted a "lack of self control" factor. Low self-controlled individuals seek for immediate pleasure and cannot control their impulses. This tendency to instant gratification leads them to commit acts of deviance.

Although in the original model (Gottfredson & Hirschi, 1990) emotional regulation or temper is proposed as being part of the construct of self control, in our study emotional control seems to constitute a separate factor, yet highly correlated to impulsivity and risk taking. Results showed that emotions affect self-control, which replicates previous findings indicating that emotion regulates cognition and changes the way people act (Posner, 2001). However, self-regulation also directly predicted antisocial behavior.

Our model contains a component of emotional stability which had not been previously included in the theory. Emotions could be developed through life span to respond more adequately to social stimuli; in this sense, emotion is also seen as part of an adaptive process aimed at adjusting people's responses to social requirements. The more the individual develops emotional regulation the more (s)he gets adapted to social life and avoids antisocial behavior. Antisocial individuals are incapable to control their behavior or emotions.

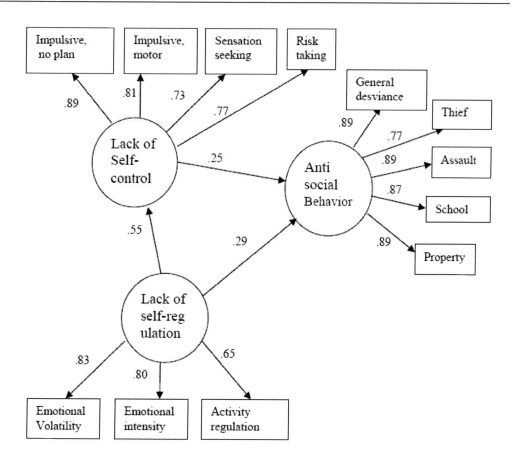

Figure 1. Model of self control and antisocial behavior. All structural coefficients and factor loadings are significant at at $p < .05$. Goodness of fit: $X^2 = 102.28$ (51 df), $p = 0.00$; NFI =. 93 NNFI =.95, CFI = .96, RMSEA= .07; R^2 =. 23.

However, the phenomenon of delinquency is complex and should instigate the searching for multiple factors explaining delinquency. This chapter analyzed some individual factors related to antisocial behavior: self-control and self-regulation, which explained almost a quarter of antisocial behavior variance.

Self control theory also assumes that ineffective childrearing practices often result in low self–control in children. Parental supervision and support help to develop cognitive and emotional regulation. In addition, negative emotions within family predict antisocial behavior in minors (Forgatch & Stoolmiller, 1994). Therefore, it is important to include in future testing of models these variables as correlates of children self-control and antisocial behavior.

Social and governmental responses to adolescents' antisocial behavior have included the creation of formal institutions for their attention and treatment; juvenile tribunals are one of them. These tribunals were firstly instituted more than a century ago; however, nowadays the question is whether or not they have been effective in preventing youth violence. It is true that children need specialized institutions. Yet, it is also true that those institutions have failed in stopping an increased juvenile criminal behavior. A change in perspective is necessary, and this can be guided by pertinent research and the participation of the diverse social and professional instances involved in this serious community problem. Sharing perspectives among psychologist, sociologists, courts, correctional institutions, defense attorneys, media, schools teachers, social workers, private institutions, and communities is crucial to find a solution (Katzmann, 2002). As a number of studies have demonstrated, using a unique theoretical perspective is not the appropriate way: the problem persists and its severity increases. Thus, the solution involves the implementation and evaluation of multiple programs containing results from scientific scrutiny. Diverse theories and approaches have to be tested, developing interventional programs based on these theories. In this chapter, the importance of emotional and cognitive self-control was demonstrated, which can provide clues for the development of treatments/interventions, in which adolescents learn to control their emotions and to be able to foresee the long-term consequence of their acts. The natural tendency to getting instant gratification could be reversed teaching them self-control through appropriate training, parental supervision and support.

REFERENCES

Abrams, D., & Hogg, M. A. (1990). Social identification, self-categorization and social influence. *European Review of Social Psychology, 1*, 195-228.

Adolphs, R. (2005). Could a robot have emotions?: Theoretical perspectives from social Cognitve Neuroscience. In J-M. Fellous & M. A. Arbib (eds), *Who Needs Emotions?: The Brain Meets the Robot.* (pp.9-25). New York,: Oxford University Press.

Avila, C., Cuenca, I., Felix, V., Parcet, M. A., & Miranda, A. (2004). Measuring impulsivity in school-aged boys and examining its relationship with ADHD and ODD ratings. *Journal of Abnormal Child Psychology*, 32, 295–304.

Baldry, A. C. (2007). "It does affect me": Disruptive behaviors en preadolescents directly and indirectly abused at home. *European Psychologist, 12,* 29-35.

Barlow, D. H. (2004). *Anxiety and its disorders: The nature and treatment of anxiety and panic*. New York: Guilford Press.

Billieux, J., Van der Linden, M., & Ceschi, G. (2007). Which dimensions of impulsivity are related to cigarette craving? *Addictive Behaviors,* 32(6), 1189-1199.

Browne, M. W., & Cudeck, R. (1993). Alternative ways of assessing model fit. In K. A. Bollen & J. S. Long (Eds.), *Testing structural equation models* (pp. 136-162). Thousand Oaks, CA: Sage.

Burfeind, J. W., & Bartusch, D. J. (2006). *Juvenile Delinquency: An integrated approach.* Ontario, Canada: Jones and Bartlett Publishers.

Cacioppo, J. T., & Gardner, W. L. (1999). Emotion. *Annual Review of Psychology, 50,* 191-214.

Campos, J.J., Mumme, D. L., Kermoian, R., & Campos, R. G. (1994). A functionalist perspective on the nature of emotion. *Monographs of the Society for Research in Child Development*, 59, 284–303.

Carrasco, M., Barker, E.D., Tremblay, R. E., & Vitaro, F. (2006). Eysenck's personality dimensions as predictors of male adolescent trajectories of physical aggression, theft and vandalism. *Personality and Individual Differences* 41, 1309–1320.

Carroll, A., Hemingway, F., Bower, J., Ashman, A., Houghton, S., & Durkin, K. (2006). Impulsivity in Juvenile Delinquency: Differences Among Early-Onset, Late-Onset, and Non-Offenders, *Journal of Youth and Adolescence,35 (4), 519–529.*

Cauffman, E., Steinberg, L., & Piquero, A. R. (2005). Psychological, neuropsychological and physiological correlates of serious antisocial behavior in adolescence: the role of self-control. *Criminology,* 43, 133-175.

Cicchetti, D., & Manly, J. T., Eds. (2001). Operationalizing child maltreatment: Developmental process and outcomes (Special issue). *Development and Psychopathology, 13.*

Crime in the United States (2007). Retrieved on July 2009 from: http://www.fbi.gov /ucr/cius2007/arrests/index.html.

Dahlen, E. R., Martin, R. C., Ragan, K., & Kuhlman, M.M. (2005). Driving anger, sensation seeking, impulsiveness, and boredom proneness in the prediction of unsafe driving. *Accident Analysis and Prevention,* 37, 341–348.

Damasio, A. R. (1995). Toward a neurobiology of emotion and feeling: Operational concepts and hypothesis. *The Neuroscientist,* 1, 19-25.

Dawes, M. A., Tarter, & R. E. Kirisci, L. (1997). Behavioral self-regulation: Correlates and 2 year follow-ups for boys at risk for substance abuse. *Drug and Alcohol Dependence,* 45, I65 – 176.

Dickman, S. J. (1990). Functional and dysfunctional impulsivity: Personality and cognitive correlates. *Journal of Personality and Social Psychology,* 58(1), 95-102.

Eisenberg N, Fabes RA. 1998. Prosocial development. In *Handbook of Child Psychology. Social, Emotional, and Personality Development,* ed. W Damon, N Eisenberg (ser. ed). 3:701–78. New York: Wiley & Sons.

Enticott, P. G., & Ogloff, J. R. P. (2006). *Elucidation of impulsivity. Australian Psychologist,* 41(1): 3-14.

Forgatch, M. S., & Stoolmiller, M. (1994). Emotions as contexts for adolescents delinquency. *Journal of Research on Adolescence,* 4(4), 601-614.

Fossati, A., Barratt, E. S., Carretta, I., Leonardi, B., Grazioli, F., & Maffei, C. (2004). Predicting borderline and antisocial personality disorder features in nonclinical subjects using measures of impulsivity and aggressiveness. Psychiatry Research, 125, 161–170.

Frías, M., Ramírez, J., Soto, R., Castell, I., & Corral, V. (2000). Repercusiones conductuales del maltrato infantil: Un estudio con grupos de alto riesgo. En AMEPSO (Ed.), *La Psicología Social en México,* Vol. 8. México: AMEPSO.

Frijda, N. H. (1986). *The emotions.* New York: Cambridge University Press.

Galambus, N. L., & Costigan, C. L. (2003). Emotional and personality development in adolescence. In R.M. Lerner, M. A. Easterbooks, and Mistry, J. (Eds), I. B. Weiner, (Ed. In chief), Handbook of Psychology, *Developmental Psychology,* vol. 6. Pp.251- 372. New Jersey, John Wiley & Sons, Inc.

Gatzke-Kopp, L. M., Raine, A., Loeber, R., Stouthamer-Loeber, M., & Steinhauer, S. (2002). Serious delinquent behavior, sensation seeking, and electrodermal arousal. *Journal of Abnormal Child Psychology,* 30, 477–486.

Golden, C. J., Jackson, M. L., Peterson-Rohne, A., & Gontkovsky, S. T. (1996). Neuropsychological correlates of violence and aggression: a review of the clinical literature. *Aggression and Violent Behavior,* 1(1), 3-25.

Gottfredson, M. R., & Hirschi. T. (1990). *A General Theory of Crime*. Stanford, CA: Stanford University Press.

Gottfredson, M. R., & Hirschi.T. (2009). The nature of criminality: Low self-control. In F. R. Scarpitti, A. L. Nielsen, & J. M. Miller (Eds.), *Crime and Criminals: Contemporary and Classic Readings in* Criminology (pp. 272-288). New York: Oxford University Press.

Grano, N., Virtanen, M., Vahtera, J., Elovainio, M., & Kivimaki, M. (2004). Impulsivity as a predictor of smoking and alcohol consumption. *Personality and Individual Differences, 37*, 1693–1700.

Grasmick, H., Title, C., Bursick., & Arneklev, B. (1993). Testing the core empirical implication of Gottfredson and Hirschi's General Theory of Crime. *Journal of Research in Crime and Delinquency, 30*, 5-29.

Grasmick, H. G., & Bursik, R. J., Jr. (1990). Conscience, significant others, and rational choice: Extending to deterrence model. *Law and Society Review, 24*, 837-861.

Herba, C. M., Tranah, T., Rubia, K., & Yule, W. (2006). Conduct Problems in Adolescence: Three Domains of Inhibition and Effect of Gender. *Developmental Neuropsychology, 30*(2), 659–695.

Hirschi, T. (2002). *Causes of delinquency*. New Jersey: Transaction publishers.

Hirschi, T. (2009). A control Theory of delinquency. In F. R. Scarpitti, A. L. Nielsen, & J. M. Miller (Eds.), *Crime and Criminals: Contemporary and Classic Readings in Criminology* (pp. 272-288). New York: Oxford University Press.

Hirschi, T., & Gottfredson, M. R. (1994). The Generality of Deviance. In T. Hirschi and M. R. Gottfredson (eds) *The Generality of Deviance*, pp. 1–22. New Brunswick, NJ: Transaction Publishers.

Hoffmann, J. P. (2002). A Contextual Analysis of Differential Association, Social Control, and Strain Theories of Delinquency. *Social Forces*, 81(3):753-785.

Hornsey, J. M. (2008). Social Identity Theory and Self-categorization Theory: A Historical Review. *Social and Personality Psychology Compass, 2*(1), 204–222.

Izard, C. E., & Read, P. B. (1982). *Measuring emotions in infants and children*. New York: Cambridge University Press.

Izard, C. E, (1998). Emotions and facial expressions: A perspective from differential emotions theory. In J. A. Russell & J. M. Fernández-Dols, G. Mandler. *The psychology of facial expression*. Cambridge, UK: Cambridge University Press.

Katzmann, G. S. (2002). *Securing Our Children's Future: New Approaches to Juvenile Justice and Youth Violence*. Washington, D.C. Brookings Institution Press.

Kelley, A. E. (2005). Neurochemical networks encoding emotion and motivation: evolutionary perspective. In J-M. Fellous & M. A. Arbib (eds), *Who Needs Emotions?: The Brain Meets the Robot*. (pp.29-77). New York,: Oxford University Press.

Krug, E. G., Dahlberg, L. L., Mercy, J. A., Zwi, A. B., & Lozano, R. (2002). World Report on Violence and Health (WHO). Retrieved on June 20, 2006, from: http://www.who.int/violence_injury_prevention/violence/world_report/en/full_en.pdf.

Lansford, J. E., Dodge, K. A., Pettit, G. S., Bates, J. E., Crozier, J., & Kaplow, J. (2002). Long-term effects of early child physical maltreatment on psychological, behavioral, and academic problems in adolescence: A 12-year prospective study. *Archives of Pediatrics and Adolescent Medicine, 156*, 824–830.

Lazarus, R. S. (1984). *On the primacy of cognition. American psychologist,* 39(2), 124-129.

Lazarus, R. S. (1991). Cognition and motivation in emotion. *American Psychologist,* 46(4), 352-367.

Leeb, R. T., Barker, L. E., & Strine, & T. W. (2007). The effect of childhood physical and sexual abuse on adolescent weapon carrying. *Journal of Adolescent Health, 40(6),* 551-558.

MacDonald, J. M., Piquero, A. R., Valois, R. F., & Zullig, K. J. (2005). The Relationship Between Life Satisfaction, Risk-Taking Behaviors, and Youth Violence. *Journal of Interpersonal Violence,* 20; 1495-1514.

Maguire, M.,Morgan, R., & Reiner, R. (2002). *Manual de Criminología.* México: Oxford University Press.

Marcus, B. (2004). Self-control in the General Theory of Crime: *Theoretical implications of a measurement problem. Theoretical Criminology,* 8(1), 33–55.

McCord, J. (2009). Family relation, Juvenile delinquency, and adult criminality. In F. R. Scarpitti, A. L. Nielsen, & J. M. Miller (Eds.*), Crime and Criminals: Contemporary and Classic Readings in Criminology* (pp. 272-288). New York: Oxford University Press.

Meeus, W., Branje, S., & Overbeek, G.J. (2004). Parents and partners in crime: a six-year longitudinal study on changes in supportive relationships and delinquency in adolescence and young adulthood. *Journal of Child Psychology and Psychiatry* 45(7),1288-1298.

Miller, E., Joseph, S., & Tudway, J. (2004). Assessing the component structure of four self-report measures of impulsivity. *Personality and Individual Differences,* 37, 349–358.

Moeller, F. G., & Dougherty, D. M. (2002). *Impulsivity and Substance Abuse: What Is the Connection? Addictive Disorders Their Treatment,* 1, 3-10.

Moffitt, T. E. (2003). Life-course-persistent and adolescence-limited antisocial behavior: A 10-year research review and a research agenda. In Benjamin B. Lahey, Terrie E. Moffitt and Avshalom Caspi (eds.). *Causes of Conduct Disorder and Juvenile Delinquency.* New York: Guilford Press.

Muraven, M., Pogarsky, & G. Shmueli, D. (2006). Self-control depletion and the General Theory of Crime. *Journal of Quantitative Criminology,* 22, 263–277.

Murray, J., & Farrington, D. P. (2005). Parental imprisonment: effects on boys' Antisocial behavior and delinquency through the life-course. Journal of Child Psychology and Psychiatry 46(12), 1269–1278.

Ngai, N., & Cheung, C. (2005). Predictors of the likelihood of delinquency: A study of marginal Youth in Hong Kong, China. Youth & Society, 36, 445-470.

Oatley, K., & Jenkins, J. M. (2006). Understanding Emotions. Oxford, UK: Wiley-Blackwell.

Ortiz, X., Ramírez, C., &Valdez, P. (2009). Ritmos circadianos en la motivación y la emoción. En P. Valdez Ramírez (Ed.), Cronobiología Respuestas Psicofisiológicas al tiempo. (pp. 213-225). Nuevo León México: Universidad Autónoma de Nuevo León.

Ortony, A., & Turner, T. J. (1990). What's basic about basic emotions? Psychological review, 97(3), 315-331.

Posner, E. A. (2001). Law and Emotions. *Georgetown Law Journal, 89,* 1977-1993.

Pratt, T. C., & Cullen, F. T. (2000). The empirical status of Gottfredson and Hirschi's general theory of crime: A meta-analysis. *Criminology, 38,* 931-964.

Putnam, F. W. (2003). Ten-year research update review: Children sexual abuse. *Journal of the American Academy of Child and Adolescent Psychiatry, 42,* 269-278.

Rafaelli, M., & Crockett, L. (2003). Sexual risk taking in adolescence: The role of self regulation and attraction to risk. *Developmental Psychology, 39,* 1036-1046.

Rebellon, C. J., & Van-Gundy, K. (2005). Can control theory explain the link between parental physical abuse and delinquency? A longitudinal analysis. *Journal of research in crime and delinquency, 42,* 247-274.

Reynolds, B., Ortengren, A., Richards, J. B., & de Wit, H. (2006). Dimensions of impulsive behavior: Personality and behavioral measures. *Personality and Individual Differences,* 40, 305–315

Reynolds, B., Richards, J. B., Horn, K., & Karraker, K. (2004). Delay discounting and probability discounting as related to cigarette smoking status in adults. *Behavioral Processes,* 65, 35-42.

Reynolds, B., Penfold, R. B., & Patak, M. (2008). Dimensions of Impulsive Behavior in Adolescents: Laboratory Behavioral Assessments. *Experimental and Clinical Psychopharmacology,* 16(2), 124–131.

Rolls, E. T. (2005). What are emotions, why do we have emotions, and what is their computational basis in the brain. In J-M. Fellous & M. A. Arbib (eds), *Who Needs Emotions? The Brain Meets the Robot.* (pp.117-146). New York,: Oxford University Press.

Roucek, J. S. (1970). *Juvenile delinquency.* New York: Philosophical reading.

Schultz, P.W. (2002). Knowledge, information, and household recycling: Examining the knowledge-deficit model of behavior change. In T Dietz & P. Stern (Eds.), *New Tools for Environmental Protection: Education, Information, and Voluntary Measures* (pp. 67-82). Washington, DC: National Academic Press.

Schwartz, S. (2002). ¿Existen aspectos universales en la estructura y contenido de los valores humanos? In M. Ros & V. Gouveia (Eds.), *Psicología Social de los Valores Humanos.* Madrid: Biblioteca Nueva.

Secretaría de Seguridad Pública de México, Consejo de Menores, (2008). *Transparencia focalizada de prevención y readaptación social: Estadísticas penitenciarias.* Retrived on June, 10, 2009, from: http://www.ssp.gob.mx/portalWebApp/ShowBinary? nodeId=/ BEARepository/365162//archivo

Sethi, A., Mischel, W., Aber, J., Shoda, Y., & Rodriguez, M. L. (2000). The role of strategic attention deployment in development of self-regulation: Predicting preschoolers' delay of gratification from mother-toddler interactions. Developmental Psychology, 36, 767–777.

Sigala, M., Burgoyne, C., & Webley, P. (1999). Tax communication and social influence: Evidence from a British simple. *Journal of Community and Applied Social Psychology, 9,* 237-241.

Simon, V. M. (1997). La participación emocional en la toma de decisiones. Psicothema, 9(2), 365-376.

Slater, M. D. (2003). Sensation-seeking as a moderator of the effects of peer influences, consistency with personal aspirations, and perceived harm of marijuana and cigarette use among younger adolescents. Substance Use and Misuse, 38, 865-880.

Stanford, M. S., Houston, R. J., Villemarette-Pittman, N. R., & Greve, K. W. (2003). Premeditated aggression: clinical assessment and cognitive psychophysiology. Personality and Individual Differences, 34, 773–781.

Taylor, C.S. (1996). *The unintended consequences of incarceration: Youth development, the juvenile corrections system, and crime.* Presented at Conf. Vere Inst. Harriman, NY.

The Political Constitution of the United Mexican States. (2009). Retrieved on March 25, 2009 from: http://www.cddhcu.gob.mx/LeyesBiblio/

Thompson, R. (1994). Emotion regulation: A theme in search of definition. In N. Fox (Ed.), The development of emotion regulation: Biological and behavioral considerations. *59*(2–3, Serial 240). *Monographs of the Society for Research in Child Development.*

Tyler, T. R. (2006). *Why People Obey The Law.* New Jersey: Princeton University Press.

Valiente, C., Lemery-Chalfant K., & Reiser, M. (2007). Pathways to Problem Behaviors: Chaotic Homes, Parent and Child Effortful Control, and Parenting. *Social Development, 16*(2), 249-267.

Vazsonyi, A., Pickering, L., Junger, M., & Hessing, D. (2001). An empirical test of a general theory of crime: a four-nation comparative study of self-control and the prediction of deviance. *Journal of Research in Crime and Delinquency, 38,* 2, 91-131.

Vigil-Colet, A., & Codorniu-Raga, M. J. (2004). Aggression and inhibition deficits, the role of functional and dysfunctional impulsivity. *Personality and Individual Differences, 37*(7), 1431-1440.

Vitacco, M. J., & Rogers ,R. (2001). Predictors of adolescent psychopathy: The role of impulsivity, hyperactivity, and sensation seeking. *Journal of American Academy of Psychology and Law* 29(4): 374–382.

White, J. R., Moffitt, T. E., Caspi, A., Bartusch, D. J., Needles, D. J., & Stouthamer-Loeber, M. (1994). Measuring Impulsivity and Examining Its Relationship to Delinquency. *Journal of Abnormal Psychology,* 103(2), 192-205.

Whiteside, S. P., & Lynam, D. R. (2001). The five factor model and impulsivity: Using a structural model of personality to understand impulsivity. *Personality and Individual Differences,* 30, 669−689.

Wortley, R., & Mazarolle, L. (2008). *Environmental Criminology and Crime Analysis.* Portland, Oregon: William Publishing.

Zajonc, R. B. (1984). On the primacy of affect. *American psychologist,* 39(2), 117-123.

Zeanah, C.H. (2005). *Handbook of Infant Mental Health.* New York: Guilford Press.

In: Psychology of Self-Regulation
Editor: Vassilis Barkoukis

ISBN: 978-1-61470-380-8
© 2012 Nova Science Publishers, Inc.

Chapter 9

HYPNOSIS, ABSORPTION AND THE NEUROBIOLOGY OF SELF-REGULATION

Graham A. Jamieson
University of New England, Australia

In memory of my mother, Agnes Fraser Jamieson

ABSTRACT

In hypnosis, suggested behaviours are characteristically accompanied by a diminished sense of effort and personal agency while suggested experiences, which strongly contradict objective reality, appear to be accepted without conflict. Dissociated control theory is a cognitive neuroscience account of hypnosis that emphasises functional disconnections (dissociations) within the predominantly anterior brain networks, which implement cognitive control. Profound alterations in the ongoing experience of the self outside the hypnotic context (labelled by Tellegen as absorption) are a key predictor of a person's ability to experience suggested distortions of reality. Tellegen (1981) defined the trait of absorption as arising from the interplay of two mutually inhibitory mental sets, the instrumental and the experiential mental sets. The capacity to set aside an instrumental set finds a clear counterpart in current neuroimaging and EEG studies of dissociated control in hypnosis. The consequent ability to adopt an experiential set has a clear counterpart in the recent discovery of a characteristic brain network during quiescent mental activity. Neuroimaging studies of suggestions used to induce hypnotic analgesia show strongly overlapping activations with the loci of this network which generates core aspects of internally focused self experience. Tellegen pointed to distinctive roles for the instrumental and experiential mental sets in psychophysiological self-regulation in order to explain the importance of the trait absorption in mediating the mixed pattern of results in earlier biofeedback studies. This account finds further support in recent studies on the roles of these mutually inhibitory neural networks in differing patterns of regulation of peripheral physiology. These findings provide an important foundation from which to understand the unique contributions of absorption and hypnosis in effective practices of self-regulation.

INTRODUCTION

One of the most characteristic features of experience during hypnosis is the loss of awareness of the immediate environment and a strong focus on the communication (words) of the hypnotist and/or the experiences they suggest. This feature of hypnosis was labeled by Shor (1959) as loss of Generalized Reality Orientation (GRO) and identified as a primary dimension of hypnotic experience in his influential 3-factor theory of hypnosis. Similar observations had been made by other observers going back to the nineteenth century. Although Shor interpreted this feature of hypnosis as an expression of a loss of contact and concern with everyday reality (indeed with the very psychological framework required to focus on that reality) others (for example Milton Eriksen) interpreted this as the expression of the development of an intense attentional focus leading to the exclusion of otherwise distracting or irrelevant stimuli from conscious awareness. Meanwhile, following the advances in the measurement of individual differences in hypnotic ability which led to the Stanford and Harvard scales psychological researchers sought to identify the personality and ability characteristics which predisposed an individual to high (or low) hypnotizability. Despite an intensive effort from the late 1950s to the early 1970s with virtually every psychological measure available these efforts were largely fruitless (a situation which remains essentially unchanged to this day).

The one notable exception to these null findings was the biographical interview work, focusing on the construct of imaginative involvement, conducted by Josephine Hilgard and her associates (Hilgard, 1974). At the same time Tellegen and Atkinson (1974) reported the development of a 'paper and pencil' personality scale which correlated significantly with hypnotic susceptibility. The items on this scale (developed from a series of similar early attempts) asked about the occurrence of a range of unusual or trancelike alterations in experience in daily life. Abstracting from the content of several items (and likely influenced by contemporary ideas in the hypnosis literature) Tellegen and Atkinson (1974) fatefully defined the trait measured by their scale as "absorption". They described absorption as a state of, "total attention involving a full commitment of available perceptual, motoric, imaginative and ideational resources to a unified representation of the attentional object" (Tellegen & Atkinson, 1974, p. 274).

HYPNOSIS AND THE SUPERVISORY ATTENTIONAL SYSTEM

Influenced by this lead, a number of neurophysiological researchers began to search for evidence of the involvement of the brains systems of attentional control in the various phenomena of hypnosis. The Supervisory Attentional System (SAS) model of Norman and Shallice (1986) elegantly summarises key elements of the thinking which guided these efforts. According to this model the selection of routine responses is the outcome of an automatic and unconscious competition amongst fixed action schemata (neural networks mapping specific inputs to specific outputs), for access to various response systems. This process, called contention scheduling is implemented predominantly in posterior cortical regions. However flexible, non-routine responses require current goals to guide the selection of task appropriate but often weak schema mappings against the competition of much stronger automatic mappings. This is implemented by the SAS which monitors the activation of task relevant schema and modulates their activation to bias the contention scheduling process in favour of the current task set. Task set representations are stored in anterior cortical regions, thus the source of top-down attentional control is activity in elements of a far frontal attentional network.

These researchers therefore searched for evidence of activity within the anterior cortical networks believed to implement top-down attentional control, which would distinguish high from low hypnotically susceptible individuals particularly during hypnosis, or when responding to specific suggestions such as hypnotic analgesia. In work with the electroencephalogram (EEG) interest focused on the theta frequency band (4-7 Hz) due to the role of theta in tasks demanding mental concentration or effort (e.g., Ishii et al., 1999). Indeed over several decades a number of studies have reported evidence of a positive relationship between hypnotizability and or the hypnosis condition and increases in EEG theta power (e.g., Ray, 1997). In addition increased prefrontal cortical activation reported in PET studies of hypnotic analgesia suggestion, a phenomenon which some have considered to be a paradigm case for the role of focused attentional control in the production of hypnotic responses, have been interpreted as further support for this view (e.g., Crawford et al., 2000).

Woody and Bowers (1994) employed the SAS model in a very different way to understand another key aspect of hypnotic experience that of effortlessness or non volition in the generation of hypnotic responses, otherwise known as 'the classic suggestion effect' (Weitzenhoffer, 1953). On the Norman and Shallice account a volitional response is a paradigm case of attentional control implemented by the SAS. Therefore, Woody and Bowers argued, if the experience of non volition in hypnosis is veridical it must be accompanied by a reduction, if not loss, of SAS control and a shift toward contention scheduling. At the level of cortical dynamics this corresponds to a weakening of the influence of prefrontal task set representations on more posterior cortical processing. Evidence for this model of hypnotic responding requires a decrease (not an increase) in the efficiency of selective attentional control in hypnotized high susceptibles and a corresponding decrease in functional connectivity between cortical regions responsible for implementing top-down attentional control.

According to Woody and Bowers hypnosis is characterized (at least in part) by dissociation between conscious volitional control implemented by the SAS and unconscious automatic control implemented by contention scheduling. A shift from the former to the latter should be evidenced by a decrement (rather than an improvement) in performance on those very tasks which are paradigm cases of executive attentional control. The Stroop task (Stroop, 1935) is without doubt the classic selective attention task in experimental psychology and has been employed in more publications than any other paradigm in the field (MacLeod & MacDonald, 2000). In the Stroop task participants view color-name stimuli presented in an actual color, which may be congruent (e.g., the color-name "red" presented in red) or incongruent (e.g., the color-name "red" printed in green) with the color-name. Participants must respond to either the color-word or the actual color. The Stroop effect is evidenced by slower reaction times (and typically a greater error rate) when responding to incongruent than congruent stimuli. An important feature of the Stroop effect is that it is greater when responding to the color of the stimulus then when responding to the color-name. Current models of the Stroop effect emphasize co activation of competing responses driven by different features of the stimulus (the color-name and the color of the word, respectively).

When these are congruent there is little response conflict. Likewise when the task is to respond to the color-name over learned and highly automatic word reading schema easily out compete schema activated by the color of the word in the contention scheduling process for access to motor response systems. However, when the task requires a response to the color of the word on incongruent stimuli additional top-down (SAS) control is required to bias response competition in favor of the weaker color response pathways (Botvinick, Cohen and Carter, 2004). A similar logic is employed in many Stroop type tasks subsequently developed in the experimental literature.

Studies of hypnosis (without further suggestion) and hypnotic susceptibility using the Stroop task have shown that high susceptibles in the hypnosis condition show a significant decline in multiple indices of the efficiency of Stoop performance on high conflict (i.e., incongruent, color naming) trials. Sheehan, Donovan and MacLeod (1988) found an increase in Stroop color naming reaction times (although high susceptibles were better able to make use of further specific suggestions to reduce Stroop conflict). Kaiser et al. (1997) found higher errors in hypnotized participants with higher hypnotic susceptibility using a Stroop type task. Nordby, Hugdhal, Jasiukaitis and Spiegel (1999) also reported greater Stroop errors in hypnotized high susceptibles. Jamieson and Sheehan (2004) employed a classic version of the Stroop task in a very large sample, rigorously assessed for hypnotic susceptibility and found a significant interaction between hypnotic susceptibility and hypnosis condition in Stroop error rates (with errors rising specifically for high susceptibles in the hypnosis condition). Collectively this evidence points very strongly towards a decrease in the efficiency of top-down SAS control of Stroop induced response conflict in the hypnotized condition for high susceptible individuals.

However Sheehan et al. (1988) found that, distinct from the effect of hypnosis per se, with specific suggestions hypnotized high susceptibles were better able to control Stroop induced response conflict than were lows. Recently Raz, Shapiro, Fan and Posner (2002) found that high susceptibles were able to eliminate the Stroop effect by means of specific hypnotic suggestions. Subsequently Raz, Kirsch, Pollard and Nitkin-Kaner (2006) also found that high susceptibles were able to use these specific suggestions to modulate Stroop interference but could do so both with and without undergoing a hypnotic induction procedure. Thus it appears that, in response to suggestion, there are effects in hypnosis which suggest enhanced control of conflicting or distracting competition for attentional resources. Earlier a series of neuropsychological studies conducted by Gruzelier and his colleagues indicated decreased performance on tasks affected by prefrontal lesions (such as letter fluency see Gruzelier and Warren, 1993) during the hypnosis condition, particularly by those higher in hypnotic susceptibility. Gruzelier (e.g., 1998) has consistently interpreted these findings as evidence for a decrease in frontal cortical activation brought about by hypnosis.

Crawford and Gruzelier (1992) proposed a synthesis of their respective focused attention and frontal inhibition accounts of hypnosis in which the hypnotic induction first engages and directs the focus of frontally mediated attentional processes followed by a gradual inhibition of frontal activation and finally a shift to a more posterior mediated flow of mental activity. In this case focused attention becomes a prerequisite for subsequent frontal inhibition. Egner and Raz (2007) have also attempted a synthesis of their recent divergent Stroop and hypnosis findings by pointing to the distinction between the effects of hypnotic induction and specific hypnotic suggestions in their respective results. On their account hypnosis is characterized by a disengagement of anterior mediated SAS control processes which in turn allows the development of sustained iterative processing loops in the absence of (more usual) disruption by frontal attentional control networks. In many respects this proposal by Egner and Raz may be considered as almost the inverse of that put forward by Crawford and Gruzelier 15 years earlier in that a sustained attentional focus, when it appears in hypnosis, is not underpinned by the activity of frontal attentional control networks but is enabled precisely as a consequence of the disengagement of these networks (see also Jamieson and Sheehan, 2004).

CONFLICT-MONITORING AND COGNITIVE CONTROL

Despite its historical importance both to the development of cognitive neuroscience and modern hypnosis research today the SAS model fails to provide a detailed account of cognitive control. For example the SAS performs both monitoring and control functions and the deficits caused by frontal lesions indicate the key role of anterior cortical networks in their implementation but beyond this the model has little to say as to where or how they are implemented in the anterior cortex or how these functions are related. While there are several leading accounts of cognitive control and/or the executive functions of the anterior cortex arguably the most clearly specified and empirically studied is the conflict-monitoring model developed by Cohen and associates (Cohen, Aston-Jones and Gilzenrat, 2004; Miller and Cohen, 2000). According to this model activity in task set or goal representations located in the lateral prefrontal cortex (PFC) biases competition between competing responses much as described in the SAS model. However activation in these task set representations is dynamically modulated by feedback about the level of conflict between competing response tendencies. Specifically response conflict is monitored by the dorsal Anterior Cingulate Cortex (dACC), a deep midline anterior cortical structure. As conflict between competing response tendencies rises (indicating a greater likelihood of an incorrect response or error) so does activation in the dACC which in turn triggers an increase in control related activation in lateral PFC task set representations which then brings about a flexible adjustment of top-down attentional control of competing response processes (Botvinick, Cohen and Carter, 2004).

Using this model MacDonald, Cohen, Stenger and Carter (2000) were readily able to distinguish regions of brain activation related to cognitive control from those related to conflict-monitoring using the Stroop paradigm in an fMRI scanner. They presented congruent or incongruent Stroop stimuli preceded by an instruction to name the color-word or to name the color in which the word appeared. Two different contrasts were performed. The first contrast was performed for the post instruction interval and was between the color naming instruction and the color-word naming instruction. This represented a contrast between high and low control demand conditions respectively and revealed significant activation in the left dorsolateral prefrontal cortex. The second contrast was made in the post stimulus period and was between incongruent (high response conflict) and congruent (low response conflict) stimulus events respectively. In this case conflict related activation occurred exclusively in the dACC.

The conflict-monitoring model functionally and anatomically fractionates monitoring and control functions and clearly specifies the relationship expected between them. In addition to strong experimental support from neuroimaging studies this model has largely been generated and tested around the Stroop task and similar response conflict paradigms making it an obvious choice for the further investigation of changes in cognitive control and the functional role of anterior cortical networks in hypnosis.

Egner, Jamieson and Gruzelier (2005) adopted a strategy similar to that used by MacDonald et al. (2000) in order to identify the specific mechanism of the dissociation in attentional control believed to occur in hypnosis. They conducted an event related fMRI study of high and low hypnotically susceptible participants in both hypnotized and non hypnotized conditions performing a Stroop paradigm requiring color naming or color-word naming responses to congruent and incongruent Stroop stimuli. Similarly to MacDonald et al. (2000) high versus low conflict contrasts revealed significant activations in dACC and a color naming versus color-word naming contrast identified significant activation in left inferior frontal gyrus (IFG). However when activity levels were examined in conflict related regions of interest a classic interaction effect was found between hypnotic susceptibility and hypnotic condition. Conflict related activation in dACC rose in high susceptibles in hypnosis but actually dropped in low susceptibles demonstrating reduced efficiency in the control of response conflict in hypnotized highs. There was no effect present for activation in the control related region of interest for high or low susceptibles in either hypnotized or non-hypnotized conditions. This is contrary to the expected relationship between conflict and control related activations where increased conflict detection should lead to an up regulation in control related activation. The absence of a similar pattern in the control related activation strongly suggests a breakdown of functional connectivity between conflict monitoring and control processes and their respective anterior cortical regions rather than between anterior and posterior cortex as suggested in the initial formulation of dissociated control theory.

In this study Egner et al. (2005) sought to directly assess functional connectivity between cortical regions through EEG coherence. We recorded EEG from the same participants performing the identical task under hypnotized and non-hypnotized conditions on a separate occasion away from the MRI scanner. We found that coherence in the gamma band (closely associated with the binding of discrete cortical processes into an integrated neural ensemble - see De Pascalis, 2007) declined between recording sites reflecting activity in dACC and left IFG (electrodes Fz and F3 respectively) for high susceptibles in the hypnotized condition. No such breakdown in cortical functional connectivity was observed for low susceptibles or for the homologous right hemisphere connection between Fz and F4. A similar breakdown in EEG gamma band coherence was found by Trippe, Weiss and Miltner (2004) between motor cortex and frontal cortical sites in hypnotized high susceptibles experiencing hypnotic analgesia. By comparison high and low susceptibles generating analgesia by attentional distraction (the mechanism proposed for hypnotic analgesia by proponents of the focused attention account of hypnotic phenomena) did not show this effect. Further EEG evidence (again from the high frequency gamma band) in support of a functional disconnection between and within anterior cortical regions in hypnosis has been reported by Croft, Williams, Haenschel and Gruzelier (2002) who found that the correlation between ACC sourced gamma and subjective pain experience broke down for higher susceptible individuals in the hypnosis condition.

An often overlooked finding from EEG research on cognitive control in hypnosis comes from the work of Kaiser et al. (1997) who examined averaged event related potentials (ERP's) to error responses on their Stroop type task (see discussion of their behavioral results above). These error related ERP's play an important role in the brains detection of and response to errors in task performance and have been the subject of intense investigation and theorizing from this perspective (Falkenstein, 2004). Kaiser et al. (1997) found that a later positive component the error related positivity or Pe, which appears to be closely related to the emotional experience of making an error (the so called "oh crap" response) and to the magnitude of subsequent behavioral corrections (Nieuwenhuis et al., 2001), is diminished in high susceptibles in hypnosis. However an earlier negative going component of the brains response to errors, the error related negativity or Ne, was not affected. In our most recent data on this topic, gathered in conjunction with Croft, Cleary, Hammond and Findlay, we have also found a significant reduction in the Pe in hypnotized highs and further a significant increase in the Ne in this same condition. Although significant we are currently extending our sample prior to a journal submission.

If correct this suggests two things. Firstly the finding of an increased Ne independently supports the finding of Egner et al. (2005) that hypnotized highs showed greater conflict related activation in dACC while performing the Stroop task. Both sets of results were produced from a Stroop paradigm, one utilized fMRI the other EEG, one studied correct responses the other error responses. Although controversial the account of conflict-monitoring in cognitive control has recently been powerfully extended to cover electrophysiological error responses by modeling the Ne as generated by the dACC post response detection of conflict between the intended correct response and the executed incorrect response (Van Veen and Carter, 2002). Note that due to the timing of its peak, approximately 100 milliseconds post error response, the Ne cannot be generated by feedback from the actual error response itself. If the conflict-detection account is correct then the enhanced Ne in the present findings has precisely the same functional interpretation as the increased dACC activation reported by Egner et al. (2005) that is increased dACC responsiveness to the detection of response-conflict in hypnotized high susceptibles. Secondly, the earlier unconscious Ne response is generated in dACC and the later Pe more closely associated with conscious awareness of error and corrective behavioral responses) appears to be generated in rostral ACC. Meta analyses of imaging studies strongly support a functional division between dorsal and rostral segments of the ACC with dorsal activations more closely associated with cognitive and behavioral tasks and rostral activations more closely associated with affective and motivational manipulations (Bush, Luu and Posner, 2000). It is likely then that functional connectivity from dorsal to rostral ACC plays a key role in the translation of detection of the likelihood of an error (arising from post error response conflict) into the mobilization of an adaptive change in top-down control to reduce the likelihood of error on subsequent trials. Consistent with the findings of Egner et al. (2005) it appears that the earlier monitoring part of this adaptive control circuit is intact (if anything it is hypersensitive) in hypnosis but that the later part of the control network is disrupted due to a dissociation between monitoring and control functions within and between key anterior cortical regions in hypnotized high susceptibles.

TWO MODES OF SELF-REGULATION

Over the last fifteen years the new discipline of cognitive neuroscience, which combines the new imaging technologies with the EEG, the rigorous experimental paradigms of cognitive psychology and the mathematical modeling of connectionism, has grown and flourished principally focusing on the issue of cognitive control. While there remains deep disagreement and controversy rapid progress has been made which no truly contemporary hypnosis researcher should ignore. For many traditional cognitive paradigms key components of the circuitry of cognitive control have been mapped along with their dynamic functional connectivity. Whist this circuitry is far from identical for disparate tasks there are common identifiable themes (sketched above) involving a dynamic interplay between dACC monitoring, prefrontal task set representations and top-down control of more posterior perceptual and motor control functions. Within this same time period the work described above has shown that, at least in part, important aspects of the change in mental organization which occurs in hypnosis can also be understood within this emerging theoretical framework, principally a breakdown in functional connectivity between monitoring (dACC) and control functions within the anterior cortex and the consequent effects of this on the integrated control of other brain-mind functions. However just as the seemingly discrete discipline of cognitive neuroscience has itself spilled over into the most recent development of cognitive-affective-social neuroscience so to related research in hypnosis is now pointing to the necessity for a wider integration with social and affective neuroscience in the understanding of hypnosis.

Conclusions from this work are necessarily more tentative but even at this point important new directions and the beginnings of new advances can be clearly identified. An early finding within imaging studies of effortful cognitive activity (the antithesis of the experience of hypnotic responding) was a ubiquitous activation within the dACC relative to various "control"conditions. However just as ubiquitous, but much less commented on, was a consistent deactivation of several other brain regions (including the rACC) in the same experimental contrasts. Subsequent meta analyses have shown that an identifiable network of (functionally connected) brain regions is more active in a variety of "resting state" control conditions than effortful cognitive processing (Raichle et al., 2001). That is just as there appears to be a broad pattern of functionally interconnected regions (with important common nodes) implementing effortful cognitive control there arguably appears to be a broad but systematic alternative pattern of brain activations and connections closely associated with effortless experience. These distinct functional networks are mutually inhibitory; implementation of one excludes implementation of the other. The dorsal and rostral divisions of the ACC are critical nodes in each network. Provocatively a previous meta analyses has also identified a mutually inhibitory relationship between activation in dorsal and rostral ACC in cognitive and affective paradigms respectively (Bush et al., 2000).

I have argued above that hypnosis is closely associated with a specific type of disruption to one of these principal networks. It is plausible then that hypnosis is also associated with some form of modulation of the alternative network engaged during other forms of effortless experience. Data from PET studies of hypnosis conducted by Faymonville et al. (2003) and by Rainville et al. (2002) may provide initial evidence of this wider possibility. Faymonville et al., (2003) conducted an investigation of the functional connectivity of a dACC region in which activity co-varied with the analgesic effects of hypnotic suggestions to relive a positive affective experience. They conducted a Psychophysiological Interaction (PPI) analysis which found regulatory interactions with key nodes of the "resting state" network, including rACC and regions of the posterior cingulate cortex and parietal association areas. Rainville et al. (2002) used self report ratings of the experience of absorption during a hypnosis procedure to identify a network of brain regions in which activation co-varied systematically with this experience. They also reported a network which featured rACC, posterior cingulate and parietal association cortex. The consistent nodes in the activation networks related to these additional components of hypnotic experience in both studies also appear as principal nodes in the meta analyses identifying the resting state network. Unlike with cognitive control I cannot offer a systematic theory of these findings but I suggest they are closely tied to the role of hypnosis, and what are more widely known as trance states, in psychophysiological (as distinct from cognitive) self-regulation (see also Woody and Szechtman, 2007). A recent series of neuroimaging studies conducted by Critchley and colleagues (Critchley et al., 2003; Nagai et al., 2004) have identified distinct networks of brain regions (each spanning across a range of higher cortical midbrain and brain stem structures) engaged in the regulation of phasic sympathetic nervous system activity and in the regulation of tonic parasympathetic nervous system activity. Activation in each network is mutually inhibitory and the dorsal and rostral ACC play a fundamental role in each. Critchley (2005) has himself observed the likely integration of these central networks of somatic regulation and the networks regulating active cognitive processes and resting self-focused mental states respectively.

Growing evidence for two functionally distinct, mutually inhibitory networks of cognitive, affective and somatic self-regulation bring us full circle to a psychobiological construct with deep roots in hypnosis research, that of absorption (Ott, Reuter, Hennig and Vaitl, 2005). Absorption has been found to play a critical role in the success of different psychological strategies for somatic self-regulation. Qualls and Sheehan (1981) attempted to understand the factors underlying the success (and failure) of biofeedback training. Across a series of important studies they found that individuals' level of trait absorption was a critical predictor of the success or failure of disparate self-regulation strategies. Looking at electromyograph activity (muscle tension) they found that low absorption individuals could learn to lower muscle tension through biofeedback protocols but that when instructed to use this same approach high absorption individuals not only failed but actually increased their state of muscular tension. High absorption individuals were readily able to lower muscular tension if allowed to adopt their preferred self-regulatory style of focusing their awareness on self generated inner experiences. When instructed to adopt this approach low absorption individuals failed to lower (and actually raised) their level of muscular tension. High and low absorption ability (the ability to engage in trance like experiences in daily life) is closely related to the ease and effectiveness of two very different styles (and associated strategies) of psychological and somatic self-regulation.

These findings led Tellegen (1981) away from his earlier account of absorption as strongly focused attention to a fundamental redefinition of the trait. Tellegen (1981) described experience as being organized around two discrete and mutually exclusive mental sets, the instrumental-mental-set and the experiential-mental-set. He (Tellegen, 1981, p.222) describes the instrumental set as "a state of readiness to engage in active, realistic, voluntary and effortful planning, decision making and goal directed behavior". A description which is immediately recognizable as active cognitive control implemented by the dACC, lateral PFC and posterior cortical networks described by cognitive neuroscience and known to be disrupted in high susceptibles during hypnosis.

By contrast, Tellegen described the experiential set as "a state of receptivity or openness to experiencing whatever events, sensory or imaginal [that] may occur … a tendency to dwell on rather than go beyond the experiences …[which] have a sense of effortlessness and involuntariness" (Tellegen, 1981, p. 222). He further emphasized the role of affective processes in the experiential-mental-set. Tellegen then conceptualized absorption as a predisposition, when circumstances permit, to set aside an instrumental set and adopt instead an experiential mental set. That is, from a contemporary cognitive-affective-social neuroscience perspective, he described absorption as the predisposition and ability to inhibit or disrupt one of two major patterns of neural functional connectivity, experience and self-regulatory organization and to adopt the other, a very different mode of organization with its own characteristic patterns of functional connectivity, experience and self-regulatory mechanisms.

CONCLUSION

The distinctive character of the changes in experience that accompany hypnosis (at least in high susceptibles) remain one of the most important features for hypnosis researchers to comprehensively catalogue, map and explain (Sheehan and McConkey, 1982). The mutual engagement between cognitive neuroscience and hypnosis research as outlined here has already proven most fruitful in this regard. However, the principal social role of hypnosis has always been and remains the self-regulation of psychological, psychophysiological and related somatic states. Therefore, the study of hypnosis must not only include but also extend beyond the purely psychological level of analysis. For example, recent studies have demonstrated the important role of hypnosis and hypnotic susceptibility in the self-regulation of stress-related endothelial dysfunction (Jambrik et al., 2005), ventricular arrhythmia (Taggart et al., 2005) and other elements of heart rate variability (Diamond, Davis and Howe, 2008). If continued vigor is shown by researchers and supported by funding bodies, the future collaboration of hypnosis with systems-level neuroscience research holds the great promise of uncovering the full nature of these underlying psychological, central and peripheral systems of self-regulation.

REFERENCES

Botvinick, M.M., Cohen, J.D. & Carter, C.S. (2004). Conflict monitoring and anterior cingulate cortex: an update. *Trends in Cognitive Science, 8*, 539-546.

Bush, G., Luu, P. & Posner, M. (2000). Cognitive and emotional influences in the anterior cingulate cortex. *Trends in Cognitive Sciences, 4*, 215-222.

Cohen, J.D., Aston-Jones, G. & Gilzenrat, M.S. (2004). A systems level theory of attention and cognitive control. In MI Posner ed. *Cognitive neuroscience of attention* (pp. 71–90). New York: Guilford Press.

Crawford, H.J. & Gruzelier, J.H. (1992). A midstream view of the neuropsychophysiology of hypnosis: recent research and future directions. In E Fromm and M Nash, eds. *Contemporary Hypnosis Research* (pp. 227-266). New York, Guilford Press.

Crawford, H.J., Horton, J.E., Harrington, G.S., Hirsch-Downs, T., Fox, K,, Daugherty, S. & Downs III, J.H. (2000). Attention and disattention (hypnotic analagesia) to noxious somatosensory TENS stimuli: fMRI differences in low and highly hypnotizable individuals. *NeuroImage, 11,* S44.

Critchley, H.D., Josephs, O., O'Doherty, J., Zanini, S., Dewar, B.-K., Mathias, C.J., Cipolotti, L., Shallice, T., & Dolan, R.J. (2003). Human cingulate cortex and autonomic cardiovascular control: converging neuroimaging and clinical evidence. *Brain, 216,* 2139– 2152.

Croft, R.J., Williams, J.D., Haenschel, C. & Gruzelier, J.H. (2002). Pain perception, hypnosis and 40 Hz oscillations. *International Journal of Psychophysiology, 46,* 101-108.

De Pascalis V. (2007). Phase-ordered gamma oscillations and the modulation of hypnotic experience. In G. A. Jamieson (Ed), *Hypnosis and conscious states: The cognitive neuroscience perspective* (pp. 67-89). New York: Oxford University Press.

Diamond, S.G., Davis, O.C., & Howe, R.D. (2008). **0** Heart rate variability as a quantitative measure of hypnotic depth. *International Journal of Clinical and Experimental Hypnosis, 56,* 1–18.

Egner, T., Jamieson, G., & Gruzelier, J. (2005). Hypnosis decouples cognitive control from conflict monitoring processes of the frontal lobes. *Neuroimage, 27,* 969-978.

Egner, T. & Raz, A. (2007). Cognitive control processes and hypnosis. In G. A. Jamieson (Ed), *Hypnosis and conscious states: The cognitive neuroscience perspective* (pp. 29-50). New York: Oxford University Press.

Falkenstein, M. (2004). ERP correlates of erroneous performance. In M Ullsperger and M Falkenstein, eds. *Errors, Conflicts, and the Brain. Current Opinions on Performance Monitoring,* pp.5-14. Leipzig, Max Planck Institute for Cognitive Neuroscience.

Faymonville, M.E., Roediger, L., Del Fiore, G., Delgueldre, C., Phillips, C., Lamy, M., Luxen, A., Maquet, P. & Laureys, S. (2003). Increased cerebral functional connectivity underlying the antinociceptive effects of hypnosis. *Cognitive Brain Research, 17,* 255 – 262.

Gruzelier, J. (1998). A working model of the neurophysiology of hypnosis: A review of evidence. *Contemporary Hypnosis, 15,* 5-23.

Gruzelier, J. & Warren, K. (1993). Neuropsychological evidence of reductions on left frontal tests with hypnosis. *Psychological Medicine, 23,* 93-101.

Hilgard, J.R. (1974). Imaginative involvement: Some characteristics of the highly hypnotizable and the nonhypnotisable. *International Journal of Clinical and Experimental Hypnosis, 22,* 138-156.

Ishii, R., Shinosaki, K., Ukai, S., et al. (1999). Medial prefrontal cortex generates frontal midline theta rhythm. *Neuroreport, 10,* 675–679.

Jambrik, Z., Sebastiani, L., Picano, E., Ghelarducci, B. & Santarcangelo, E.L. (2005). Hypnotic modulation of flow-mediated endothelial response to mental stress. *International Journal of Psychophysiology, 55,* 221– 227

Jamieson, G.A. & Sheehan, P.W. (2004). An empirical test of Woody and Bower's dissociated control theory of hypnosis. *International Journal of Clinical and Experimental Hypnosis, 52,* 232-249.

Kaiser, J., Barker, R., Haenschel, C., Baldeweg, T. & Gruzelier, J. H. (1997). Hypnosis and event related potential correlates of error processing in a stroop- type paradigm: A test of the frontal hypothesis. *International Journal of Psychophysiology, 27,* 215-222.

MacLeod, C.M & MacDonald, P.A. (2000). Interdimensional interference in the Stroop effect: uncovering the cognitive and neural anatomy of attention. *Trends in Cognitive Sciences, 4,* 383-391.

MacDonald, A.W., Cohen, J. D., Stenger, V. A. & Carter, C. S. (2000) Dissociating the role of dorso-lateral prefrontal cortex and anterior cingulate cortex in cognitive control. *Science, 288,* 1835-1838.

Miller, E.K. & Cohen, J.D. (2001). An integrative theory of prefrontal cortex function. *Annual Review of Neuroscience, 24,* 167-202.

Nagai, Y., Critchley, H.D., Featherstone, E., Trimble, M.R. & Dolan, R.J. (2004). Activity in ventromedial prefrontal cortex covaries with sympathetic skin conductance level: a physiological account of a "default mode" of brain function. *Neuroimage, 22,* 243–251.

Nieuwenhuis, S., Ridderinkhof, K.R., Blom, J.B., Blom, G.P. & Kok, A. (2001). Error-related brain potentials are differentially related to awareness of response errors: evidence from an antisaccade task. *Psychophysiology, 38,* 752-760.

Nordby, H., Hugdhal, K., Jasiukaitis, P. & Spiegel, D. (1999). Effects of hypnotizability on performance of a Stroop task and event –related potentials. *Perceptual and Motor Skills, 88,* 819-830.

Norman, D.A. & Shallice, T. (1986). Attention to action: Willed and automatic control of behaviour. In R. J. Davidson, G.E. Schwartz, & D. Shapiro (Eds.) *Consciousness and self-regulation, Vol.4* (pp. 1-18). New York: Plenum Press.

Ott, U., Reuter, M., Hennig, J. & Vaitl, D. (2005). Evidence for a common biological basis of the Absorption trait, hallucinogen effects, and positive symptoms: Epistasis between 5-HT2a and COMT polymorphisms. *American Journal of Medical Genetics (Neuropsychiatric Genetics), 137B,* 29-32.

Raichle, M.E., MacLeod, A.M., Snyder, A.Z., Powers, W.J., Gusnard, D.A. & Shulman, G.L. (2001). A default mode of brain function. *Proceedings of the National Academy of Sciences U S A, 98,* 676–682.

Rainville, P., Hofbauer, R.K., Bushnell, M.C., Duncan, G.H. & Price, D.D. (2002). Hypnosis modulates activity in brain structures involved in the regulation of consciousness. *Journal of Cognitive Neuroscience, 14,* 887-901.

Ray, W.J. (1997). EEG concomitants of hypnotic susceptibility. *International Journal of Clinical and Experimental Hypnosis, 45,* 301-313.

Raz A, Shapiro T, Fan J and Posner MI (2002). Hypnotic suggestion and the modulation of Stroop interference. *Archives of General Psychiatry, 59,* 1155-1161.

Raz, A., Kirsch, I., Pollard, J., & Nitkin-Kaner, Y. (2006). Suggestion Reduces the Stroop Effect. *Psychological Science, 17,* 91-95.

Sheehan, P. W., Donovan, P. B., & MacLeod, C. M. (1988). Strategy manipulation and the stroop effect in hypnosis. *Journal of Abnormal Psychology, 97,* 455-460.

Sheehan, P.W. & McConkey, K.M. (1982). *Hypnosis and experience: the exploration of phenomena and process.* Hillsdale N.J., Erlbaum.

Shor, R.E. (1959). Hypnosis and the concept of generalized reality orientation. *American Journal of Psychotherapy, 13,* 582-602.

Stroop, J. (1935). Studies of interference in verbal reactions. *Journal of Experimental Psychology, 18,* 643-661.

Taggart P., Sutton, P., Redfern, C., Batchvarov, V.N., Hnatkova, K., Malik, M., James, U., & Joseph, A. (2005). The Effect of Mental Stress on the Non-Dipolar Components of the T Wave: Modulation by Hypnosis. *Psychosomatic Medicine, 67,* 376–383.

Tellegen, A. (1981). Practicing the two disciplines for relaxation and enlightenment: Comment on 'Role of the feedback signal in electromyograph biofeedback: The relevance of attention' by Qualls and Sheehan. *Journal of Experimental Psychology: General, 110,* 217-226.

Tellegen, A., & Atkinson, G. (1974). Openness to absorbing and self-altering experiences: Absorption, a trait related to hypnotic susceptibility. *Journal of Abnormal Psychology, 83,* 268-277.

Trippe, R.H., Weiss, T., & Miltner, W.H.R. (2004). Hypnotisch-induzierte Analgesie - Mechanismen. *Anästhesiologie & Intensivmedizin, 45,* 642-647.

Van Veen, V. & Carter, C.S. (2002). The timing of action-monitoring processes in the anterior cingulate cortex. *Journal of Cognitive Neuroscience, 14,* 593-602.

Weitzenhoffer, A.M. (1953). *Hypnotism: An objective study in suggestibility.* New York, Grune and Stratton.

Woody, E. & Bowers, K. (1994). A frontal assault on dissociated control. In S. J. Lynn & J. W. Rhue (Eds.), *Dissociation: Clinical and theoretical perspectives* (pp. 52-79). New York: Guilford.

Woody, E. & Szechtman, H. (2007). To See Feelingly: Emotion, Motivation, and Hypnosis. In G. A. Jamieson (Ed), *Hypnosis and conscious states: The cognitive neuroscience perspective* (pp. 241-255). New York: Oxford University Press.

Reviewed by Professor Adrian P. Burgess, Department of Psychology, Aston University, Birmingham UK, and by Dr Nick Cooper, University of Essex, Colchester, UK.

INDEX

A

absorption, x, 169, 170, 176, 177, 178
abstraction, 64, 151
abuse, 149, 152
academic, 105, 116, 130, 164
ACC, 174, 175, 176, 177
access, 9, 19, 20, 77, 112, 113, 156, 170, 172
accounting, 3, 5, 11
activation, 171, 172, 173, 174, 175, 176, 177
adaptation, 1, 7, 8, 9, 25, 26, 31, 32, 35, 79, 85, 103, 134, 154, 155
adaptive functioning, 148, 153
ADHD, 162
adjustment, 35, 56, 101, 105, 114, 119, 173
adolescent, 36, 79, 96, 98, 109, 116, 118, 134, 148, 150, 152, 153, 161, 162, 163, 166, 167
adulthood, 26, 150, 155, 165
adults, viii, 61, 63, 109, 114, 166
affective experience, 176
affective meaning, 155
age, 11, 24, 25, 88, 92, 106, 108, 155, 159
aggression, 104, 106, 116, 150, 152, 163, 166
aggressiveness, 63, 72, 74, 163
alcohol, 36, 99, 104, 152, 153, 164
alternative, 176
analgesia, x, 169, 171, 174
anger, 21, 28, 29, 30, 115, 152, 163
anterior cingulate cortex, 178, 180, 181
antisocial, ix, 147, 148, 149, 150, 152, 155, 156, 157, 159, 160, 161, 163, 165
anxiety, 2, 23, 25, 36, 63, 72, 74, 104, 131, 132, 133, 150, 162
appraisals, 3, 4, 27
Aristotle, 129, 144
arrest, 148, 163
arrhythmia, 178
asocial, 149

assault, 148, 157, 181
assessment, viii, 58, 83, 88, 142, 143
assets, vii, 1, 2, 3, 5, 8, 9, 10, 11, 12, 13, 14, 15, 17, 20, 23, 24, 25, 31, 32
athletes, 134, 143, 144
attachment, 65, 150, 151
attribution, 51, 52, 53, 55
Australia, 169
authority, 20, 21, 28, 30, 64, 65, 76, 159
automatic processes, 123
automaticity, 127, 128
autonomy, 8, 18, 20, 25, 35, 71, 78, 131, 134, 137, 138, 139, 140
avoidance, 22, 72, 130, 132, 133, 134, 136, 137, 138, 139, 142, 143
awareness, vii, 2, 4, 16, 18, 19, 20, 21, 22, 23, 24, 26, 29, 31, 32, 34, 57, 69, 74, 126, 153, 170, 175, 177, 180

B

background information, 4
barriers, 112, 113
beer, 2
behavior, viii, x, 3, 4, 39, 41, 42, 44, 46, 47, 49, 50, 83, 84, 85, 86, 87, 88, 89, 90, 92, 93, 95, 96, 97, 98, 100, 130, 132, 147, 152, 153, 162, 169, 177
behavioral change, 33, 44, 55
behavioral dimension, 152
behavioral sciences, 100
beneficial effect, 8, 22, 52
benefits, 22, 85, 114, 151
bias, 31, 51, 53, 54, 171, 172
biofeedback, x, 169, 177, 181
blindness, 65
blood, 25, 45
bonds, 127, 149, 150, 151
borderline personality disorder, 117

boredom, ix, 129, 133, 135, 139, 141, 142, 163
brain, x, 10, 34, 166, 169, 173, 176, 177, 180
breakdown, 174, 176
bullying, 114
buttons, 40, 49

C

cannabis, viii, 83, 88, 89, 90, 92, 93, 94, 95, 96, 98
capacity, x, 169
carbon, 66
case study, 11, 15, 28, 29, 30, 31
catalyst, 26, 29
categorization, 151, 162, 164
category b, 13
Caucasians, 133
causal relationship, 51, 117
causality, 53, 97
causation, 44, 56
CDC, 47
cerebral function, 179
challenges, 24, 27, 42, 108, 119, 127, 153
Chicago, 33, 34, 100
child abuse, 149
child maltreatment, 118, 163
child rearing, 119, 149, 161
childcare, 106, 114
childhood, ix, 26, 35, 36, 103, 104, 108, 113, 114,
    116, 117, 119, 150, 155, 165
children, ix, 7, 20, 22, 36, 103, 104, 106, 107, 108,
    109, 110, 111, 114, 115, 118, 119, 135, 148, 149,
    150, 153, 154, 161, 164
China, 40, 165
clarity, 29, 101, 107
classes, 71, 75, 88, 143, 144, 145
classification, 56, 64
classroom, 16, 28, 88, 142, 144
climate, vii, ix, 37, 129, 131, 132, 133, 134, 137,
    138, 139, 140, 141, 142, 143, 144, 145
clinical application, 104
clinical assessment, 166
clinical psychology, 112
cognition, 3, 9, 36, 47, 58, 69, 127, 128, 155, 160,
    165
cognitive, x, 169, 173, 174, 175, 176, 177, 178, 179,
    180, 181
cognitive dissonance, 27, 28, 29
cognitive effort, 132
cognitive function, 3, 62
cognitive performance, 58
cognitive perspective, 10, 32, 34, 36, 145
cognitive process, vii, viii, 2, 3, 4, 5, 9, 14, 45, 47,
    61, 62, 125, 155, 176, 177

cognitive psychology, 39, 48, 176
cognitive skills, 130
cognitive theory, 55, 105, 116
coherence, 66, 75, 86, 112, 174
collaboration, 78, 178
color, 171, 172, 173, 174
communication, 15, 49, 63, 68, 72, 73, 79, 118, 154,
    155, 166, 170
community, x, 62, 63, 66, 70, 106, 107, 147, 150,
    155, 162
comparative analysis, 116
Comparative Fit Index (CFI), 157, 161
competition, 51, 75, 170, 172, 173
complement, 43, 66
complexity, 19, 51, 58, 66, 70
components, 176, 177
conceptualization, 7, 10, 32
conditioning, 69
conflict, x, 7, 29, 30, 41, 50, 169, 172, 173, 174, 175,
    179
confrontation, 21, 73
congruence, 113, 140
connectivity, 171, 174, 175, 176, 178, 179
conscious awareness, 123, 170, 175
consciousness, ix, 4, 32, 58, 65, 121, 122, 123, 124,
    125, 126, 128, 180
construct validity, 156, 159
construction, 35, 77, 89
consumption, 84, 90
contingency, 51, 54, 127, 132
control, x, 169, 170, 171, 172, 173, 174, 175, 176,
    177, 178, 179, 180, 181
control condition, 176
control group, 71, 155, 156
controversial, 41, 62, 80, 175
conviction, 43
cooperation, 19, 75
cooperative learning, 131, 134, 137, 138, 139, 140,
    141, 143, 144
coping strategies, 4, 6, 35, 97, 153
correlation, 99, 100, 135, 136, 174
correlation analysis, 99, 100
cortex, 173, 174, 176, 178, 179, 180, 181
cost, 57, 115, 127, 151
counterbalance, 3, 10
craving, 152, 162
criminal acts, 148, 150, 151
criminal behavior, 117, 149, 150, 151, 160, 161
criminality, 151, 164, 165
critical period, 114
critical thinking, 62, 76
criticism, 64, 66, 118
CRP, 79

cues, 4, 6, 27, 28, 40, 103

D

danger, 27, 66, 150, 155
decision making, 24, 25, 85, 177
deficit, 74, 166, 173
delinquency, ix, 117, 119, 147, 148, 149, 150, 151, 152, 153, 161, 163, 164, 165, 166
delinquent behavior, x, 147, 160, 163
delinquent group, 155
demographic data, 157
depression, 2, 28, 30, 55, 63, 72, 74, 104, 118, 150
depth, 10, 14, 15, 17, 22, 31, 32, 123, 179
Diamond, 178, 179
dimensionality, 152
disorder, 3, 27
dissatisfaction, 8, 44, 77
dissociation, 171, 174, 175
distortions, x, 169
distress, 9, 25, 153
dorsolateral prefrontal cortex, 173
double bonds, 66
dream, 66
drug addict, 73
drug consumption, 152
drug treatment, 38
drugs, 101, 152
duality, 33, 65

E

education, viii, ix, 35, 61, 62, 71, 74, 75, 76, 80, 88, 104, 129, 130, 131, 134, 139, 140, 141, 142, 144, 145, 151
educational objective, 77
educational practices, 75, 78
educational settings, vii, 2
educational system, 70
educators, 140, 141, 144
elaboration, viii, 5, 61, 132
electroencephalogram (EEG), x, 169, 171, 174, 175, 180
electromyograph, 177, 181
e-mail, 2, 61
emotion, 19, 20, 28, 33, 36, 109, 133, 153, 154, 155, 158, 160, 162, 163, 164, 165, 167
emotion regulation, 154, 167
emotional, 175, 178
emotional disorder, 1, 3, 4, 5, 6, 7, 27, 36
emotional dispositions, 154
emotional experience, 153, 175
emotional intelligence, 10
emotional problems, 106, 116, 118, 119
emotional processes, 2, 10, 12
emotional reactions, 71, 153, 155
emotional stability, 160
emotional state, 7, 69, 153, 154, 155
emotional well-being, 117
empathy, 75, 105, 153
employment, 24, 30, 114
endothelial dysfunction, 178
energy, 18, 124
England, 119, 148, 169
environment, vii, 8, 37, 38, 39, 40, 41, 42, 43, 44, 45, 46, 47, 48, 49, 50, 51, 53, 54, 56, 59, 67, 69, 71, 97, 107, 118, 131, 132, 148, 149, 154, 170
environmental factors, ix, 48, 147, 151
environmental resources, 130
environmental stimuli, 7, 108, 122, 153
epistemology, 63, 70, 75, 81
equilibrium, 1, 10
equipment, 20
everyday life, 75, 127
evidence-based practices, 112
evolution, 58, 67, 76
exclusion, 75, 170
execution, ix, 38, 50, 104, 121, 122
executive function, 173
exercise, 33, 84, 101, 106, 118, 140, 142, 143, 145
exertion, 84
expertise, 39, 46
exploitation, 50
exposure, 7, 9, 46, 86
expressivity, 8, 23
extinction, 27, 28, 30
extraversion, 152
extrinsic motivation, 132, 141, 142, 143, 145

F

facial expression, 155, 164
factor analysis, 156
failure, 177
families, 112, 114, 118, 150
family relationships, 74, 105
family support, 106, 117, 118
family violence, 149
fanaticism, 65
FBI, 148
fear, 16, 28, 73, 75, 151
fears, 8, 65, 68
feedback, 173, 175, 181
feelings, 12, 16, 23, 28, 65, 67, 68, 70, 71, 72, 73, 74, 84, 86, 130, 132, 133, 153, 158

fertilizers, vii, 37
financial, 20, 21, 41, 56, 113
flexibility, 6, 8, 9, 18, 24, 27, 48, 117, 153
flow, 172, 179
fluctuations, 45, 48, 49
fMRI, 173, 174, 175, 179
focusing, 170, 176, 177
force, 26, 56
formation, 66, 78, 79, 80, 121, 122, 126, 141, 142
foundations, 35, 108, 116
Fox, 179
framing, 98, 101
France, 61, 72, 74, 75, 76, 80, 83, 88
free choice, 14, 32
freedom, 64, 65
frontal cortex, 50
frontal lobe, 10, 179
future orientation, 86, 96, 97, 101, 102

G

gambling, 51, 53
general education, ix, 129, 130
generalizability, 59
generalized anxiety disorder, 3
generation, 171
genes, 106
goal attainment, 29, 30, 55, 105
goal directedness, 105
goal setting, 6, 8, 17, 19, 20, 29, 30, 39, 43, 56, 58,
    112, 114, 115, 141
goal-directed behavior,
goals, 170
government expenditure, 114
grades, ix, 119, 129
Greece, ix, 129, 132, 133, 144, 145
Greeks, 64
growth, 7, 9, 131
guidance, 25, 109, 111
guidelines, 12, 34, 89, 113, 141

H

happiness, 26, 54, 104
health, ix, 8, 24, 25, 26, 29, 32, 34, 36, 84, 85, 86,
    87, 96, 98, 99, 100, 101, 103, 104, 106, 113, 115,
    117, 153
health care, 106
health problems, 104
health promotion, 96
health psychology, 100
heart, 178, 179

helplessness, 55, 73
high school, viii, ix, 70, 71, 83, 88, 129, 132, 135,
    156
history, 42, 66, 70, 78, 149
HIV, 25
homeostasis, 29, 154
homework, 109, 159
host, vii, 37, 121
human, 32, 33, 42, 45, 56, 57, 59, 64, 66, 111, 113,
    123, 130, 131, 149, 151, 154
husband, 20, 21
hyperactivity, 153, 167
hypersensitive, 175
hypnosis, x, 169, 170, 171, 172, 173, 174, 175, 176,
    177, 178, 179, 180
hypnotic, x, 169, 170, 171, 172, 174, 176, 178, 179,
    180, 181
hypothesis, 8, 10, 26, 32, 40, 55, 63, 66, 71, 73, 85,
    86, 96, 97, 104, 128, 133, 139, 140, 151, 163, 180

I

ideal, 65, 130
identification, 12, 34, 132, 151, 162
illegal drug use, 99
illusion, viii, 37, 38, 51, 53, 54, 55, 57, 59, 127
image, 53, 62
imagery, 58, 128
imaging, 175, 176
immediate gratification, 152
immune function, 34
immune system, 8
implementation, 173, 176
imprisonment, 150, 165
improvements, 106, 114
impulses, 84, 152, 160
impulsive, 27, 28, 29, 72, 123, 148, 152, 160, 166
impulsiveness, 31, 163
impulsivity, x, 84, 97, 147, 152, 153, 157, 158, 160,
    162, 163, 165, 167
inattention, 48, 152, 153
income, 104, 108
independence, 107, 155
independent variable, 137, 139
indirect effect, 93, 101, 157
individual differences, 28, 101, 170
individuals, ix, 3, 4, 5, 6, 7, 8, 25, 27, 29, 31, 32, 36,
    43, 45, 52, 53, 69, 84, 85, 86, 89, 95, 103, 105,
    130, 131, 132, 149, 150, 151, 153, 155, 160, 171,
    172, 174, 177, 179
inferior frontal gyrus (IFG), 174
information processing, 2, 4, 74
informed consent, 11, 135

infrastructure, 114, 117
inhibition, 149, 167, 172
inhibitory, x, 169, 176, 177
injury, 148, 164
insecurity, 26
institutions, 150, 161, 162
integration, 9, 36, 56, 115, 122, 125, 126, 127, 176, 177
integrity, 27, 72, 131
intelligence, 9, 66
intentionality, 65
interaction, 172, 174, 176
interaction effect, 88, 93, 95, 174
interference, 172, 180, 181
internal consistency, 33, 88, 134, 135, 141, 157
internal mechanisms, 48
internalization, 150, 151
interpersonal relations, 8, 9, 62, 71, 78, 104
interpersonal skills, 107, 114
intervention, viii, ix, 2, 38, 50, 57, 83, 96, 97, 103, 104, 105, 106, 107, 109, 111, 113, 114, 115, 118, 119, 130, 142
intrinsic motivation, 9, 16, 18, 19, 24, 30, 35, 132, 133, 134, 137, 139, 141, 144
investment, vii, 37, 142
Ireland, 121
isolation, 30
Israel, 148
issues, 21, 62, 80, 87, 97, 100

J

junior high school, 132, 133
juvenile delinquency, vii, x, 148, 149, 150, 151
juvenile delinquents, x, 147, 155
juveniles, 148, 151, 156

L

lead, viii, 42, 43, 44, 46, 47, 50, 61, 66, 84, 87, 96, 97, 98, 112, 141, 170, 174
learners, vii, 2
learning environment, 38, 47, 48, 49, 54, 130, 141
learning process, ix, 39, 75, 77, 129, 130, 141
learning task, 38, 46, 47
leisure, 8, 142, 151
lesions, 172, 173
lifetime, 16, 90
light, 1, 5, 8, 10, 19, 20, 21, 24, 26, 27, 30, 40, 41, 51, 52, 62, 66, 125
likelihood, 173, 175
linear model, 118

living conditions, 96
loci, x, 169
locus, 9, 40, 52, 55, 59, 90, 100
longitudinal study, 59, 135, 149, 152, 165

M

magnitude, 17, 30, 50, 55, 175
major depressive disorder, 3
majority, 2, 4, 14, 30, 66, 122
management, 33, 43, 47, 55, 105, 107, 112, 113, 114, 117, 118, 130
mapping, 170
marijuana, 166
measurement, 57, 98, 100, 125, 143, 165, 170
media, 69, 113, 114, 162
mediation, 73, 90, 155
medical, vii, 37
memory, 16, 40, 56, 118, 122, 127, 128, 169
mental activity, x, 70, 71, 169, 172
mental health, 29, 34, 104
mentoring, 16
meta-analysis, 58, 102, 117, 118, 165
metacognition, vii, 2, 3, 4, 19, 20, 41, 58, 143
metacognitive skills, 57
methodology, 70, 101
Mexico, 147, 148
midbrain, 177
minors, 155, 156, 161
mission, 74, 78, 113
modeling, 57, 65, 68, 69, 175, 176
models, viii, x, 2, 3, 31, 61, 67, 74, 87, 90, 97, 98, 101, 148, 161, 162, 171
moderators, 58, 86, 101
modulation, 176, 179, 180
momentum, 123, 125
moral development, 105, 116
morality, 116
motion sickness, 11, 19
motivation, 9, 16, 17, 19, 22, 23, 29, 30, 43, 44, 54, 55, 56, 58, 62, 72, 84, 87, 90, 127, 130, 131, 132, 133, 134, 137, 138, 139, 140, 141, 142, 143, 144, 154, 164, 165
motor control, 123, 176
MRI, 174
multiple regression, 93, 94, 99, 100
muscles, 69, 124

N

naming, 68, 72, 172, 173, 174
National Academy of Sciences, 180

negative effects, 140, 141
negative emotions, 5, 7, 10, 20, 28, 32, 36, 153, 161
negative outcomes, 52, 131
negative relation, 93, 95, 149
negotiating, 21, 110
nervous system, 177
network, x, 169, 171, 175, 176
neural function, 178
neural network, x, 169, 170
neurobiology, 163
neuroimaging, x, 169, 173, 177, 179
neurophysiology, 179
neuroscience, x, 123, 169, 173, 175, 177, 178, 179, 181
neutral, 29, 133, 142
New England, 169
New York, 178, 179, 180, 181
New Zealand, 117
NFI, 161
nodes, 176
nonconscious, ix, 84, 86, 121, 122, 123, 124, 126, 127
Non-Normed Fit Index (NNFI), 157, 161
Nuevo León, 147, 165

O

objective reality, x, 169
objectivity, 62, 65, 67, 70
obsessive-compulsive disorder (OCD), 3, 6
obstacles, 9, 19, 27, 28, 30, 32, 111, 114
open-mindedness, 65, 67, 70
operations, 4, 24, 25, 124
opportunities, 7, 19, 131, 141
optimal resource allocation, 23
optimism, 2, 8, 17, 33, 101, 111
optimists, 9, 20
organism, 42, 154
organization, 176, 178
organizational behavior, 33, 34

P

pain, 149, 174
parasympathetic nervous system, 177
parenting, vii, ix, 99, 103, 104, 105, 106, 107, 109, 110, 111, 112, 113, 114, 115, 117, 118, 119, 149, 154
parents, 24, 25, 32, 104, 105, 106, 107, 109, 110, 111, 112, 114, 115, 118, 135, 149, 150, 156

participants, x, 1, 2, 10, 11, 12, 14, 19, 27, 31, 32, 33, 50, 52, 53, 88, 89, 107, 113, 115, 122, 124, 125, 131, 147, 155, 156, 157, 171, 172, 174
pathology, 119, 152
pathways, 96, 98, 172
perceived control, 55, 56, 89, 92, 93
perceived self-efficacy, 47
perception, 179
perceptions of control, 99
performance, 171, 172, 175, 179, 180
permission, 11, 20, 22, 28, 30, 159
personal, x, 169
personal control, ix, 9, 24, 103
personal goals, 7, 130
personality, 1, 2, 3, 5, 10, 11, 12, 15, 17, 18, 19, 20, 21, 22, 23, 25, 32, 35, 36, 56, 100, 101, 152, 162, 163, 167, 170
personality constructs, 12, 19
personality factors, 1, 10, 17, 19, 22, 32
personality traits, 35, 101, 152
PET, 171, 176
PFC, 173, 177
phenomenology, 58, 65, 76
physical activity, 142, 145
physical aggression, 162
physical education, ix, 129, 130, 131, 132, 133, 134, 135, 139, 140, 141, 142, 143, 144, 145
physical health, 108
physical well-being, 8
physics, 75, 78, 143
physiological, 180
physiological correlates, 163
physiology, x, 169
playing, 51, 135, 174, 177
pleasure, 19, 87, 89, 132, 141, 149, 160
police, 148, 150
policy, 104, 112, 113, 119
polymorphisms, 180
population, 33, 87, 91, 100, 113, 114, 115, 118, 119, 155
positive emotions, 2, 8, 9, 10, 22, 25, 27, 28, 36, 153
positive mood, 16
positive relationship, 171
positivism, 65, 76
posterior cortex, 174
power, 171
power plants, vii, 37, 38
PPI, 176
preadolescents, 162
precedent, 151
predictability, 39, 49
prediction models, 87
predictive validities, 90

predictive validity, 144
prefrontal cortex (PFC), 173, 179, 180
preparation, 11, 16, 17, 22, 23, 118
preschool, 117, 119
preschoolers, 114, 166
prevention, viii, 52, 72, 76, 83, 90, 98, 109, 118, 150, 164
primacy, 165, 167
primary school, 62, 70, 74
priming, 1, 10, 12, 31, 123, 126, 127, 128
principles, ix, 34, 58, 103, 107, 110, 111, 112, 113, 115
prior knowledge, 40
probability, 41, 51, 166
problem behavior, 86
problem solving, 7, 8, 9, 27, 28, 29, 40, 44, 55, 58, 59, 104, 107, 109, 118
problem-focused coping, 21
production, 171
professionals, 11, 73
project, 11, 12, 14, 15, 17, 18, 19, 20, 31, 54, 67, 69, 74
property crimes, 149, 157
proposition, 28, 42
protective factors, 5, 8
protective mechanisms, 35
protective role, 96
protocols, 177
psychiatry, 3
psychological phenomena, 38
psychological processes, 44
psychological stress, 33
psychological well-being, 1, 5, 29, 32
psychologist, 162, 165, 167
psychology, vii, 1, 3, 15, 31, 33, 34, 35, 45, 58, 63, 84, 99, 101, 104, 116, 128, 143, 145, 164, 171, 176
psychometric properties, 100, 134, 144
psychopathology, vii, 2, 3, 118, 150
psychosocial interventions, 116
Psychosomatic, 181
psychoticism, 152
public health, 114, 117, 118
public safety, 117
punishment, 131, 132, 133, 134, 138, 150

Q

Queensland, 103
questioning, 68
questionnaire, 36, 88, 89, 98, 135

R

range, 170, 177
reaction time, 171, 172
reactions, 71, 72, 123, 181
reactivity, x, 147, 149, 153
reading, 166, 172
real estate, vii, 37
reality, x, 6, 29, 65, 66, 77, 124, 169, 170, 180
reasoning, 62, 65, 75
recall, 1, 12, 19, 31
recognition, 12, 29, 57, 121, 126, 131, 133, 134, 136, 137, 138, 139, 140, 149, 150
reduction, 171, 175
regression, ix, 90, 92, 93, 129, 137, 139
regulation, x, 129, 133, 134, 137, 138, 139, 141, 142, 169, 174, 175, 177, 178, 180
reinforcement, 35
relationship, 114, 171, 173, 174, 176
relaxation, 181
relevance, 8, 13, 19, 32, 112, 181
reliability, 40, 43, 66, 88, 92, 134, 135
relief, 27, 28
reputation, 74, 151
requirements, 28, 148, 153, 160
research, 173, 174, 176, 177, 178
researchers, 4, 19, 62, 66, 88, 107, 113, 115, 152, 154, 155, 170, 171, 178
resilience, vii, 2, 5, 7, 8, 9, 10, 13, 14, 15, 17, 18, 19, 22, 24, 25, 26, 31, 34, 35, 36, 106
resource allocation, 57, 59
resources, vii, 3, 5, 7, 8, 10, 12, 18, 27, 31, 41, 62, 85, 97, 99, 101, 106, 113, 128, 132, 170, 172
response, 11, 31, 42, 50, 88, 90, 103, 130, 152, 154, 155, 156, 157, 170, 171, 172, 173, 174, 175, 179, 180
responsiveness, 153, 175
restructuring, 6, 7, 8
rewards, 132, 151, 154, 155
risk, x, 5, 7, 9, 10, 15, 17, 25, 30, 84, 85, 86, 87, 96, 97, 98, 99, 147, 148, 149, 150, 151, 152, 153, 157, 159, 160, 163, 166
RMSEA, 157, 161
root, 98, 118, 177, 157
routines, 6, 7, 127
rules, 40, 66, 77, 150, 151

S

sample, 172, 175
SAS, 170, 171, 172, 173
scheduling, 170, 171

schema, vii, 3, 4, 5, 24, 170, 172
school, viii, 25, 26, 61, 62, 63, 64, 69, 71, 72, 74, 75, 78, 88, 108, 110, 114, 119, 130, 133, 135, 144, 145, 150, 153, 156, 157, 162
school learning, viii, 61, 63
science, 18, 34, 62, 64, 65, 66, 67, 70, 76, 78, 80, 81
scoliosis, 11, 24, 25
scope, 6, 10, 13, 32, 123, 124
secondary schools, ix, 129
Self, 169, 175
self-assessment, 42, 43, 77
self-awareness, 4, 13, 19, 26, 28, 29, 32
self-confidence, 23
self-consciousness, 27
self-control, vii, viii, x, 29, 73, 83, 84, 85, 86, 87, 97, 99, 101, 102, 104, 108, 116, 117, 118, 119, 128, 147, 148, 149, 150, 151, 152, 155, 157, 159, 160, 161, 162, 163, 164, 167
self-efficacy, 8, 9, 16, 17, 18, 24, 29, 36, 38, 43, 44, 45, 55, 56, 59, 106, 115, 119
self-evaluations, 108
self-knowledge, 6
self-monitoring, 38, 39, 41, 46, 47, 50, 51, 54, 105, 114, 115, 130
self-presentation, 97
self-reflection, 18
self-reports, 145
self-schemata, 6
self-sufficiency, 106
semi-structured interviews, 10
sensation, x, 73, 86, 87, 132, 147, 152, 153, 157, 163, 167
sensitivity, 132
series, 170, 172, 177
service provider, 107, 115
services, 106, 112, 113
sexual abuse, 165, 166
showing, 40, 86, 87, 92, 93, 109, 140, 154
sibling, 107, 109
signals, 40, 44, 155
simulation, 55
skill acquisition, 59
skin conductance, 180
slavery, 66
smoking, 36, 101, 152, 153, 164
smoothing, 20
social behavior, vii, 128, 155
social behaviour, 62, 104, 113, 115
social class, 101, 108
social cognition, 47, 54, 127
social comparison, 9
social competence, 105
social context, 21, 32, 97, 98

social control, 150, 151
social desirability, 90, 97, 101
social development, 35, 144
social environment, 3, 32, 97, 105, 154
social group, 155
social identity, 151
social inequalities, 98
social influence, 109, 162, 166
social insecurity, 97
social interactions, 32
social learning, 21, 32, 105, 111, 115
social life, 63, 160
social network, 8, 106
social norms, 9, 98, 149, 150, 151
social problems, 73, 104
social psychology, 39, 56, 57, 98
social relations, 9
social status, 151
social structure, 98
social support, 5, 8, 23, 32
social workers, 162
socialization, 72, 75, 154
society, 62, 65, 69, 75, 115, 148, 150, 151
socioeconomic status, 98, 100
Socrates, 64
solution, 29, 162
somatosensory, 179
species, 151, 154
speech, 64, 65
stability, 5, 15, 17, 31, 32, 48, 62, 72
stabilization, viii, 61, 68
standard deviation, 91, 157, 159
state, 3, 4, 6, 7, 16, 29, 39, 43, 44, 45, 48, 52, 53, 67, 78, 97, 108, 126, 131, 141, 154, 155, 170, 176, 177, 178, 179, 181
statistics, 66, 135, 136, 157, 158, 159
stigma, 150
stigmatized, 25
stimulus, 9, 77, 123, 154, 155, 156, 171, 173
stress, 2, 5, 6, 8, 9, 25, 27, 33, 34, 48, 85, 102, 132, 150, 178, 179
structural equation modeling, x, 147
structure, 3, 40, 59, 66, 80, 98, 112, 135, 152, 165, 173
style, 16, 29, 63, 177
subjective, 45, 46, 47, 48, 49, 54, 174
subjectivity, 62, 65, 66, 67, 68, 71, 76, 98
substance abuse, vii, 108, 152, 153, 163
substance use, viii, 83, 84, 85, 86, 87, 88, 89, 91, 96, 98, 101, 102
substrates, 128
supervision, 112, 113, 117, 149, 150, 151, 161, 162
supervisor, 30, 112

survival, 144, 154
susceptibility, 51, 170, 172, 174, 178, 180, 181
Switzerland, 72, 74, 75, 76
synthesis, 116, 172
systemic lupus erythematosus, 102
systems, 170, 172, 178

T

tactics, 17, 56
target, 42, 43, 47, 50, 96, 105, 111, 114, 124
task conditions, 51
task demands, 42
task difficulty, 56
task performance, 56, 57, 58, 84, 124, 127, 175
TBP, 92
teacher thinking, 81
teacher training, 74, 75, 78
teachers, viii, 61, 62, 63, 70, 72, 73, 74, 75, 76, 77, 78, 104, 142, 162
teaching experience, 15
techniques, 1, 64, 78
technology, 114, 119, 175
tension, 8, 69, 177
testing, 40, 66, 69, 75, 86, 90, 125, 161
theory, x, 169, 170, 174, 177, 178, 179, 180
therapeutic relationship, 73
therapist, 106, 112
therapy, 104, 115, 117, 118
theta, 171, 179
think critically, 62
thoughts, viii, 3, 4, 6, 9, 12, 13, 27, 28, 29, 61, 62, 63, 66, 69, 70, 84, 121, 124, 127, 130, 152
time, 25, 31, 85, 96, 170, 176
timing, 175, 181
top-down, 171, 172, 173, 175, 176
tracks, 19, 65
training, 11, 12, 22, 23, 43, 58, 62, 63, 71, 72, 73, 74, 75, 76, 107, 108, 113, 115, 118, 119, 162, 177
traits, 3, 152
transcripts, 1, 10, 13
translation, 80, 112, 175
trauma, 7, 25
treatment, 116, 117, 148, 161, 162
trial, 53, 118

triggers, 5, 48, 173

U

ubiquitous, 176
underlying mechanisms, 50
United Kingdom (UK), 1, 2, 33, 36, 37, 164, 165, 181
United States (USA), 117, 148, 163

V

valence, 51, 52, 55, 134, 154
validation, 33, 35, 62, 100
variability, 178, 179
variables, ix, 34, 40, 63, 85, 86, 88, 90, 93, 118, 129, 132, 135, 136, 137, 139, 141, 147, 148, 151, 160, 161
ventricular arrhythmia, 178
versatility, ix, 103
victims, 74, 150
violence, viii, 61, 63, 69, 70, 72, 73, 74, 76, 79, 116, 148, 152, 161, 163, 164
violent behavior, ix, 62, 70, 71, 74, 147
violent crime, 148
volatility, x, 147, 156, 157
vulnerability, 5, 73, 96, 98

W

Washington, 34, 35, 144, 164, 166
weakness, 73, 87, 149
wealth, 54, 115, 117
web, 114, 115
well-being, 5, 8, 9, 31, 34, 35, 101, 117, 131, 144
WHO, 164
word naming, 173, 174
worry, 4, 6, 7, 16, 18, 21, 27, 28, 29, 30, 134

Y

young people, ix, 103, 109, 148